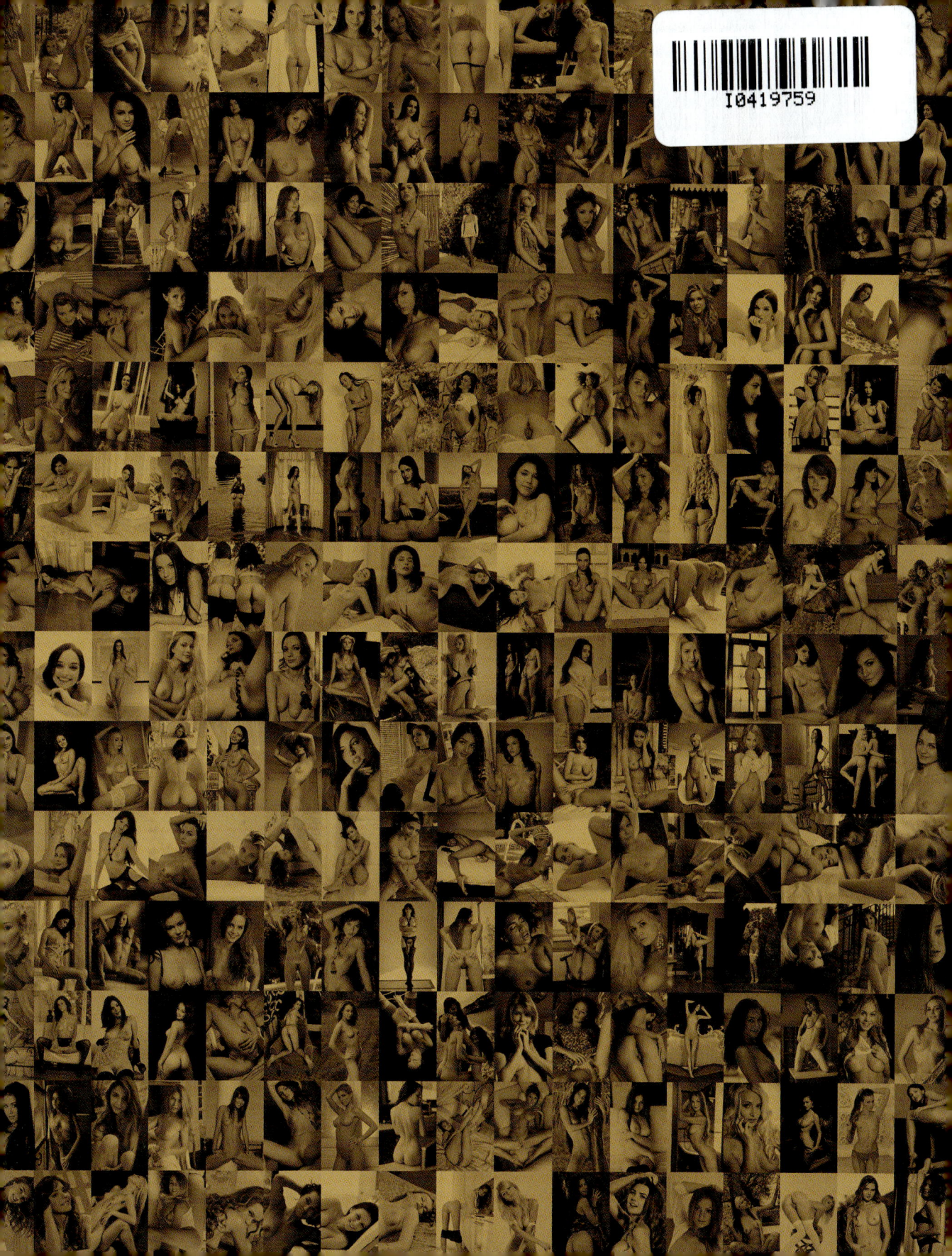

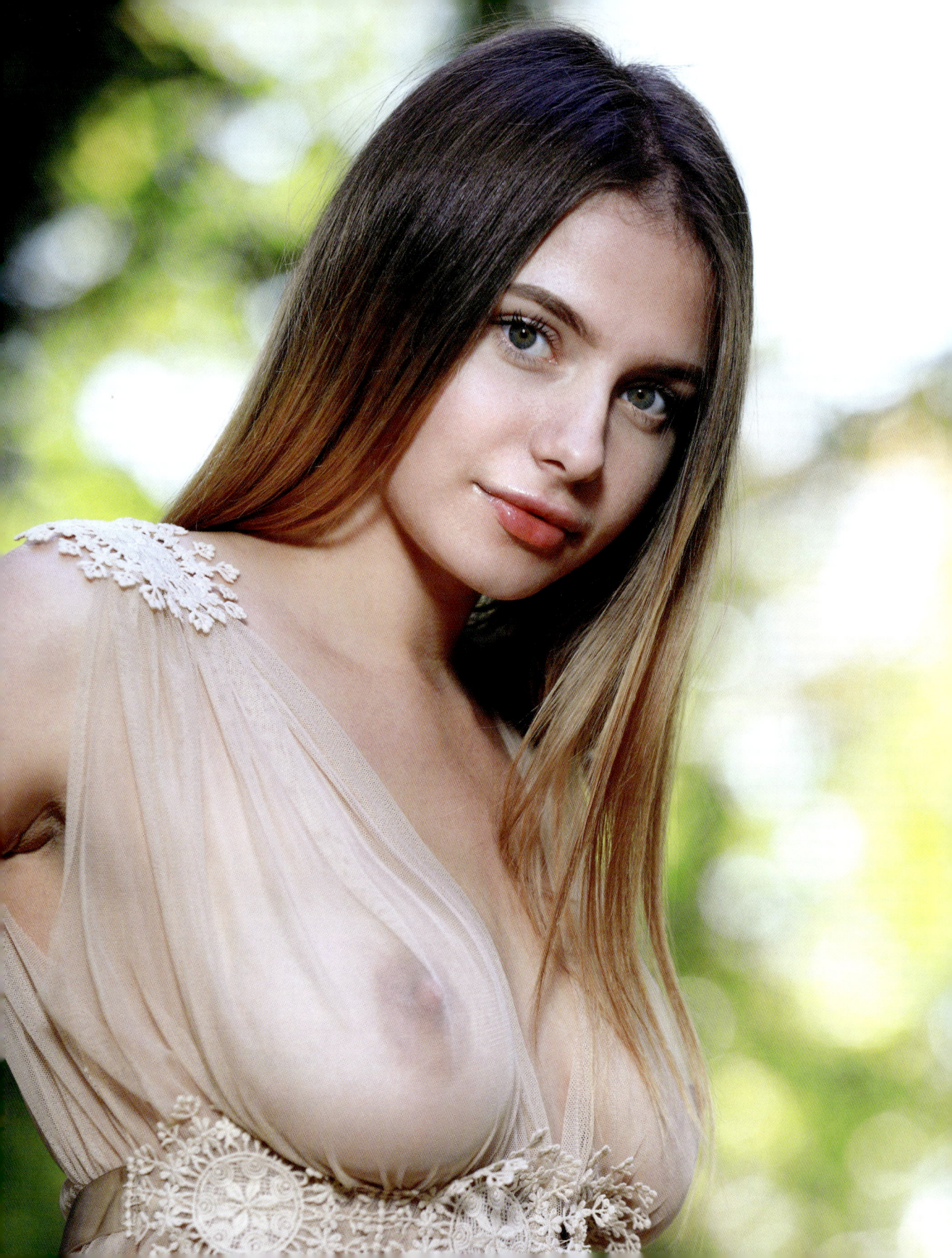

TOP MODELS OF
MetArt.com
WHERE FLAWLESS BEAUTY MEETS ART

DAKOTA PINK

COLLECTED AND EDITED BY ISABELLA CATALINA

EDITION Skylight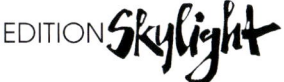

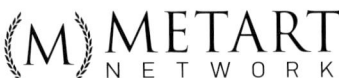

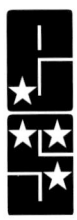

First edition 2025
Copyright © 2025 by Edition Skylight

EDITION SKYLIGHT
Rosengartenstrasse 13B
CH-8608 Bubikon / Zürich
Switzerland
info@edition-skylight.com
www.edition-skylight.com

ISBN 978-3-03766-706-4

Bibliographic information published by Die Deutsche Bibliothek
Die Deutsche Bibliothek lists this publication in the
Deutsche Nationalbibliografie; detailed bibliographic data
are available in the Internet at http://dnb.ddb.de.

Printed in Bosnia and Herzegovina

YOU WILL FALL IN LOVE WITH THIS PRETTY LOOKING AND REALLY SHY GIRL SHOWING HER AMAZING BODY SHAPES!

Stunning **Dakota Pink** became the 73rd MetArt model to join the 50+ Club at the end of May 2024. This is an honor reserved for those few elite stars that have made 50 or more appearances in their modeling career. The voluptuous Russian beauty debuted at the age of 19 in August 2018 and has been featured 51 times to date, all shot by Matiss. She has over 6,100 photos on MetArt, but not one video in her portfolio. Dakota has been exclusive to top artist Matiss across the MetArt Network with just one explicit photoset each on MetArt X and SexArt. Matiss is an artist known for his preference to shoot in scenic outdoor locations, and 34 of Dakota's MetArt sets are in alfresco settings.

No doubt her large, firm breasts, full thighs and butt and delicious shaved pussy are all attributes that members appreciate. Her hair has varied from brunette to blonde, but her huge green eyes and irresistible curves remain a constant enticement. Though Dakota has been sharing her nude beauty on MetArt for six years, she gives no indication of quitting just yet. As we congratulate her on her milestone achievement, may we look forward to much more from her in the years to come.

IN EIN SOLCHES MODEL MIT DIESEN RUNDUNGEN KANN MAN SICH BLITZARTIG VERLIEBEN!

Die atemberaubende **Dakota Pink** wurde als 73. MetArt Model Ende Mai 2024 in den 50+ Club aufgenommen. Dies ist eine Ehre, nur den wenigen elitären Stars vorbehalten, die 50 oder mehr Auftritte in ihrer Modelkarriere absolviert haben. Die üppige russische Schönheit debütierte im Alter von 19 Jahren im August 2018 und wurde bis heute in 51 Shootings abgelichtet, alle von Matiss. Sie hat über 6.100 Fotos auf MetArt, aber kein einziges Video in ihrem Portfolio. Dakota modelt im gesamten MetArt Network exklusiv für den Top-Künstler Matiss, mit jeweils nur einem expliziten Fotoset auf MetArt X und SexArt. Matiss ist ein Künstler, der mit Vorliebe an malerischen Orten im Freien fotografiert, und so sind 34 von Dakotas MetArt-Sets im Freien aufgenommen.

Zweifellos sind ihre großen, festen Brüste, ihre vollen Oberschenkel und ihr Hintern sowie ihre köstlich rasierte Muschi Attribute, die Mitglieder zu schätzen wissen. Ihr Haar hat sich von brünett zu blond verändert, aber ihre großen grünen Augen und unwiderstehlichen Kurven bleiben eine ständige Verlockung. Obwohl Dakota ihre nackte Schönheit schon seit sechs Jahren auf MetArt zeigt, gibt es keine Anzeichen dafür, dass sie jetzt aufhört. Wir gratulieren ihr zu ihrem Meilenstein und freuen wir uns auf viel mehr von ihr in den den kommenden Jahren.

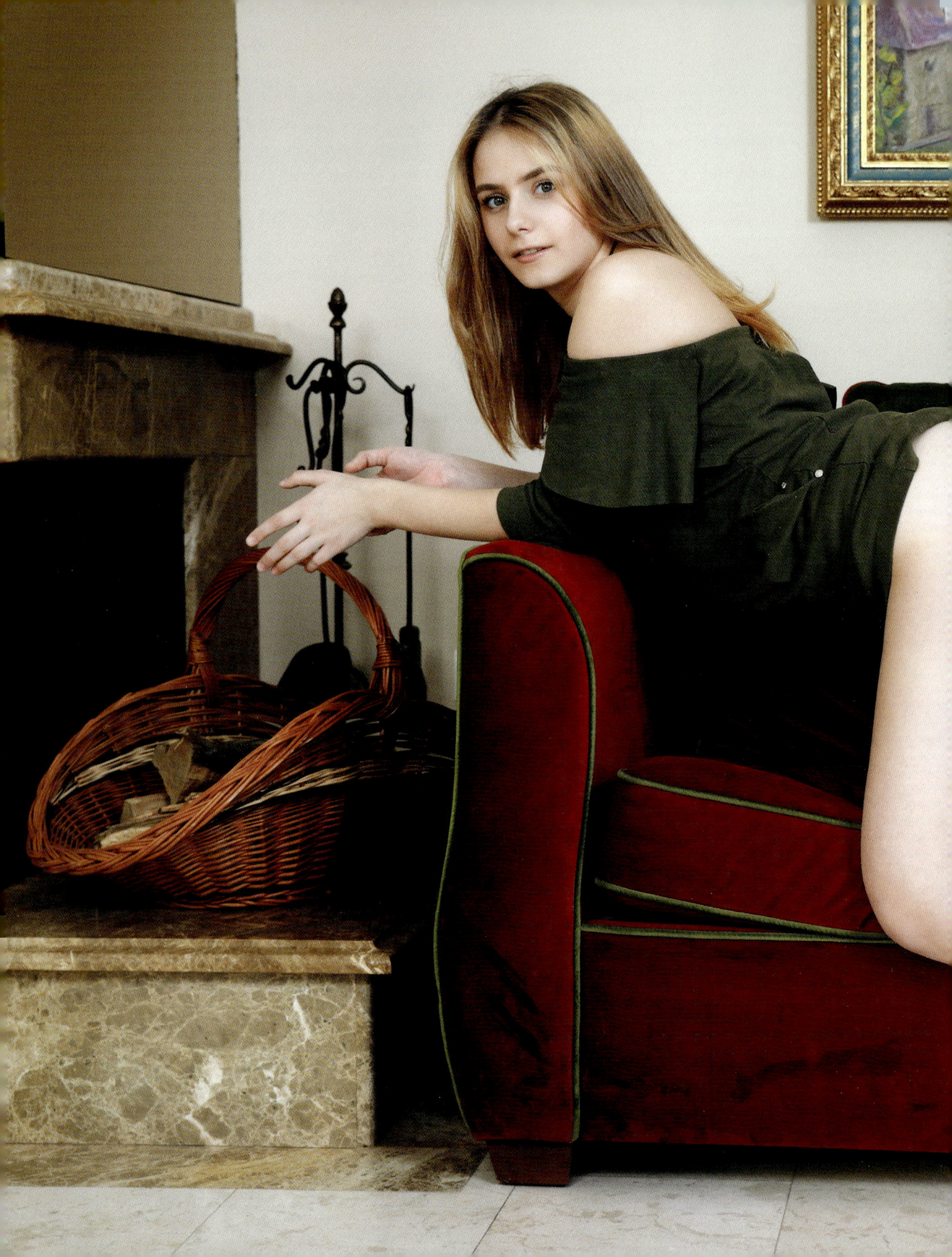

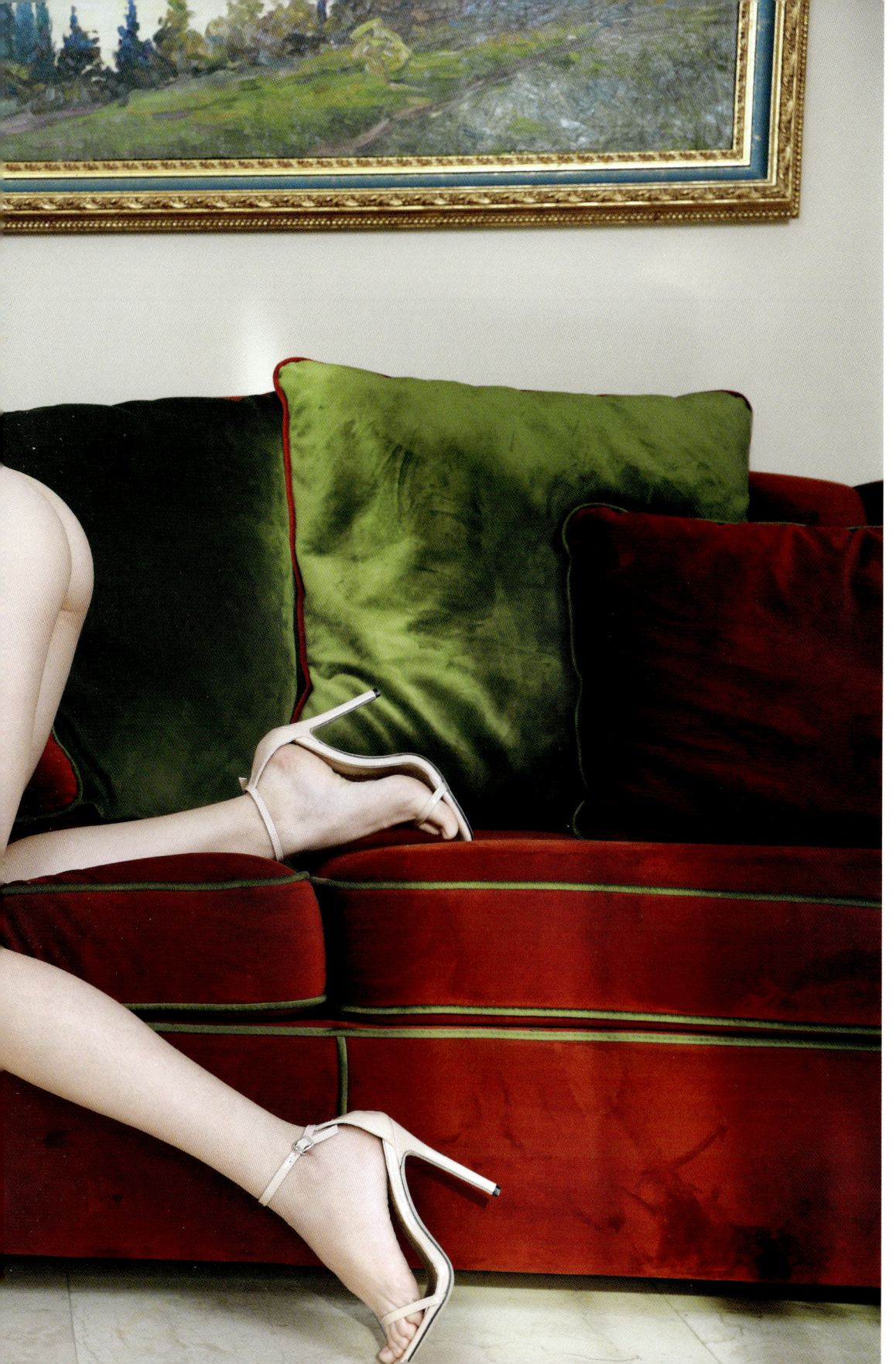

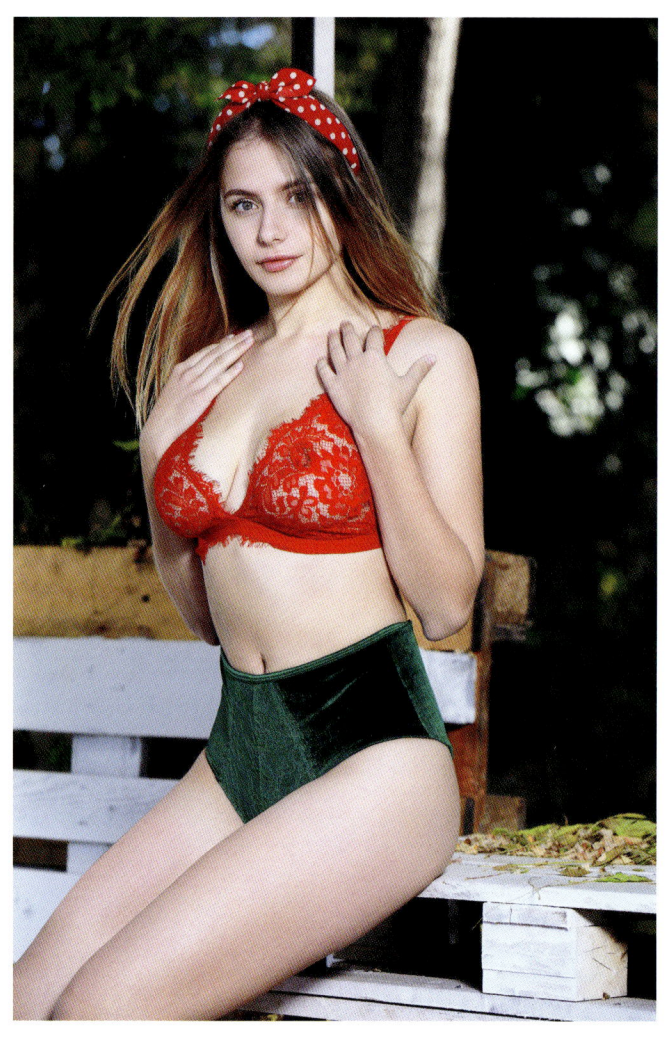

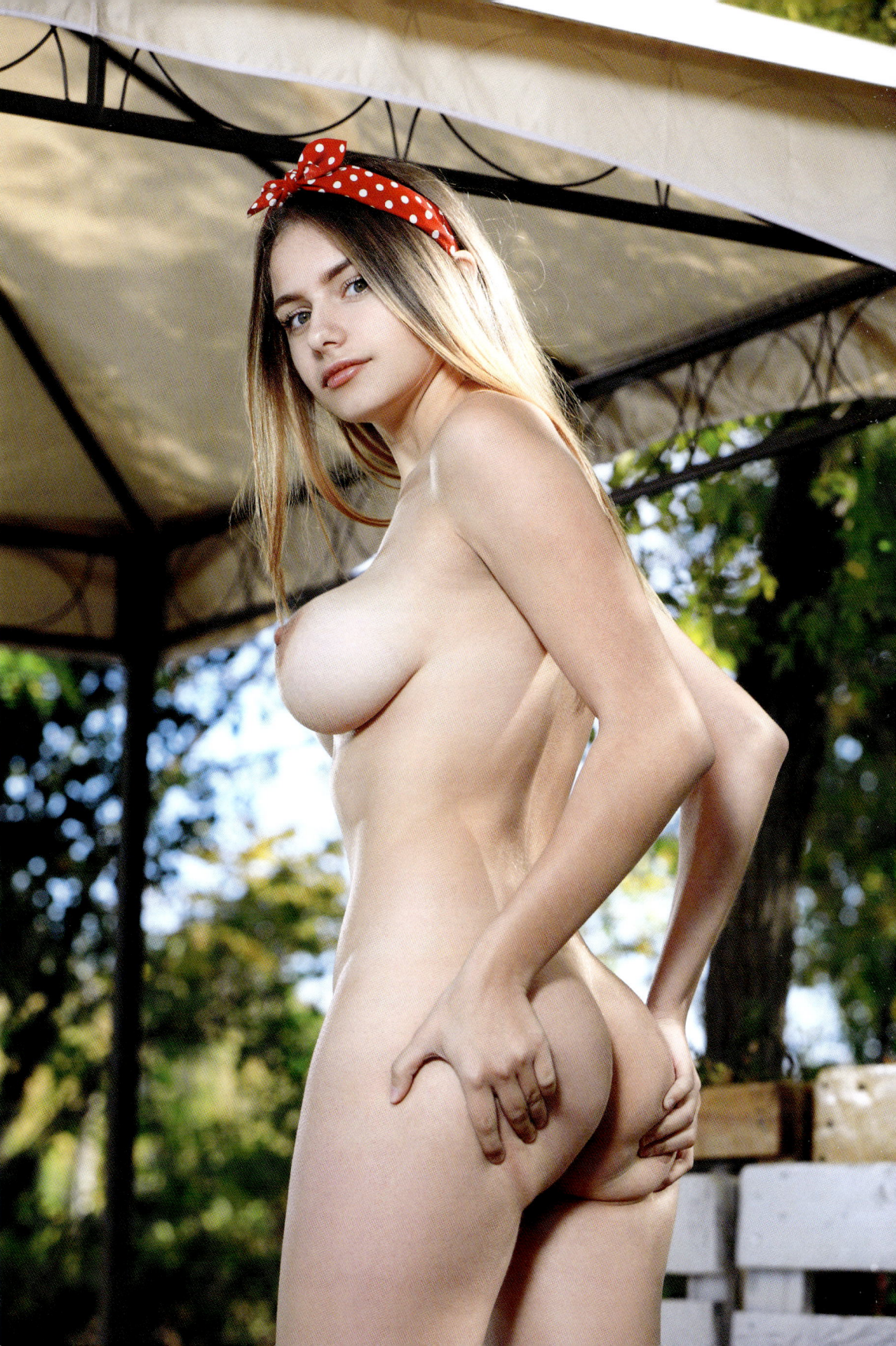

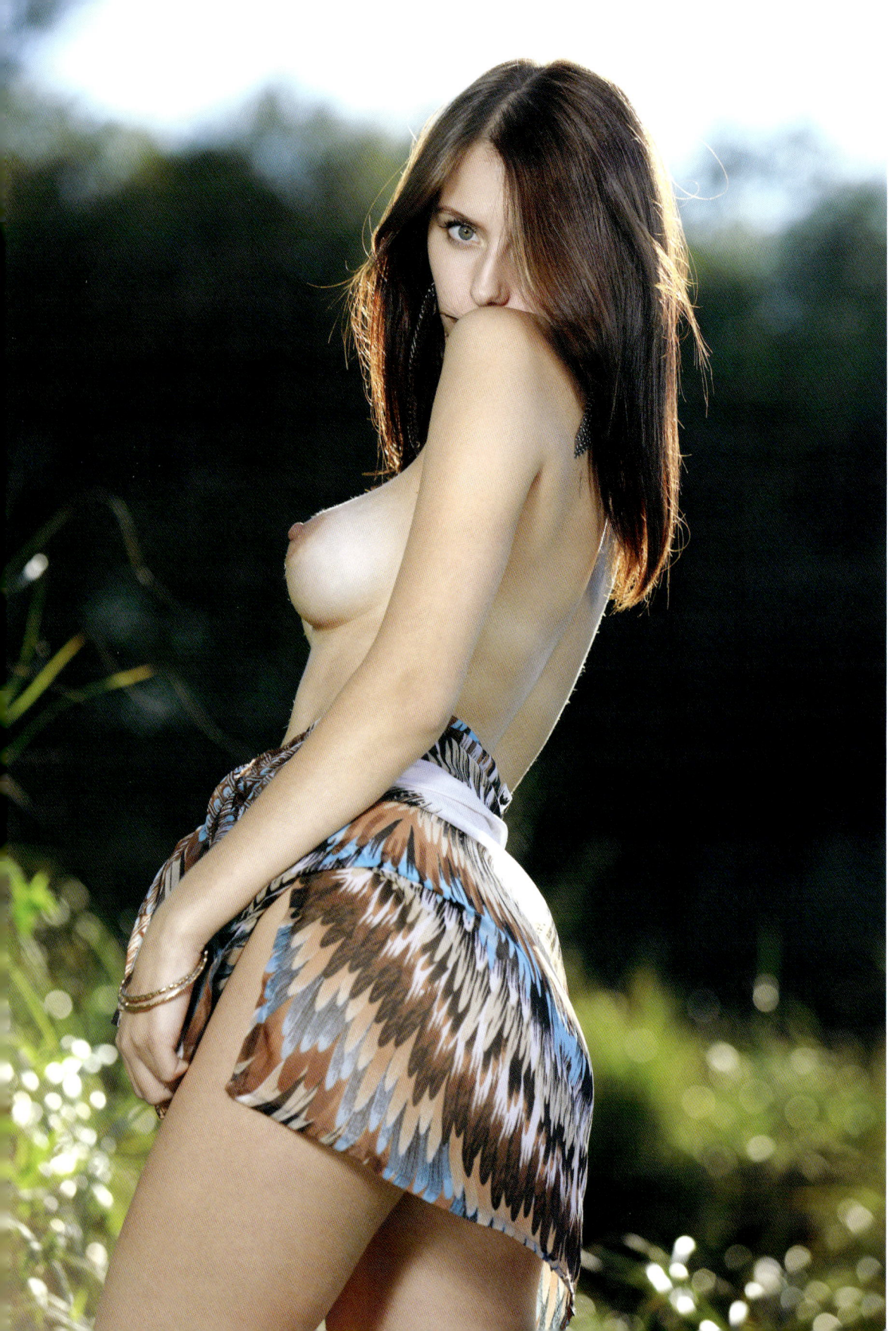

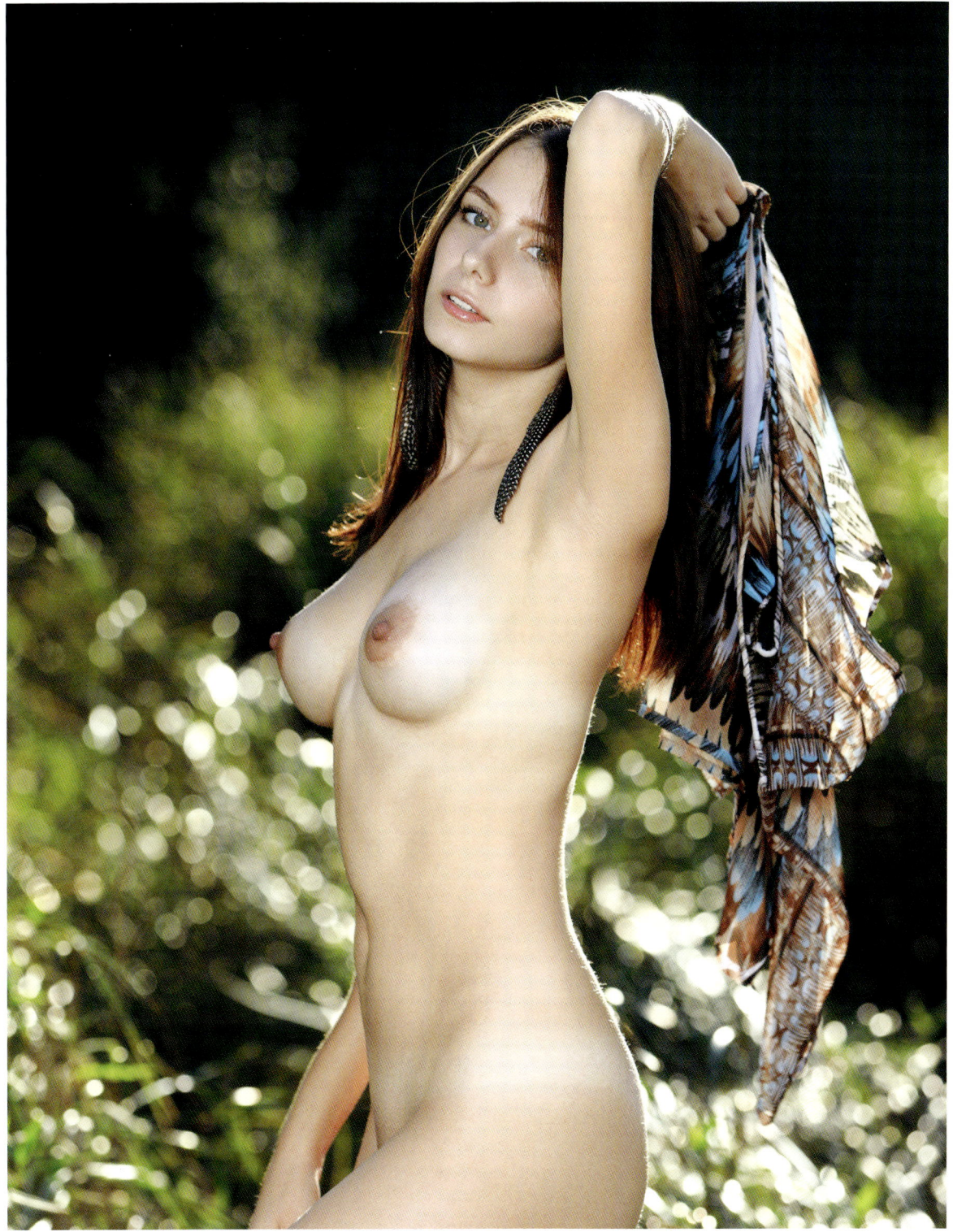

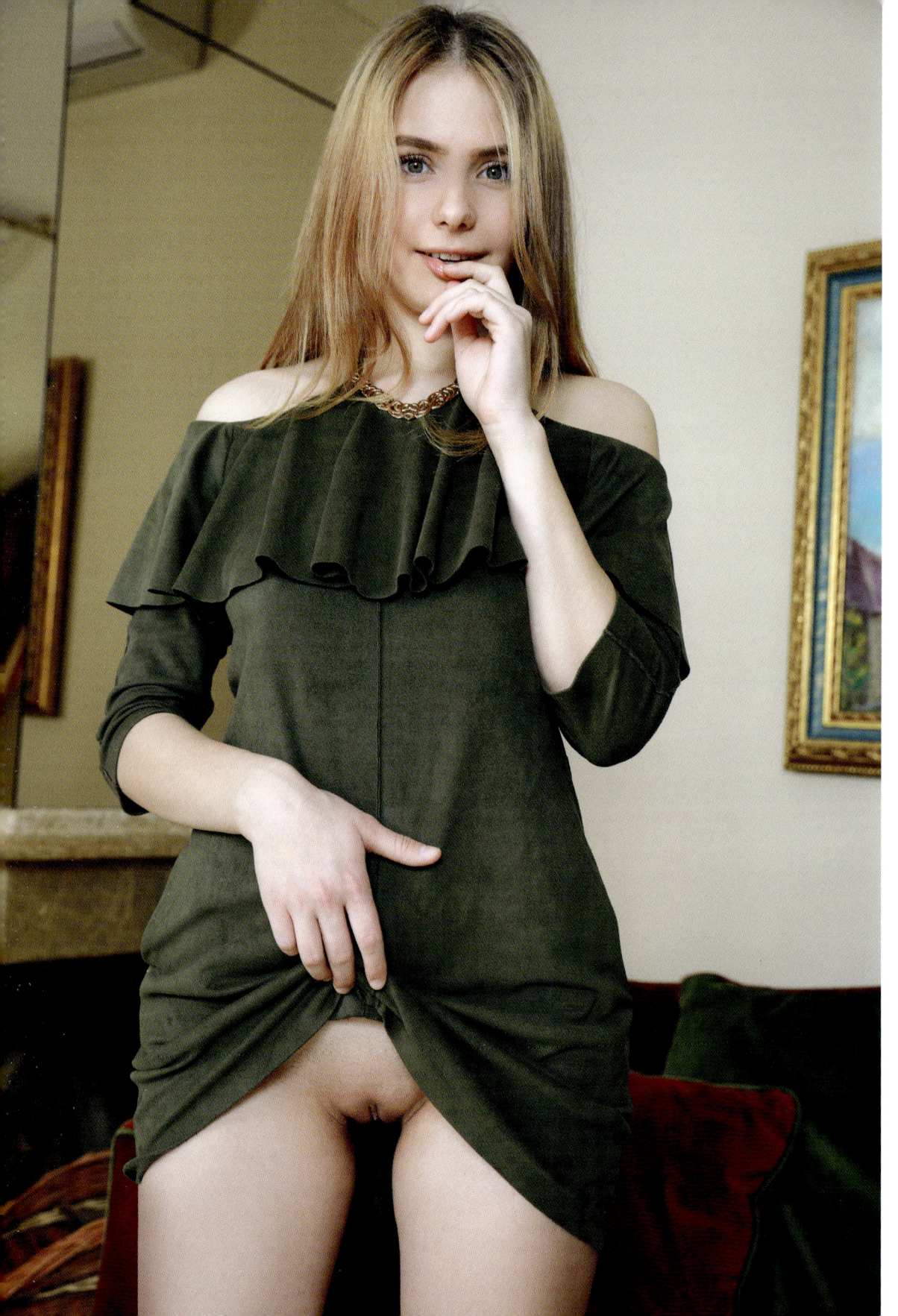

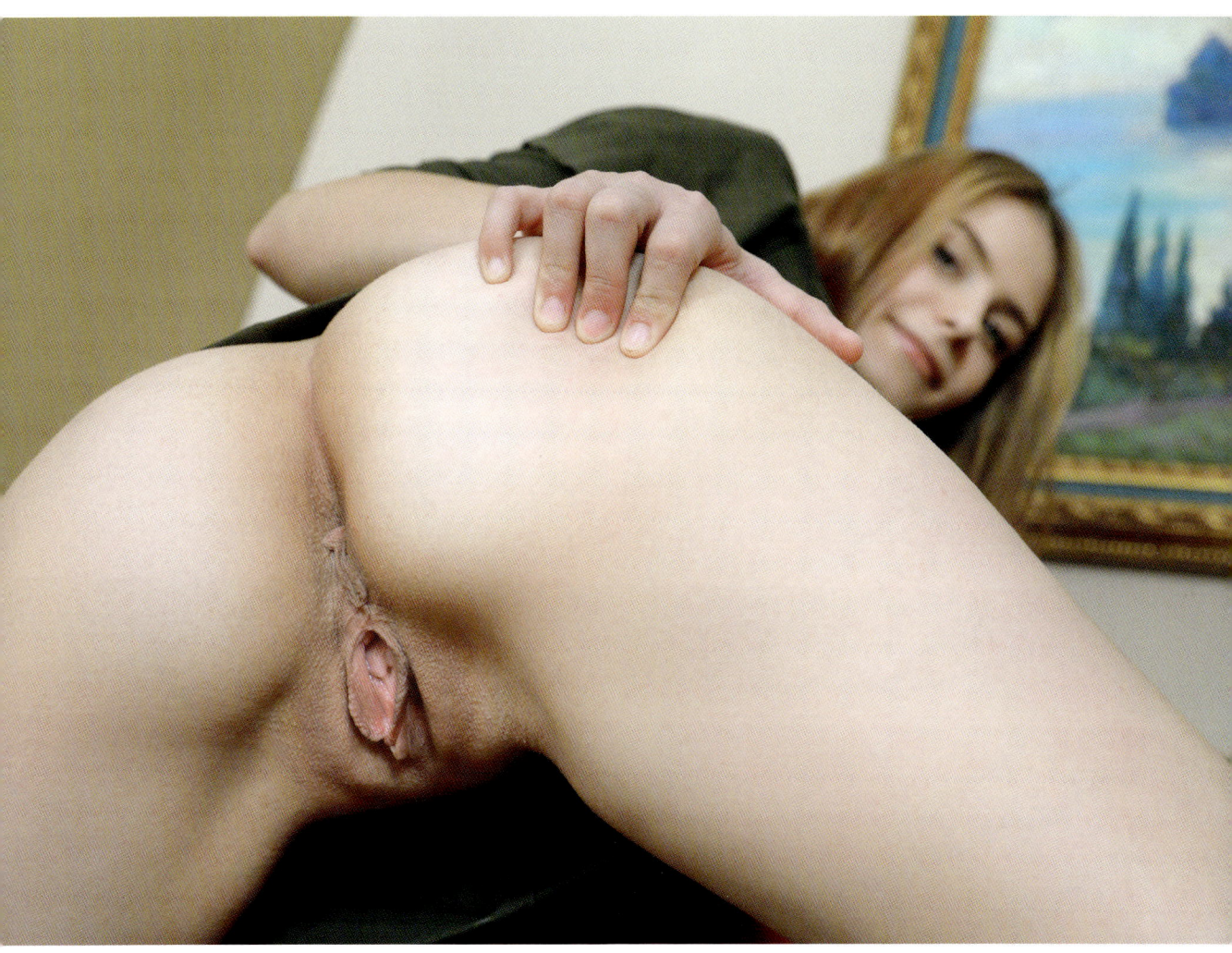

15

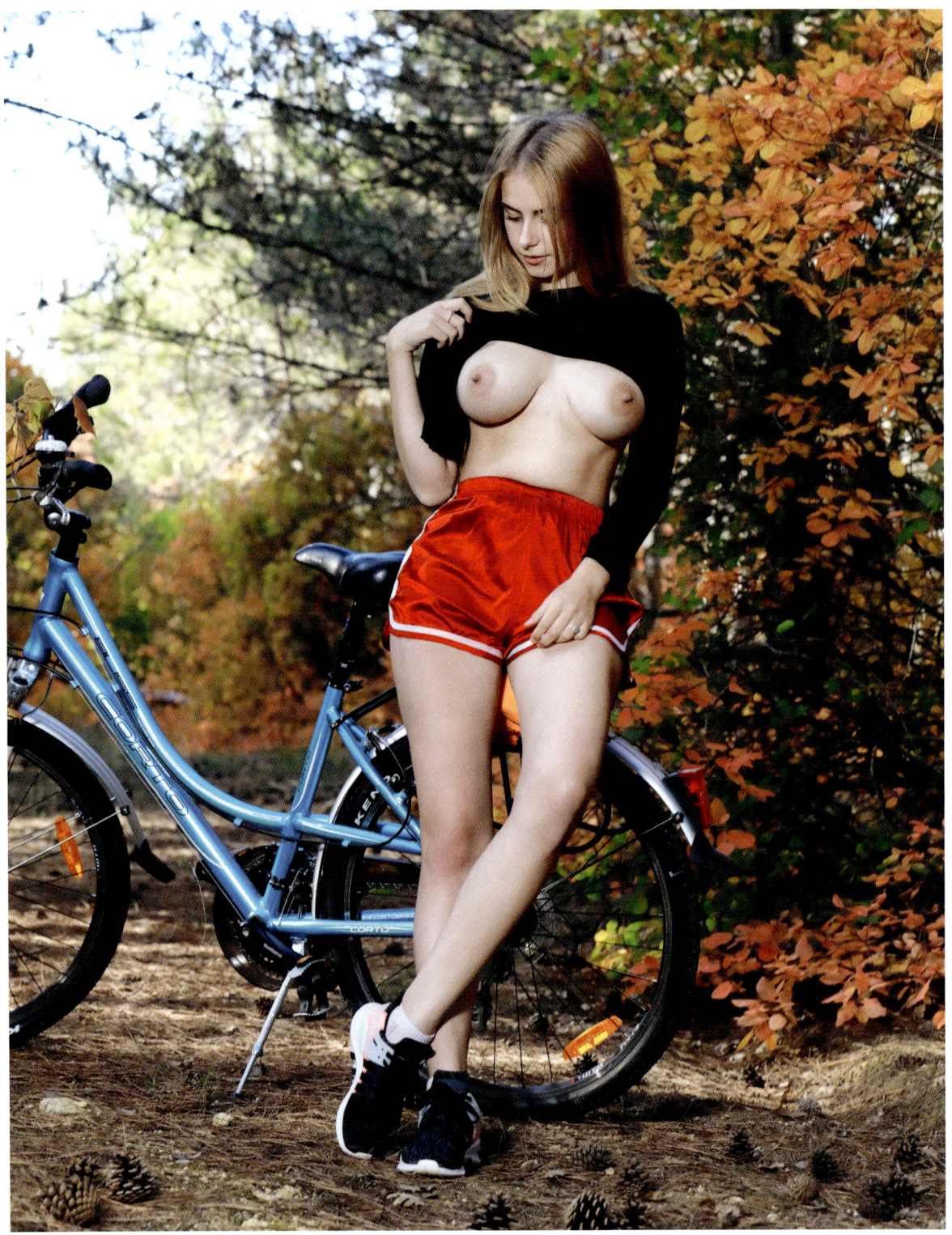

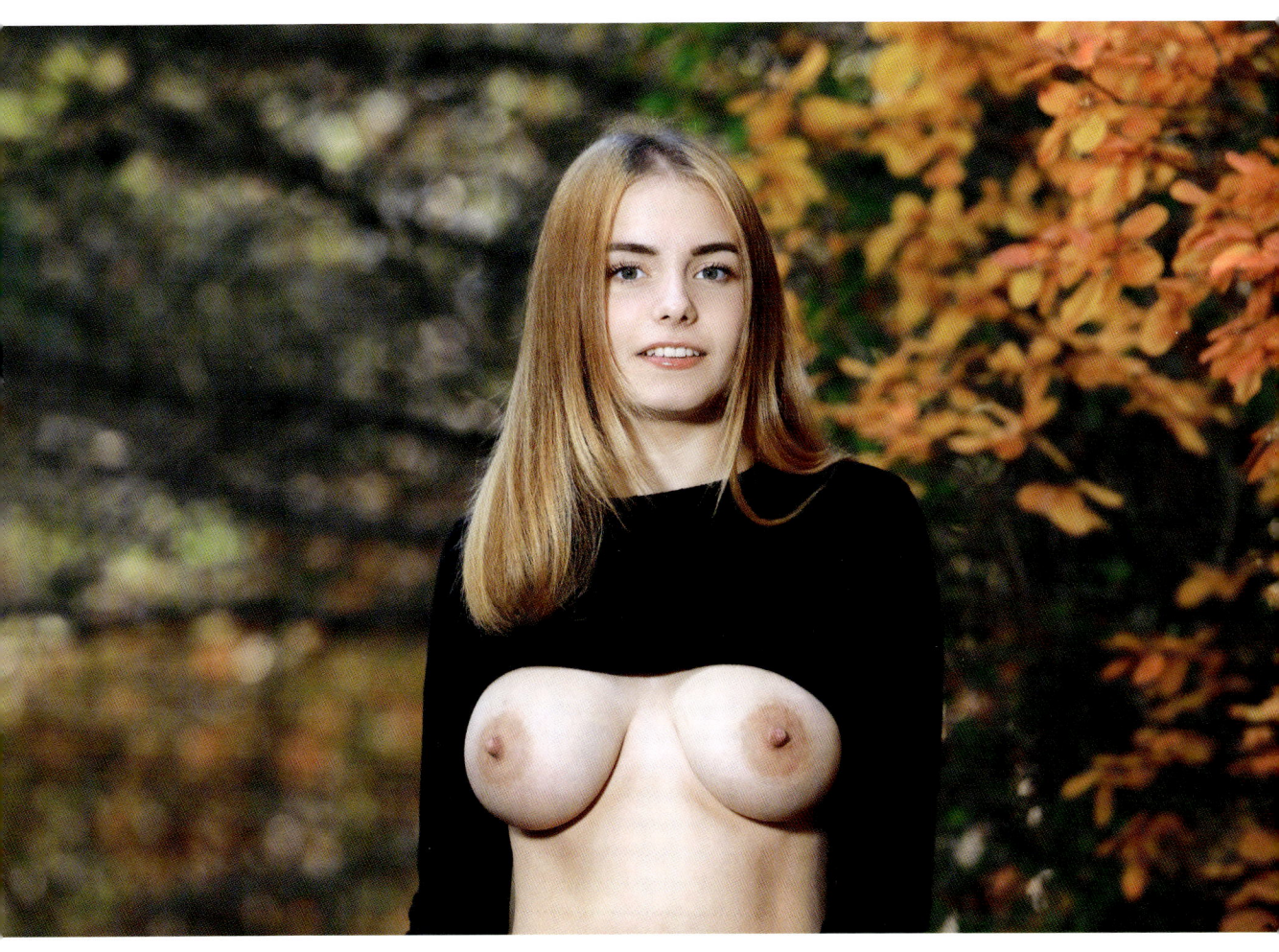

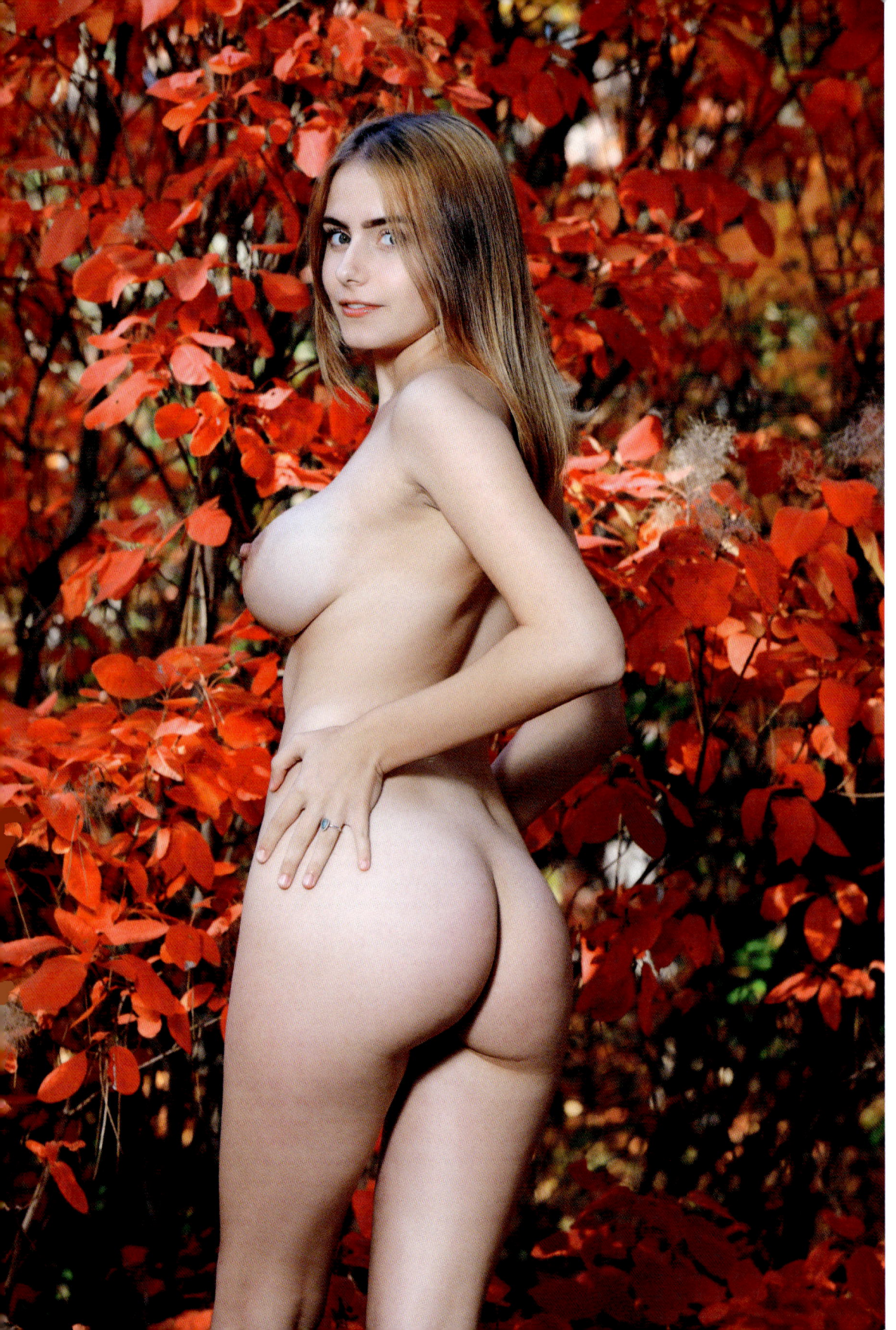

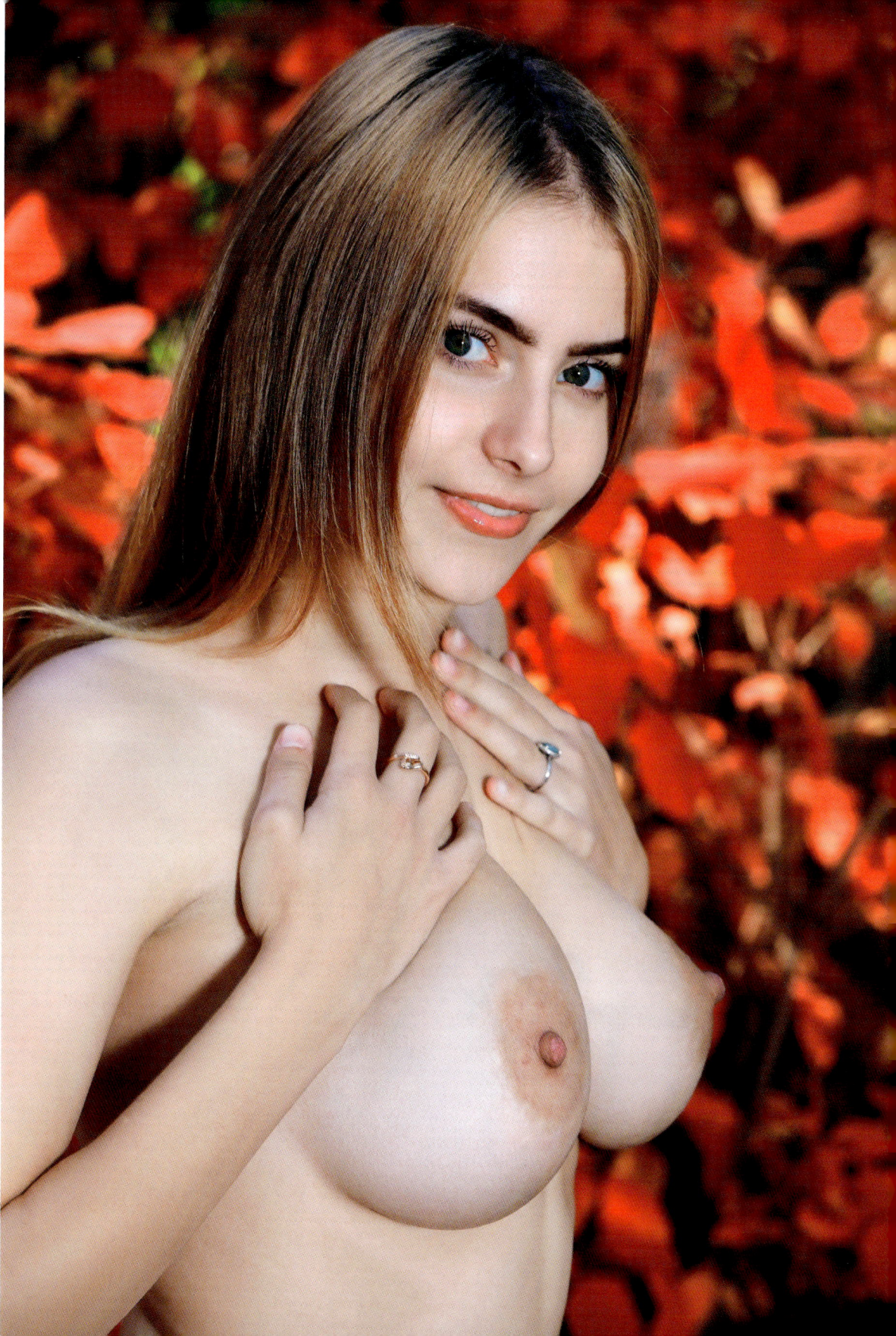

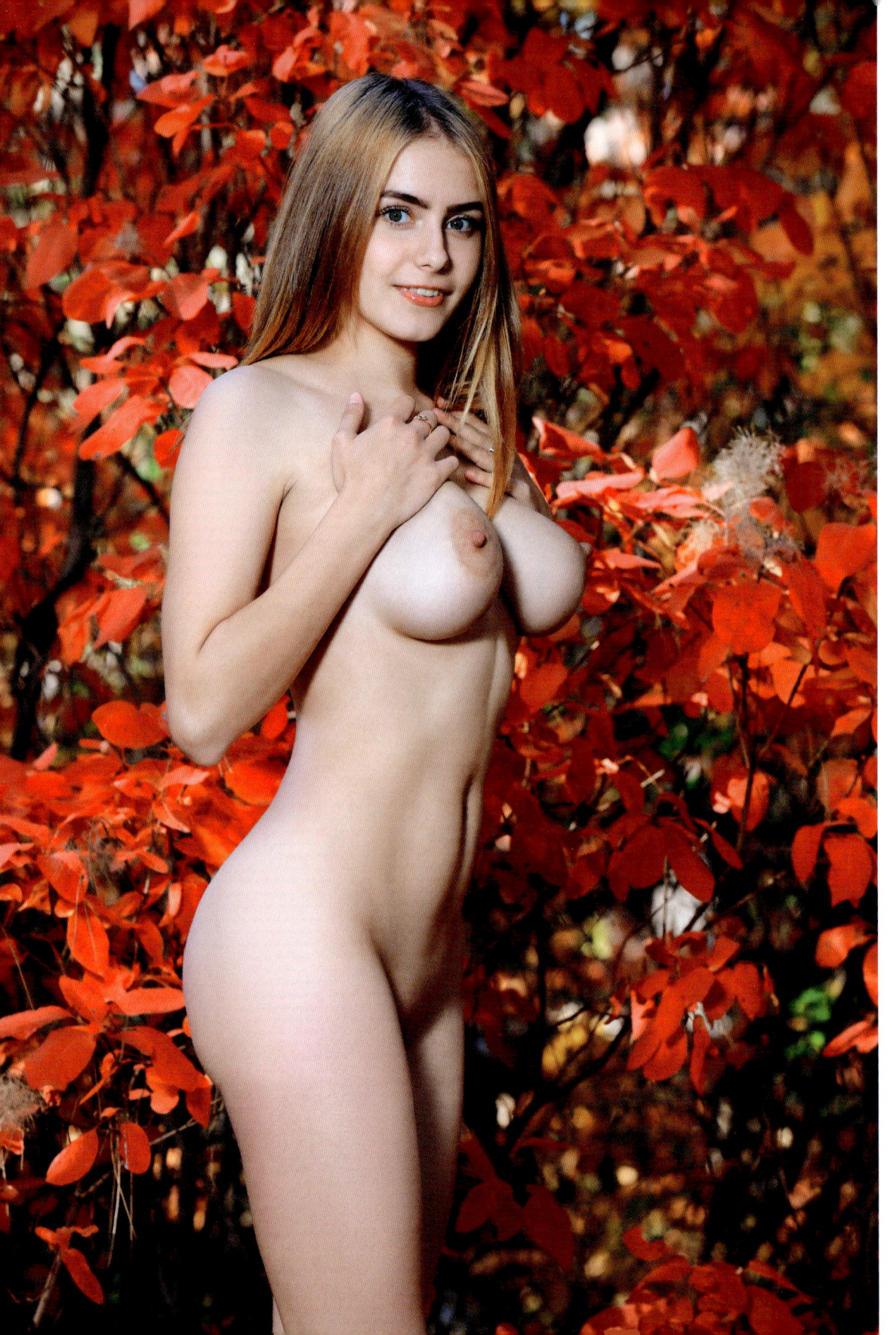

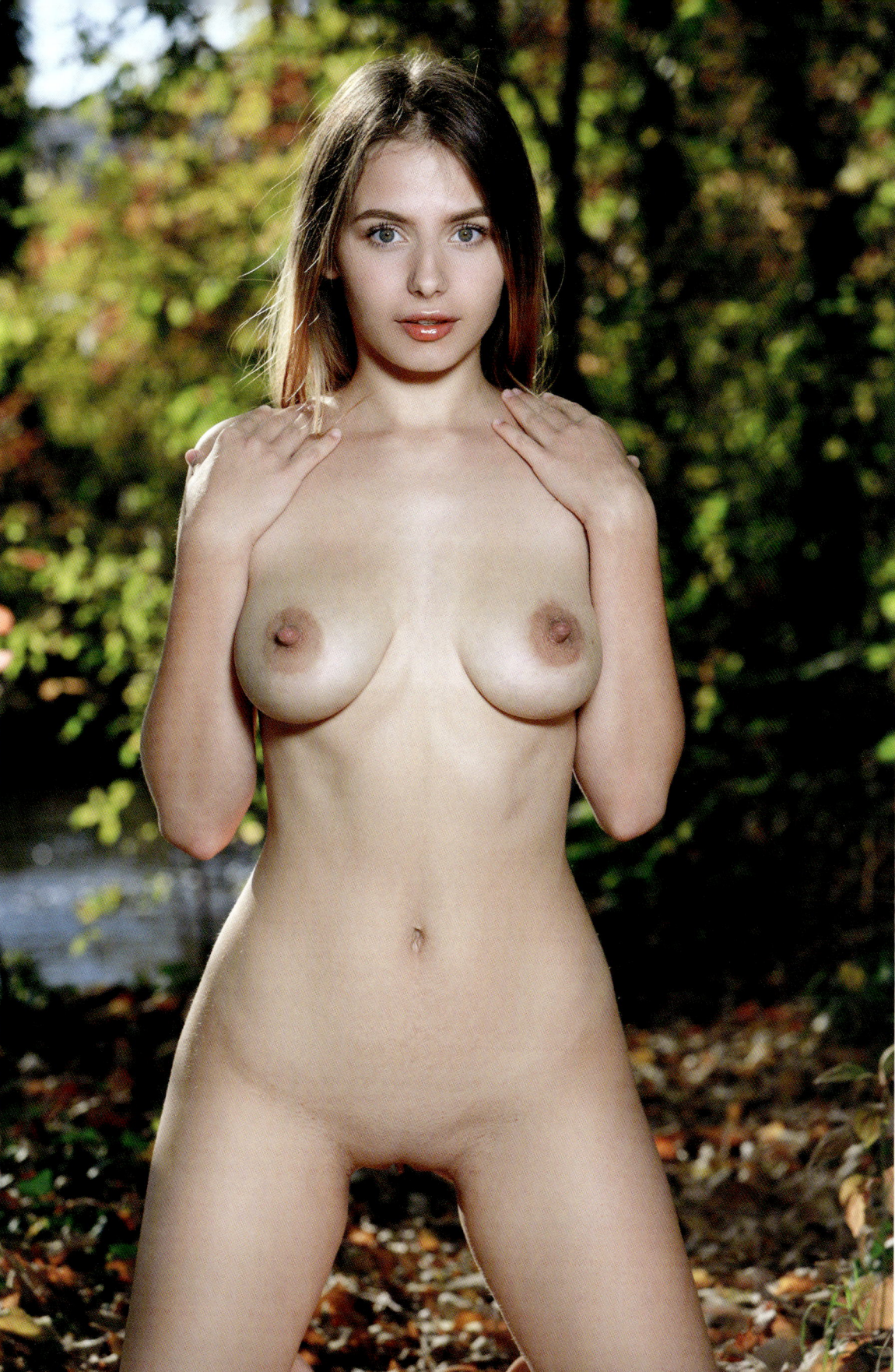

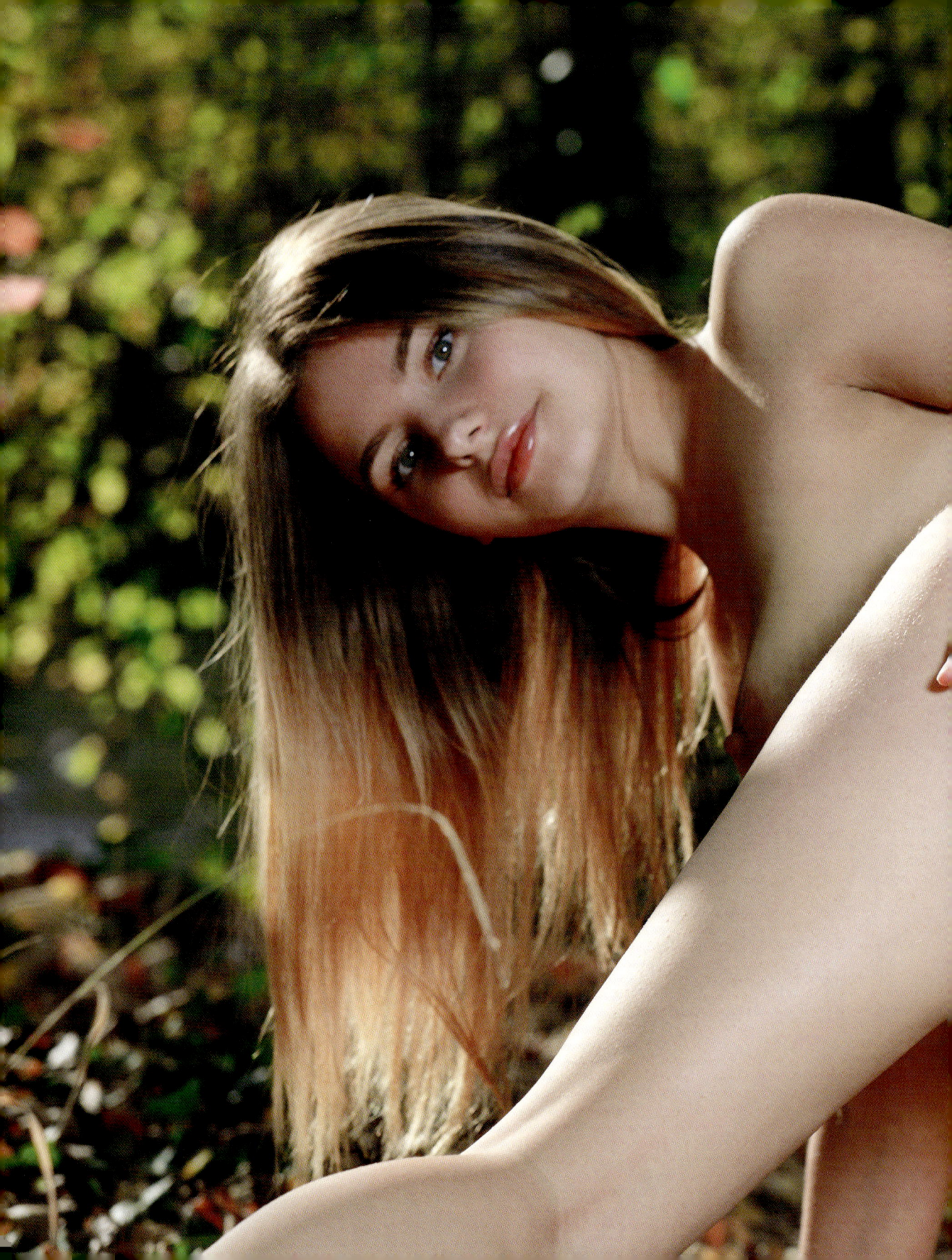

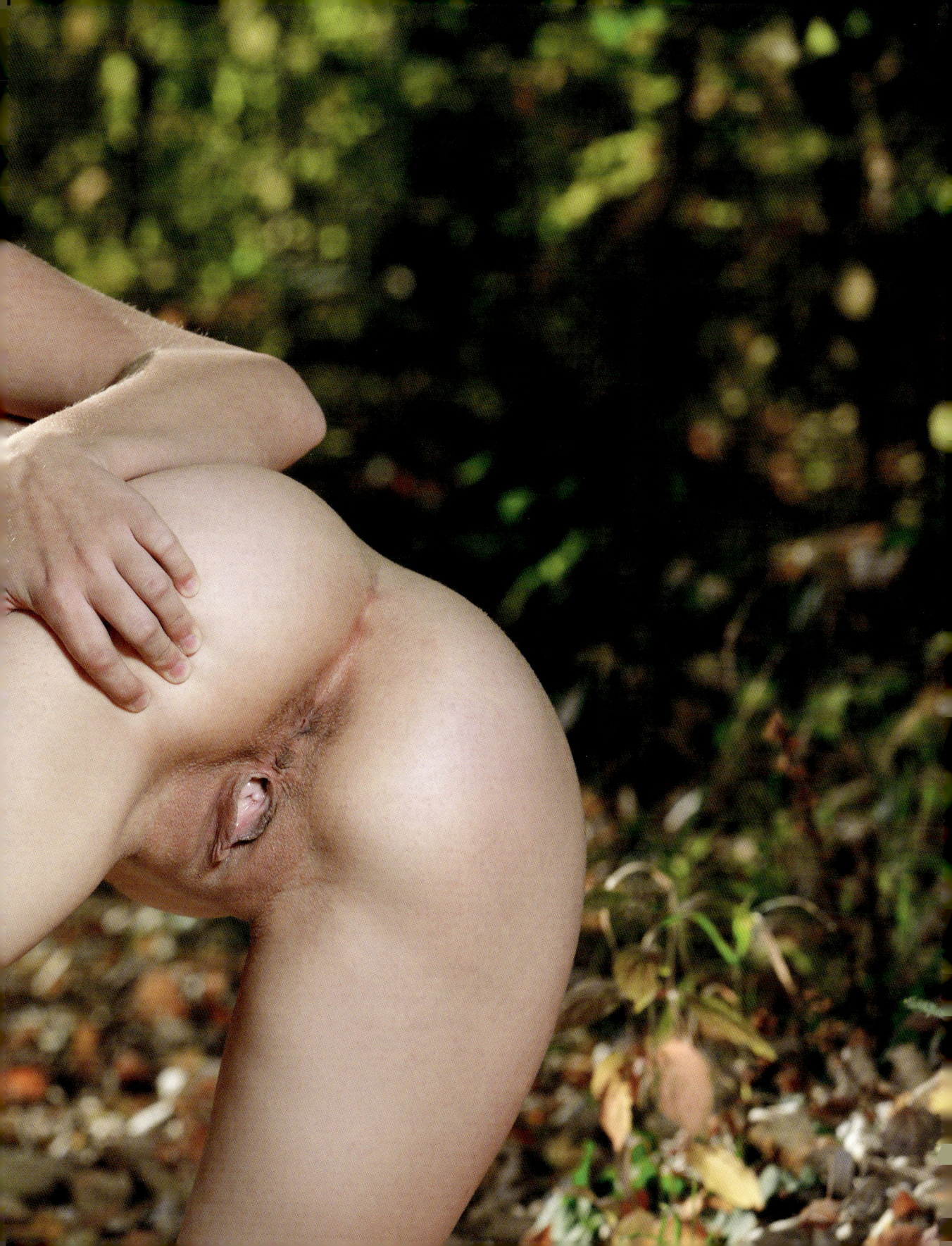

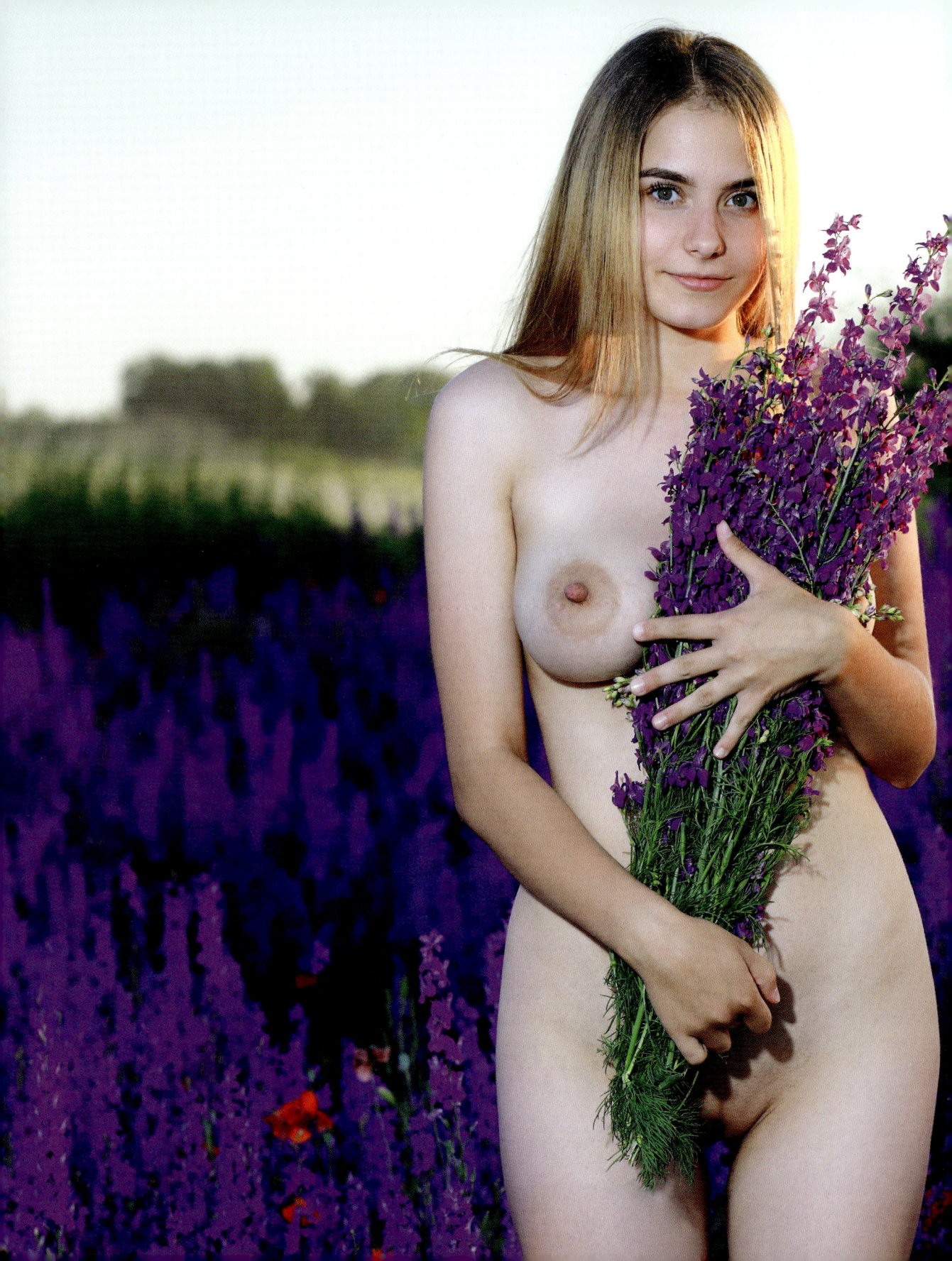

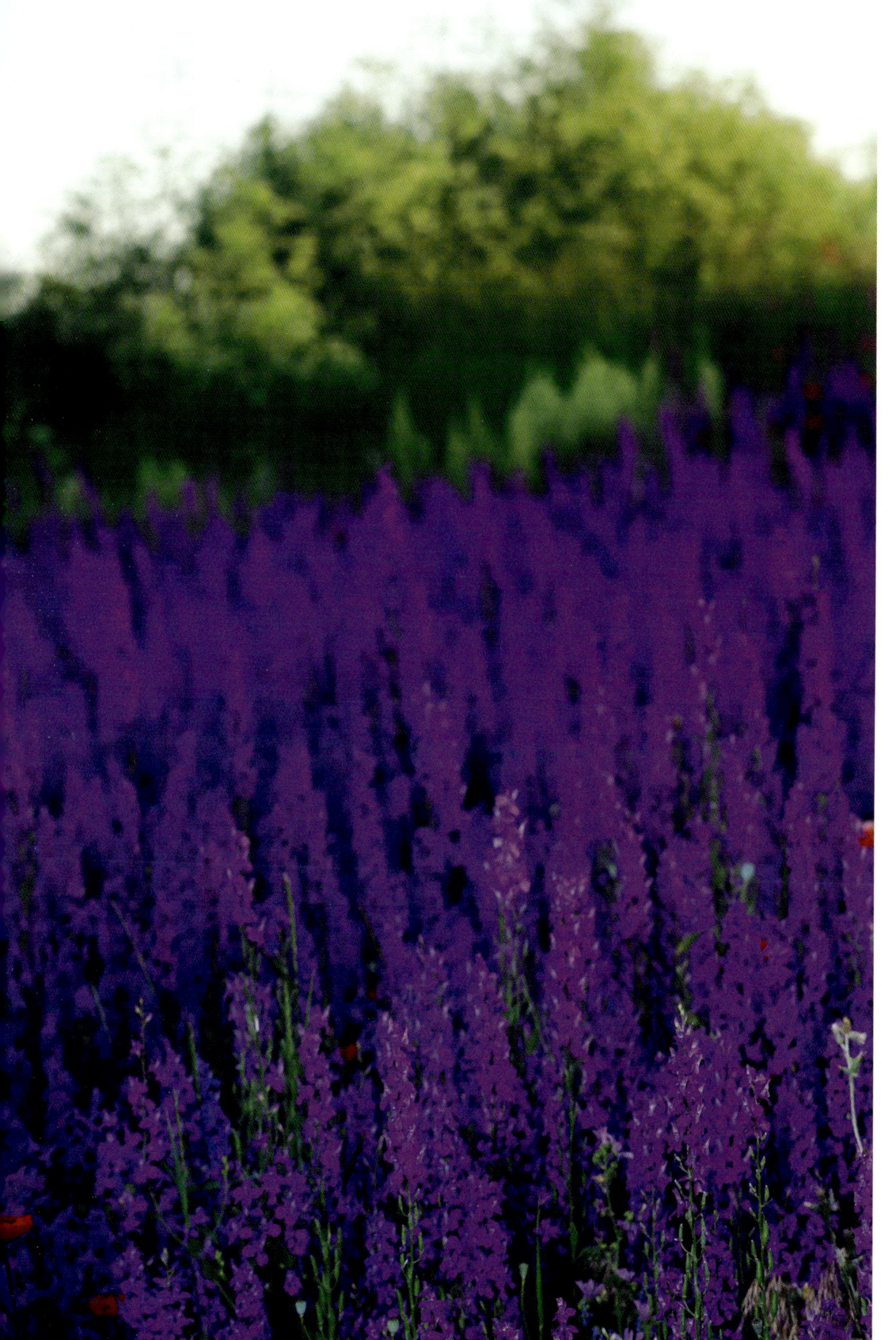

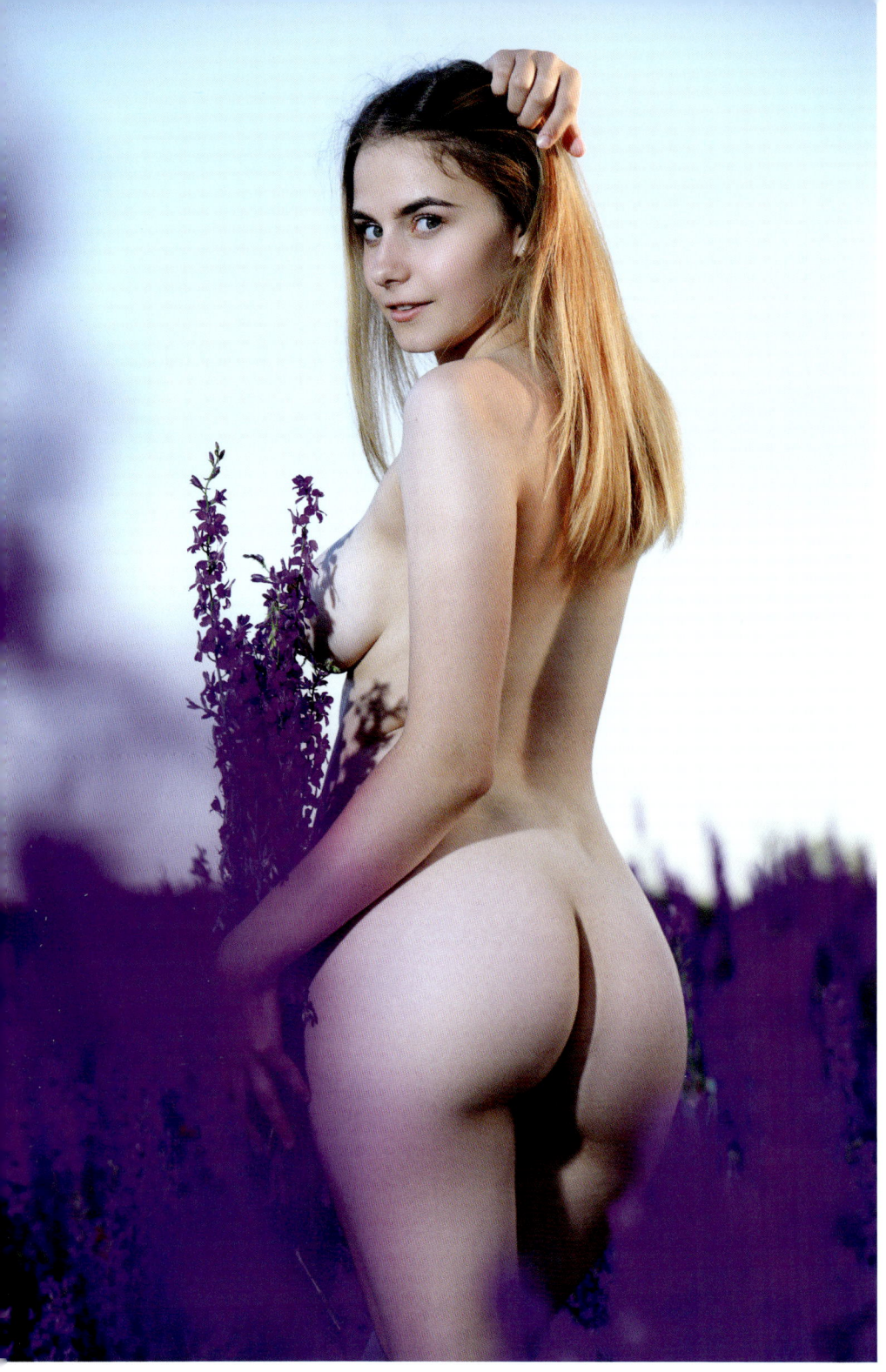

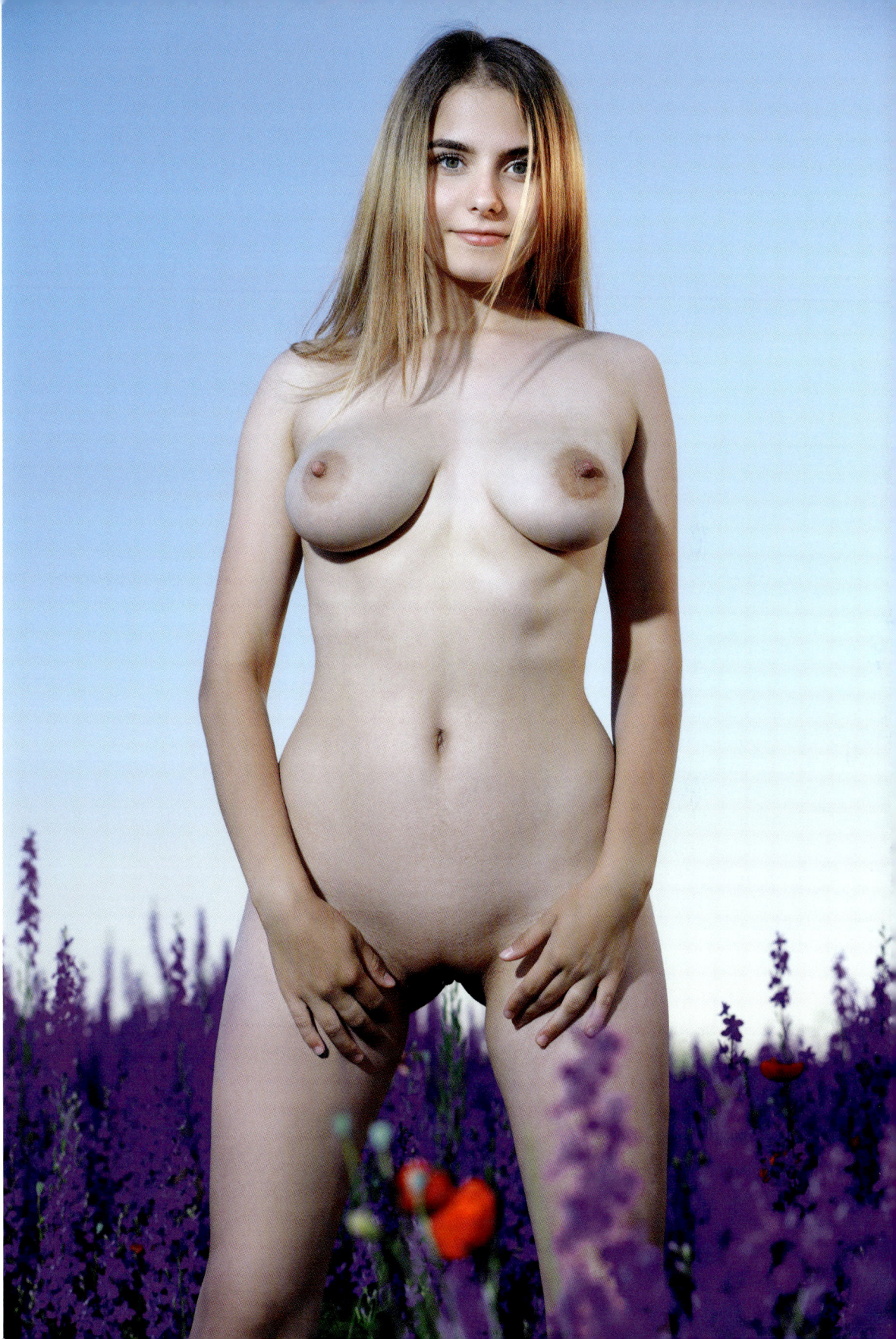

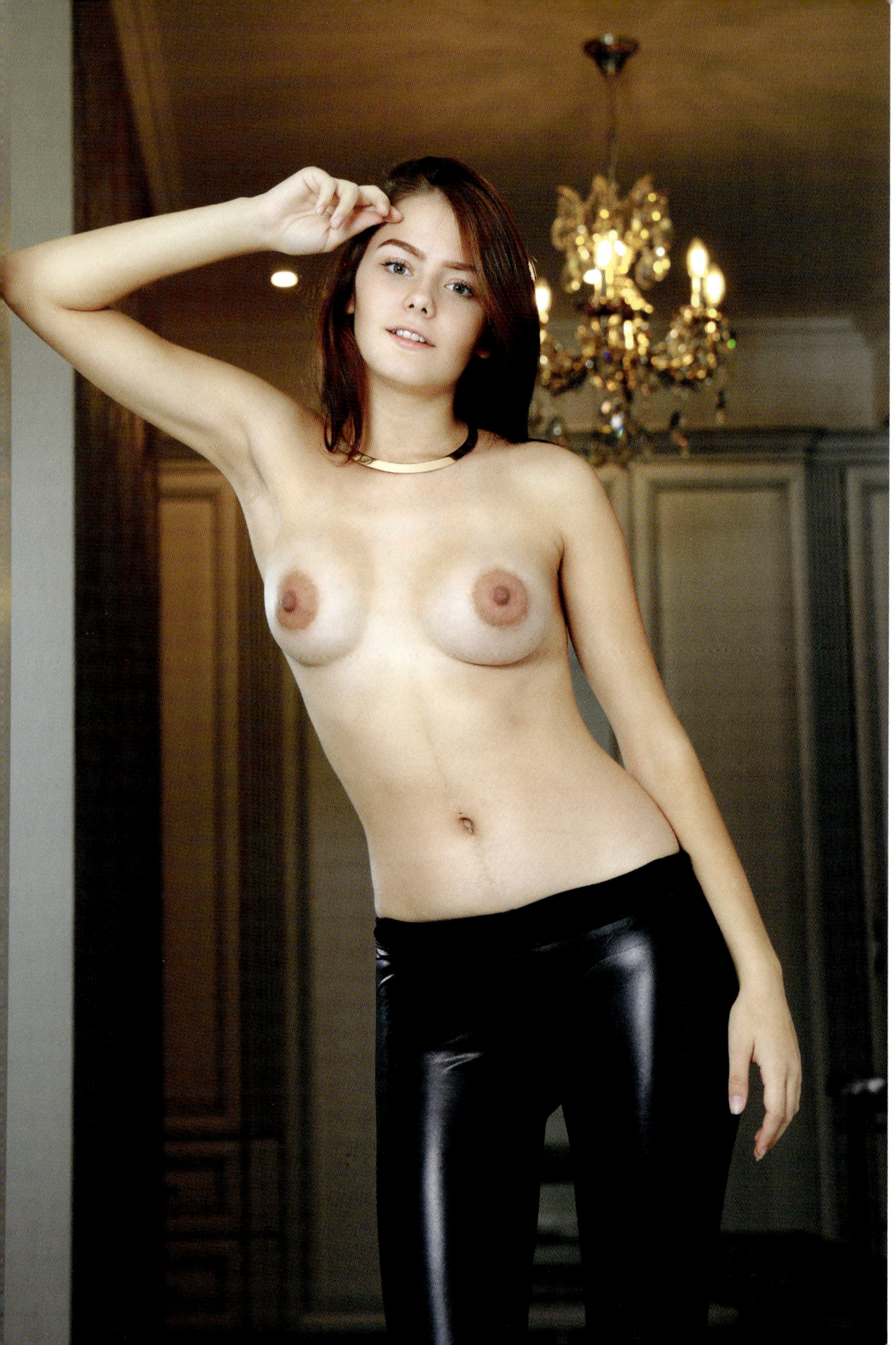

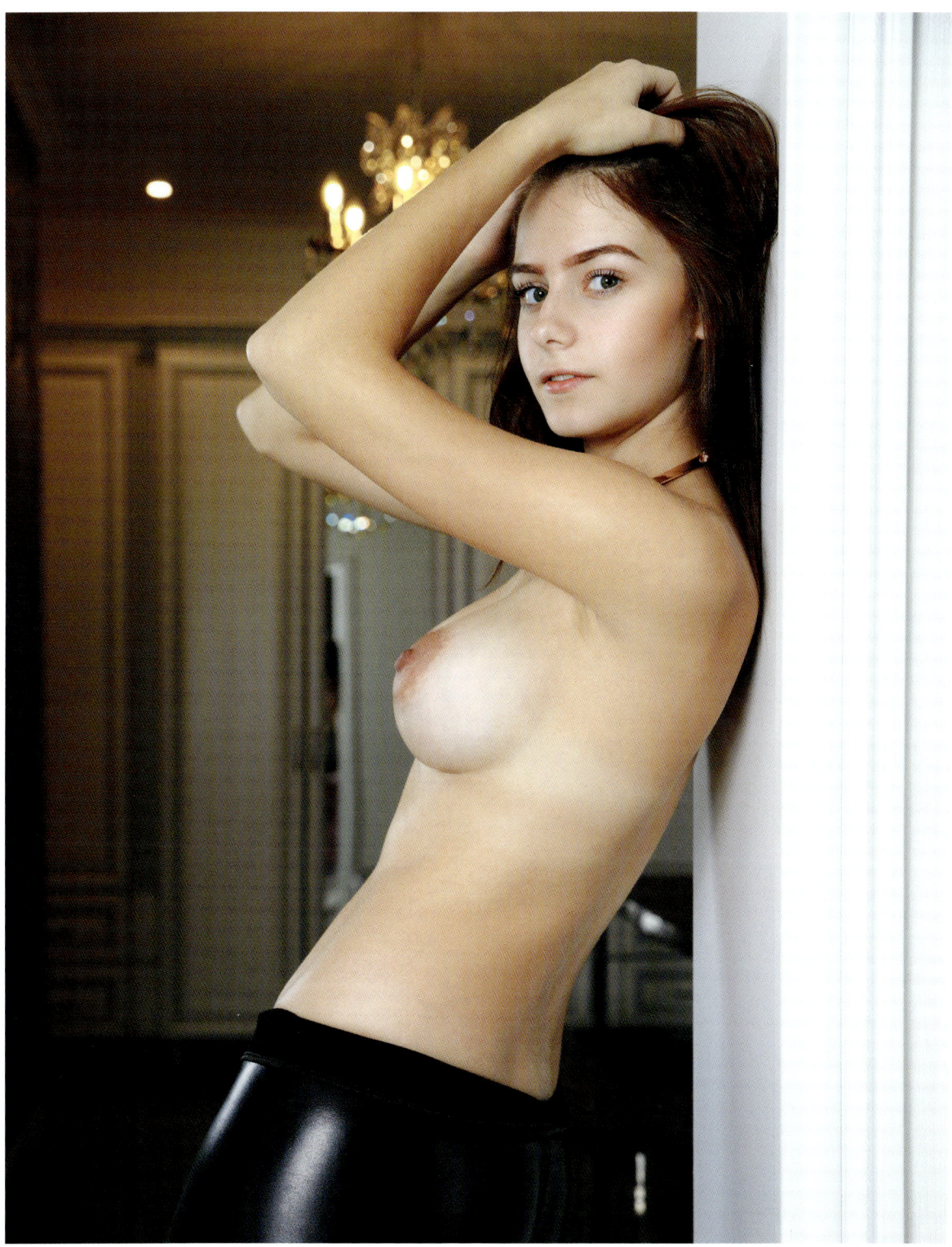

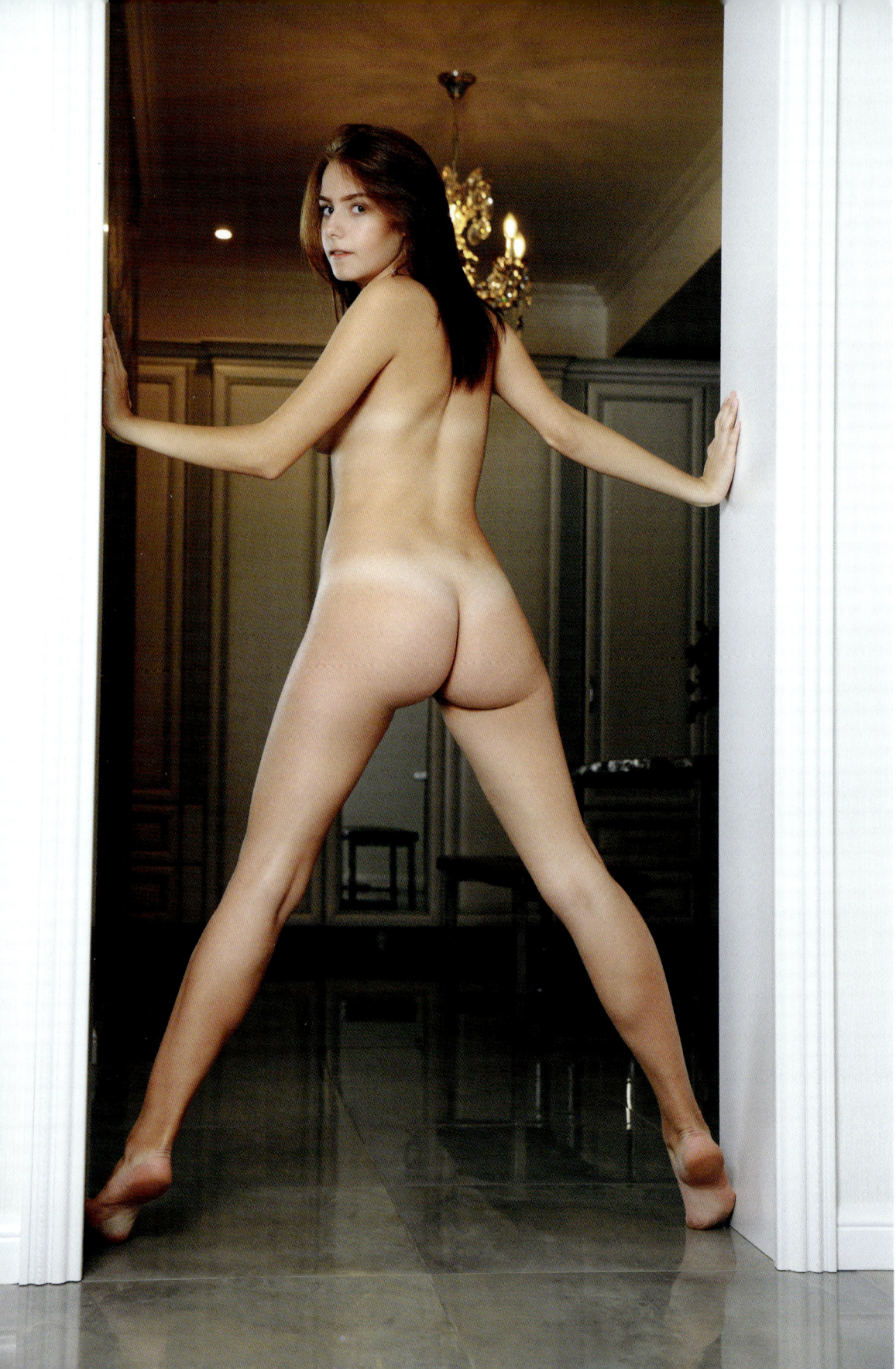

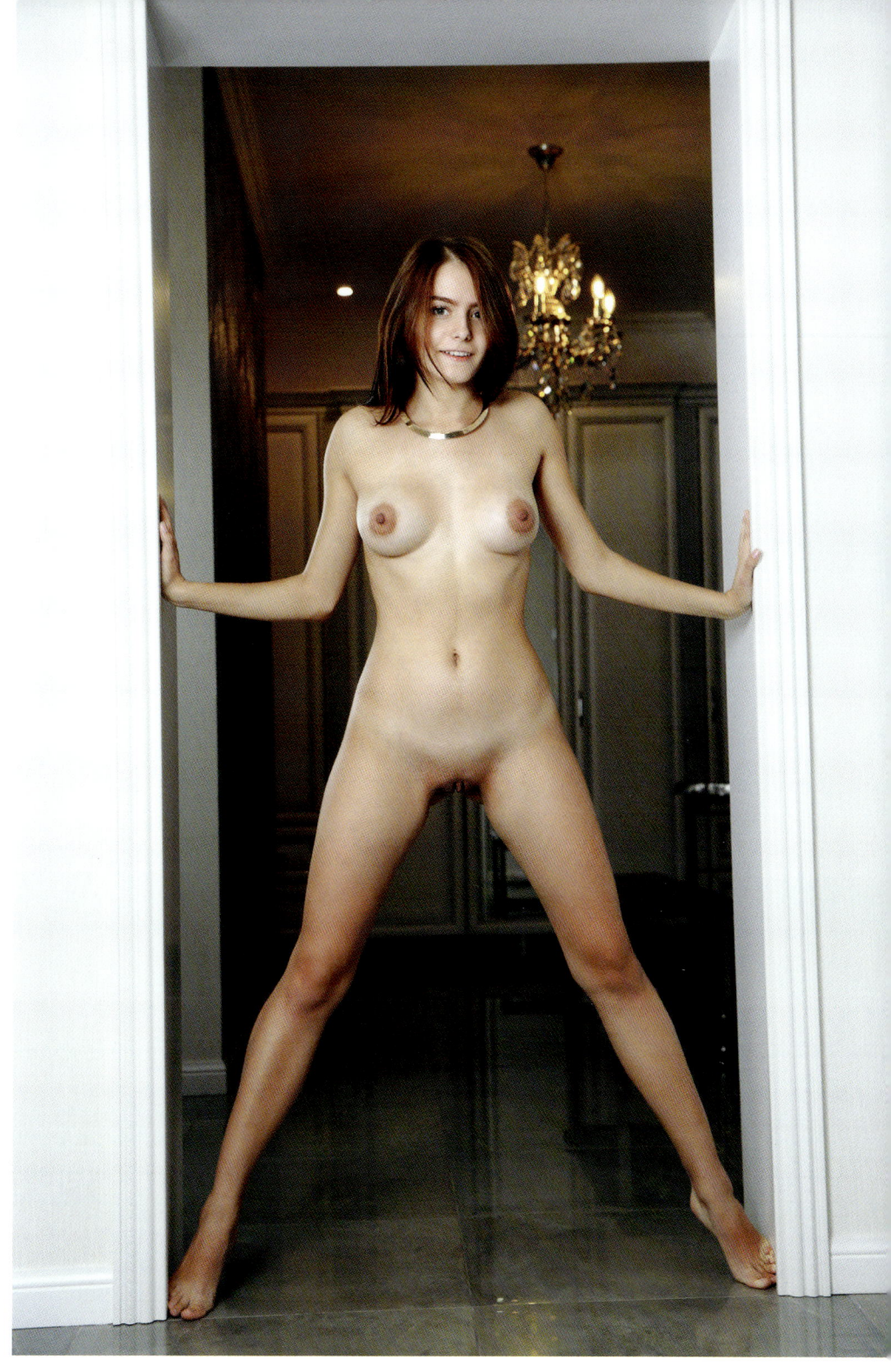

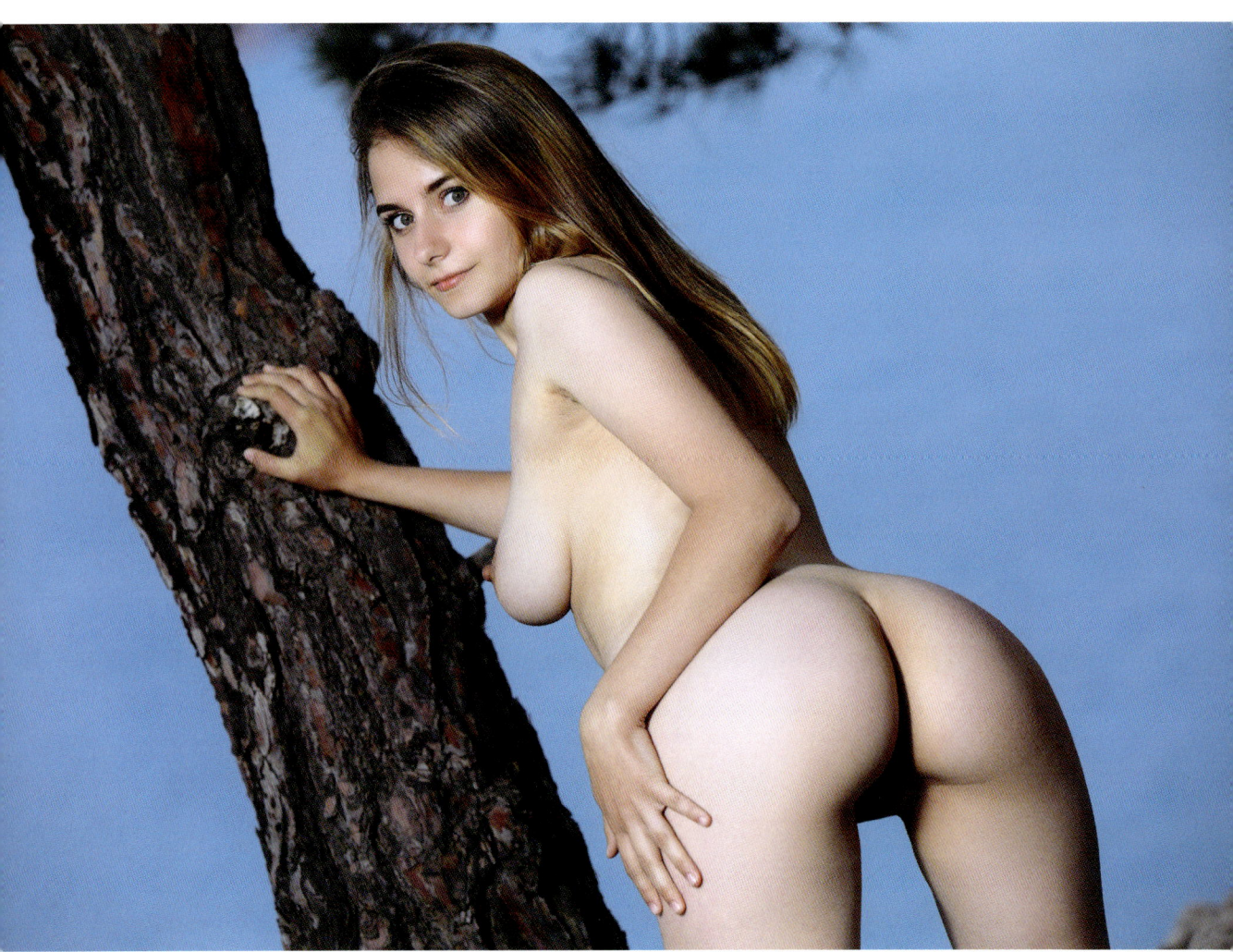

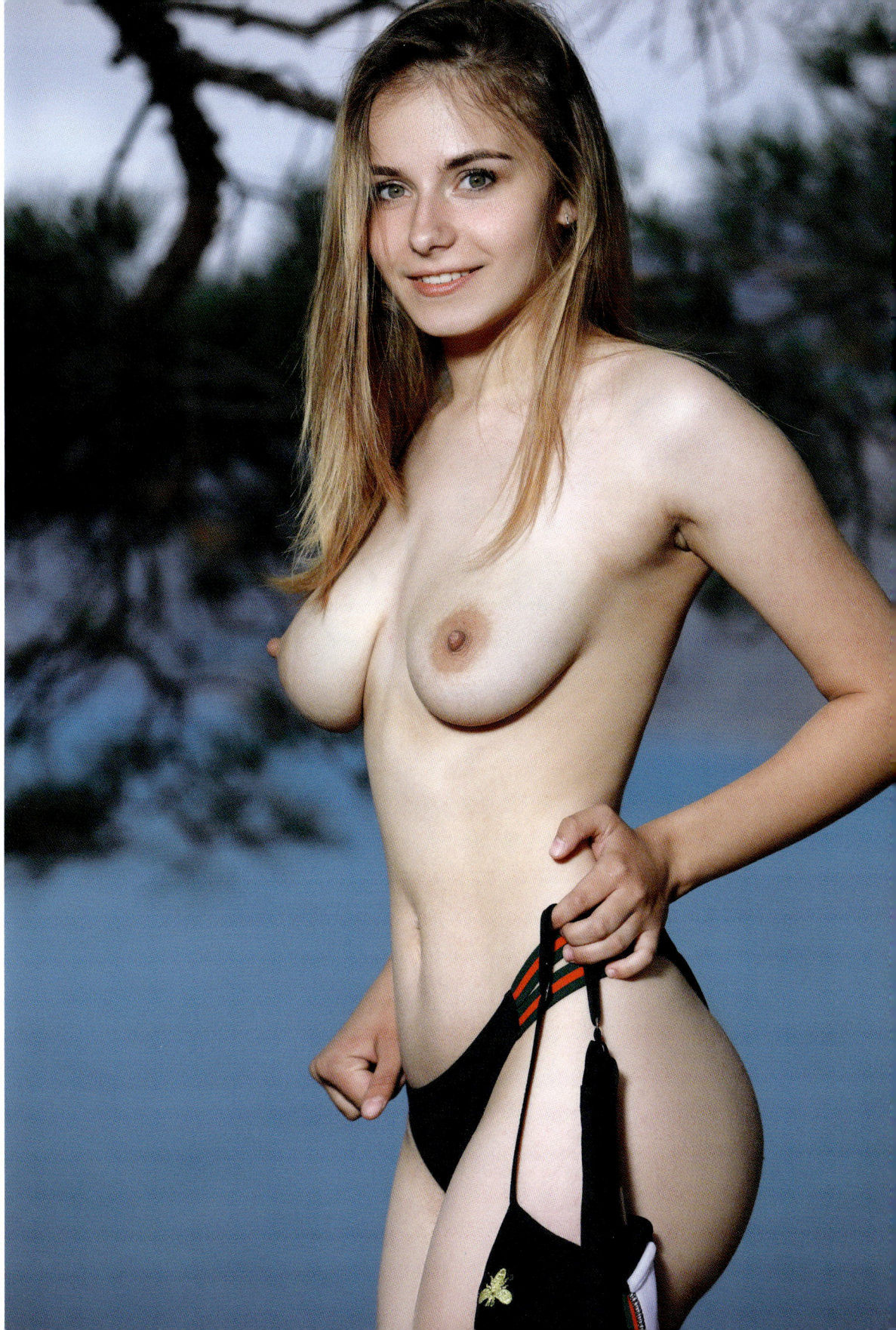

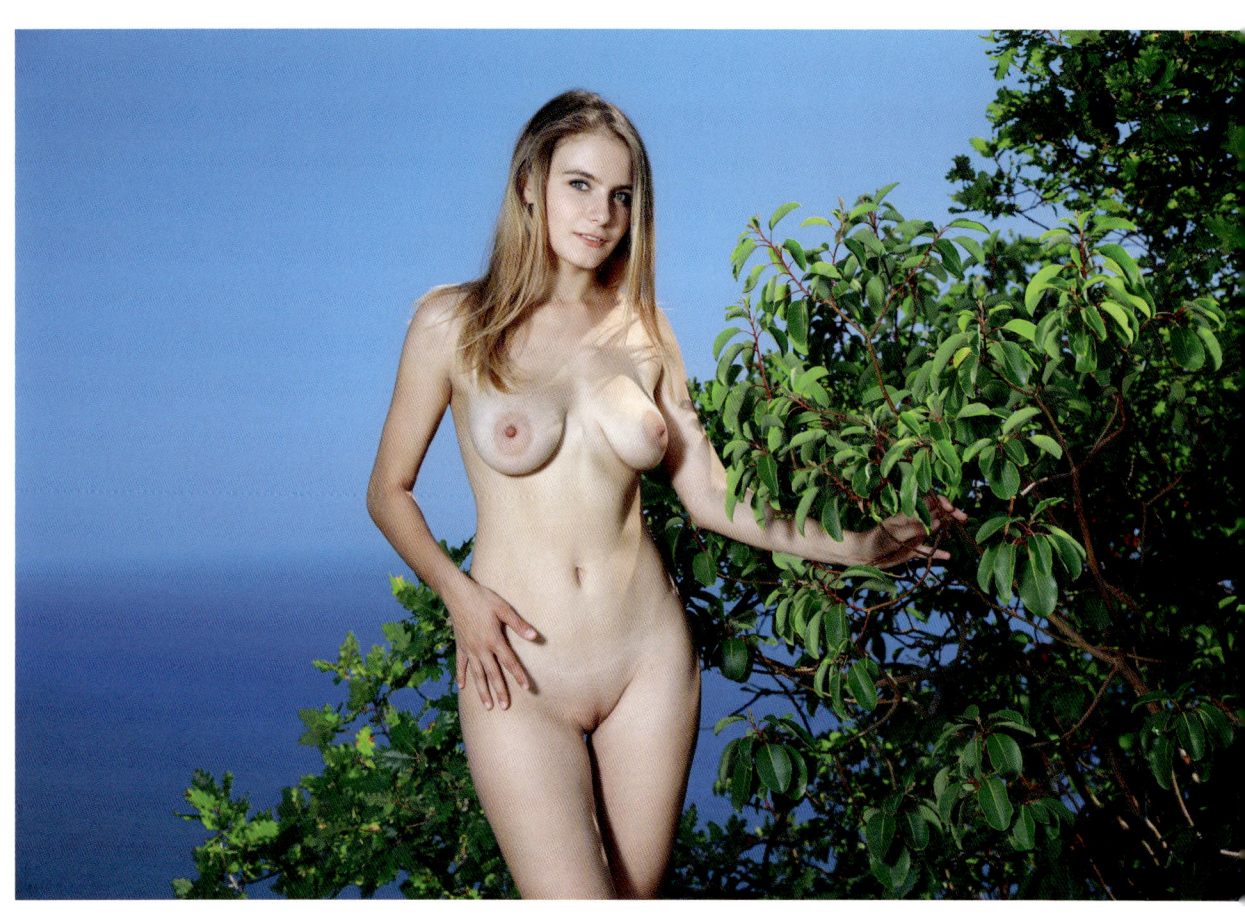

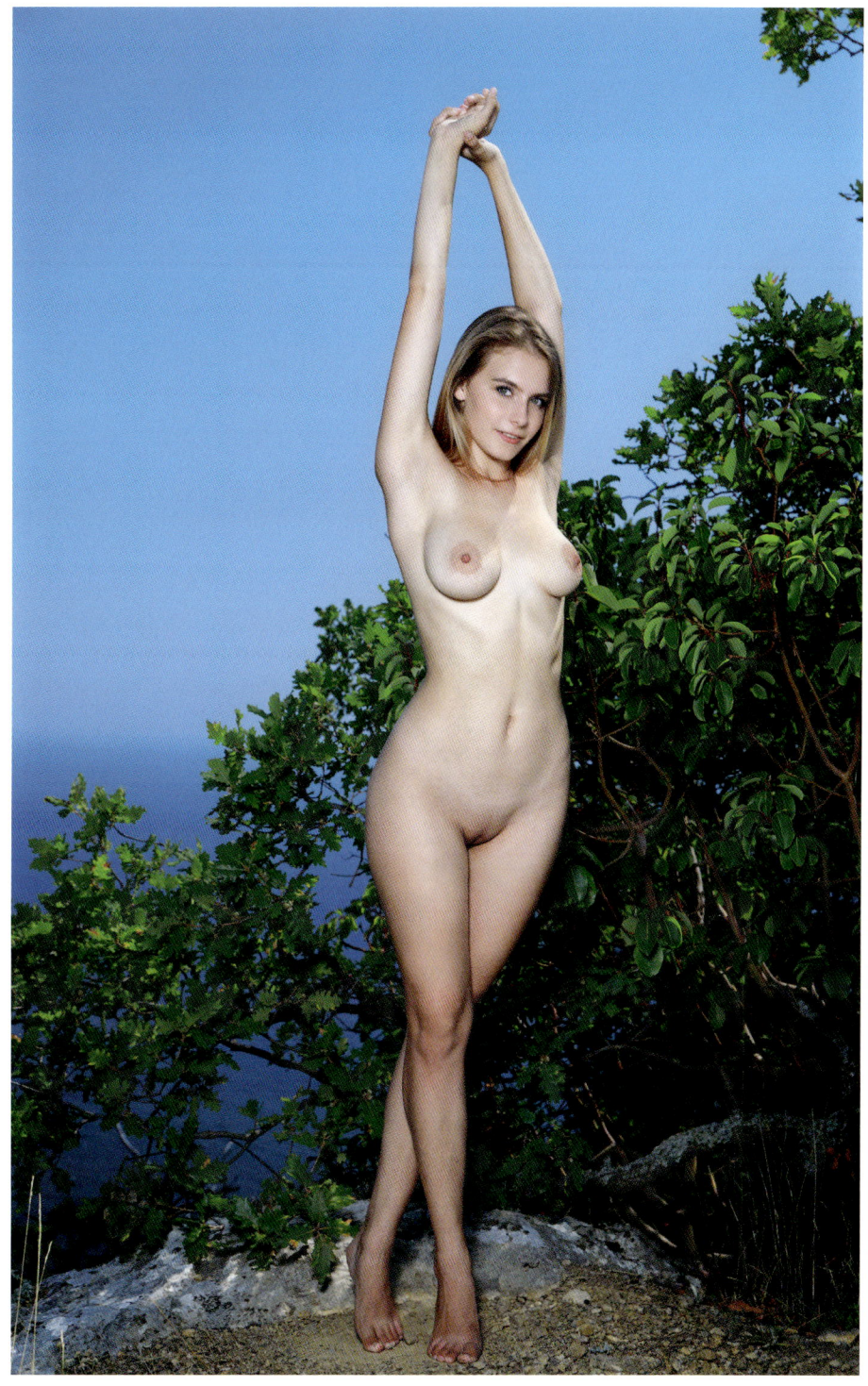

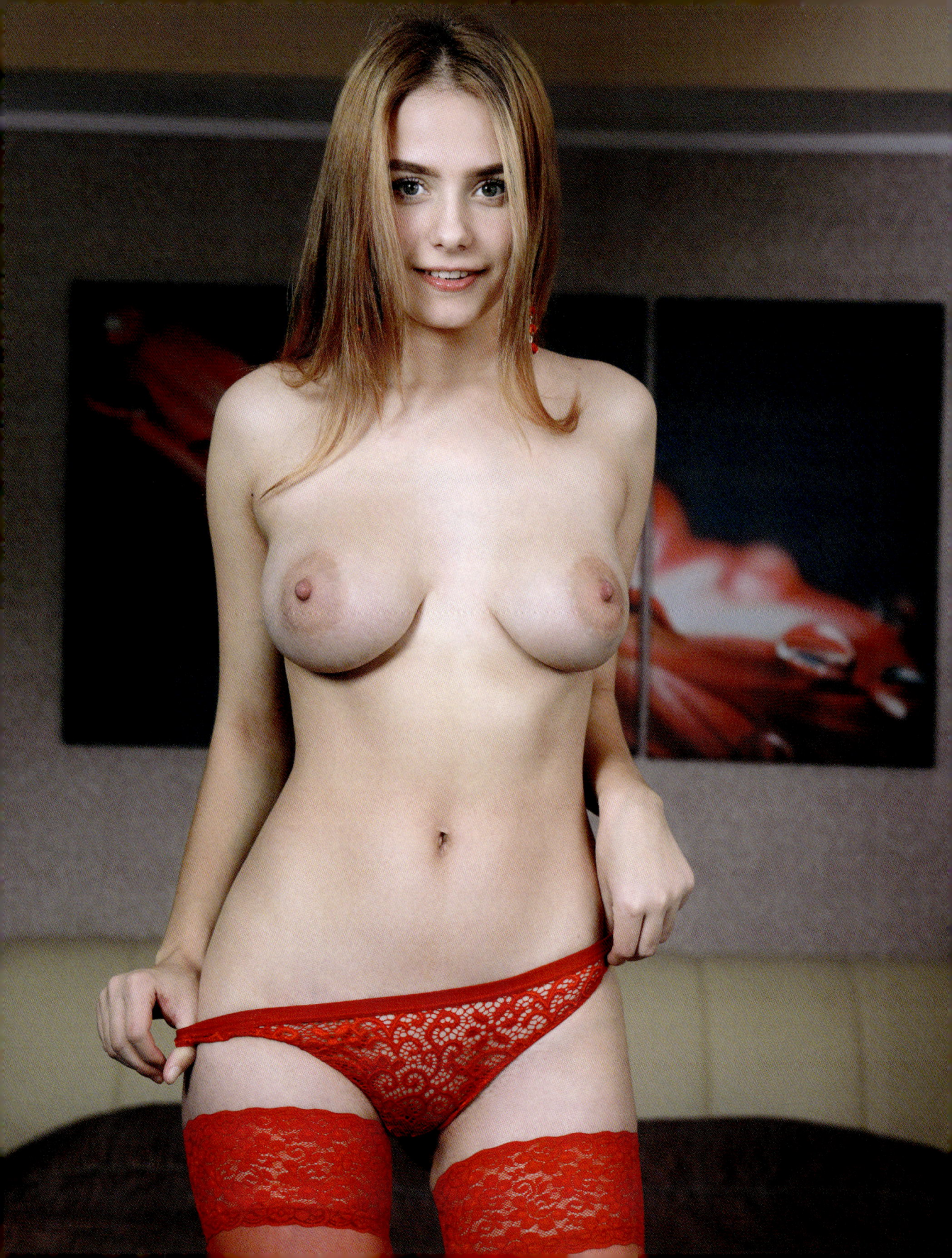

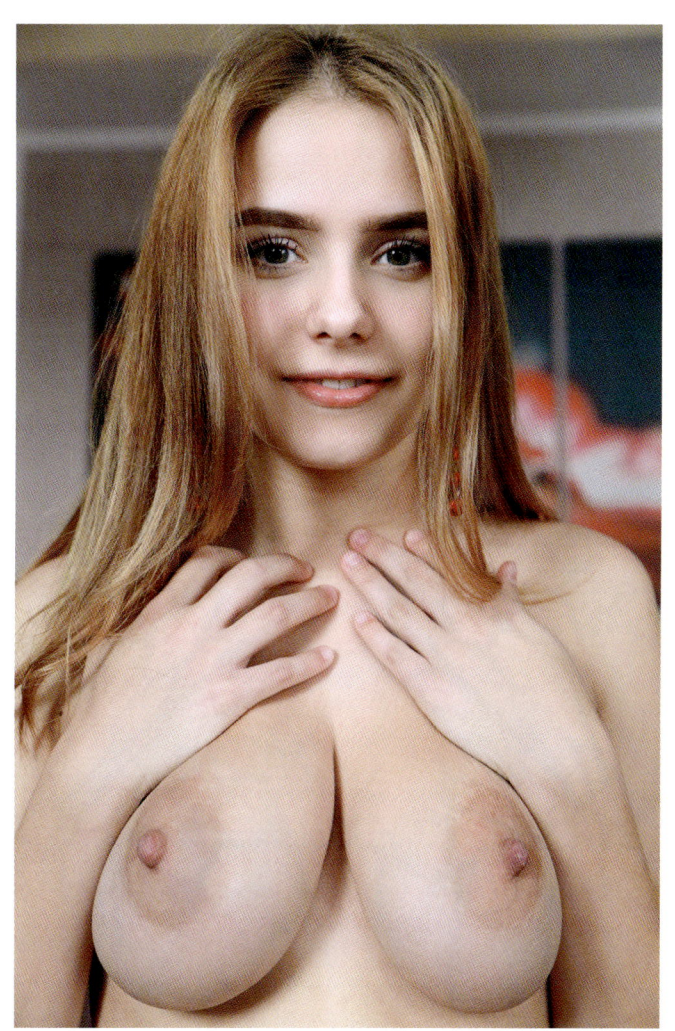

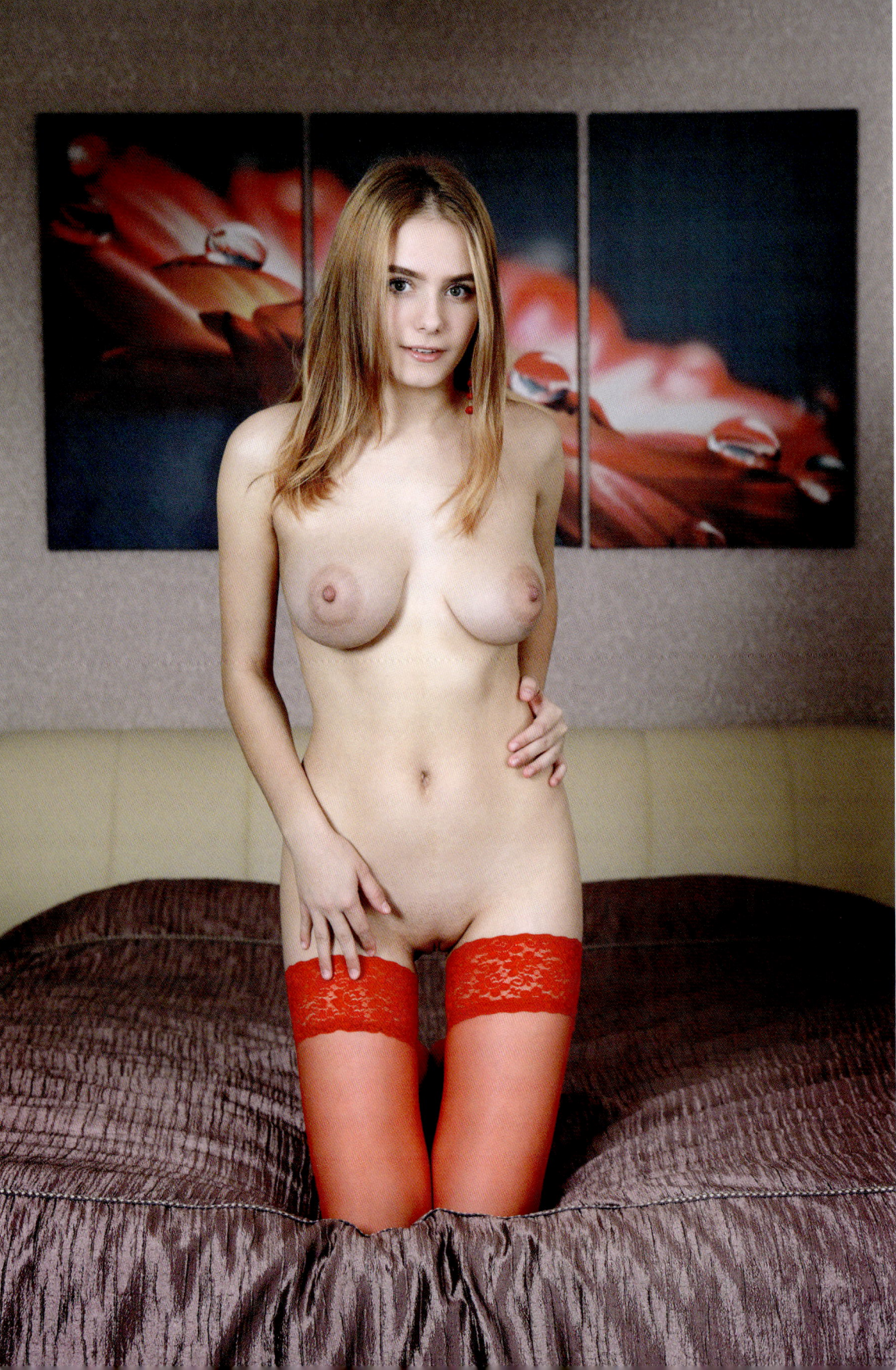

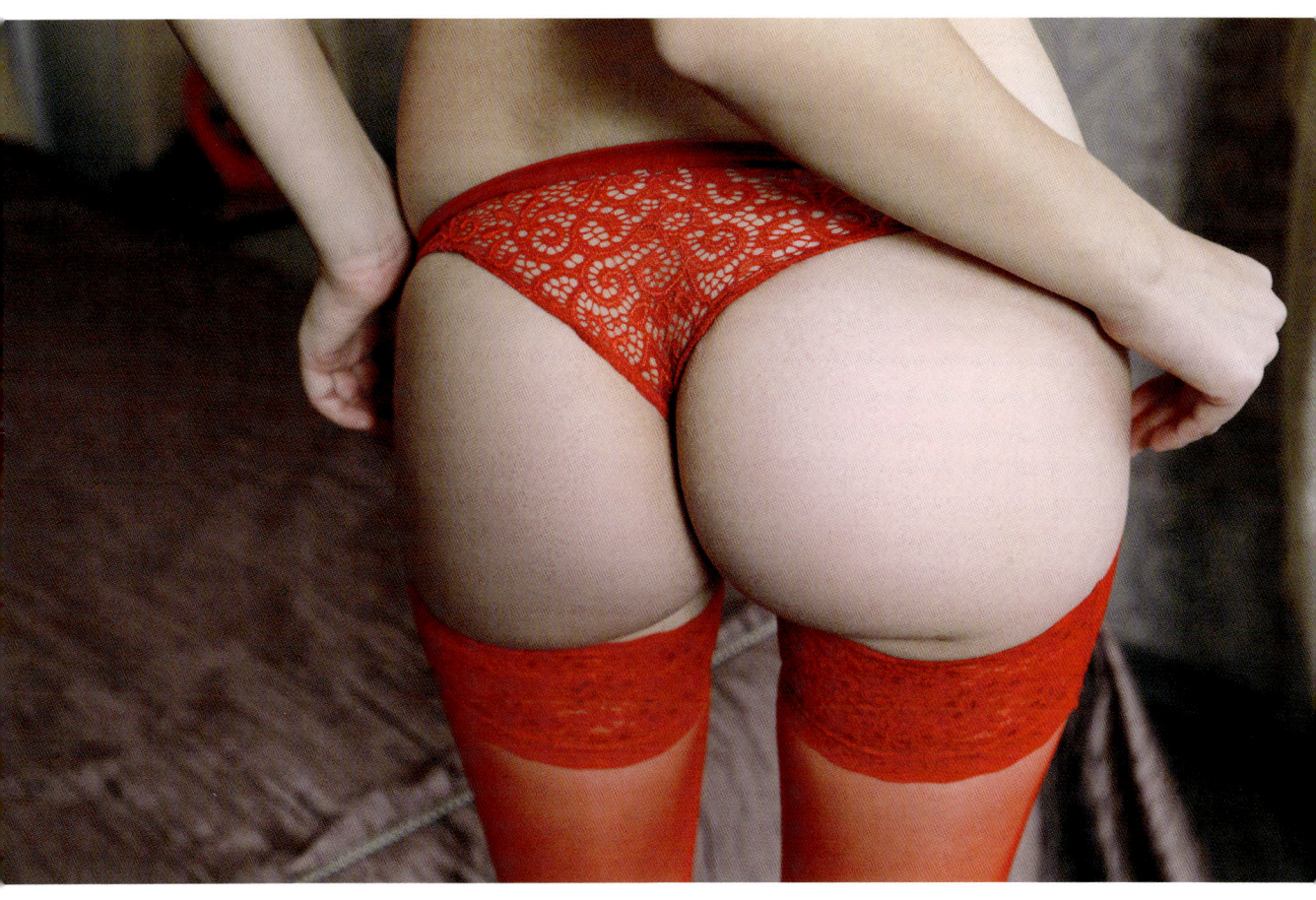

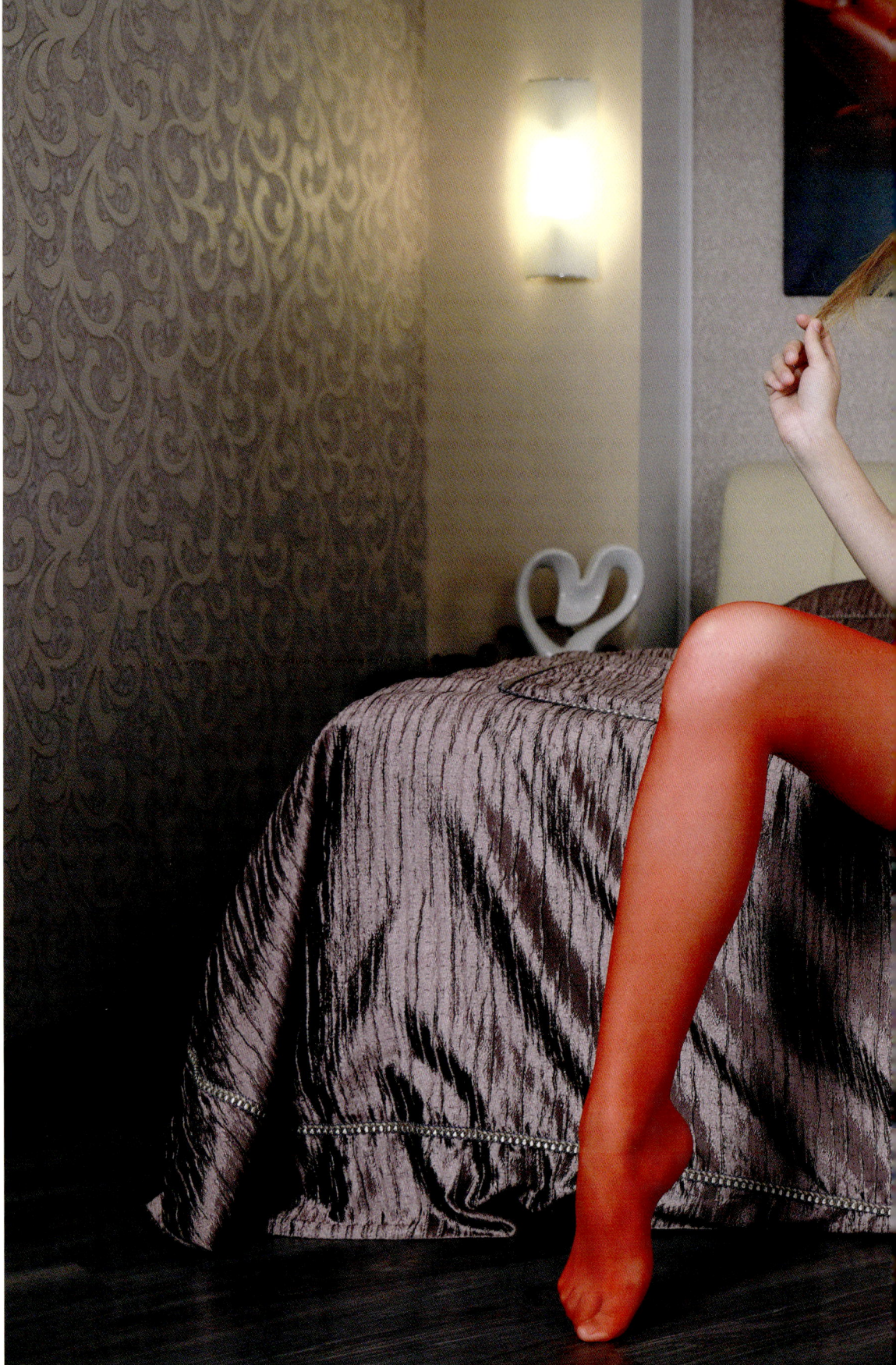

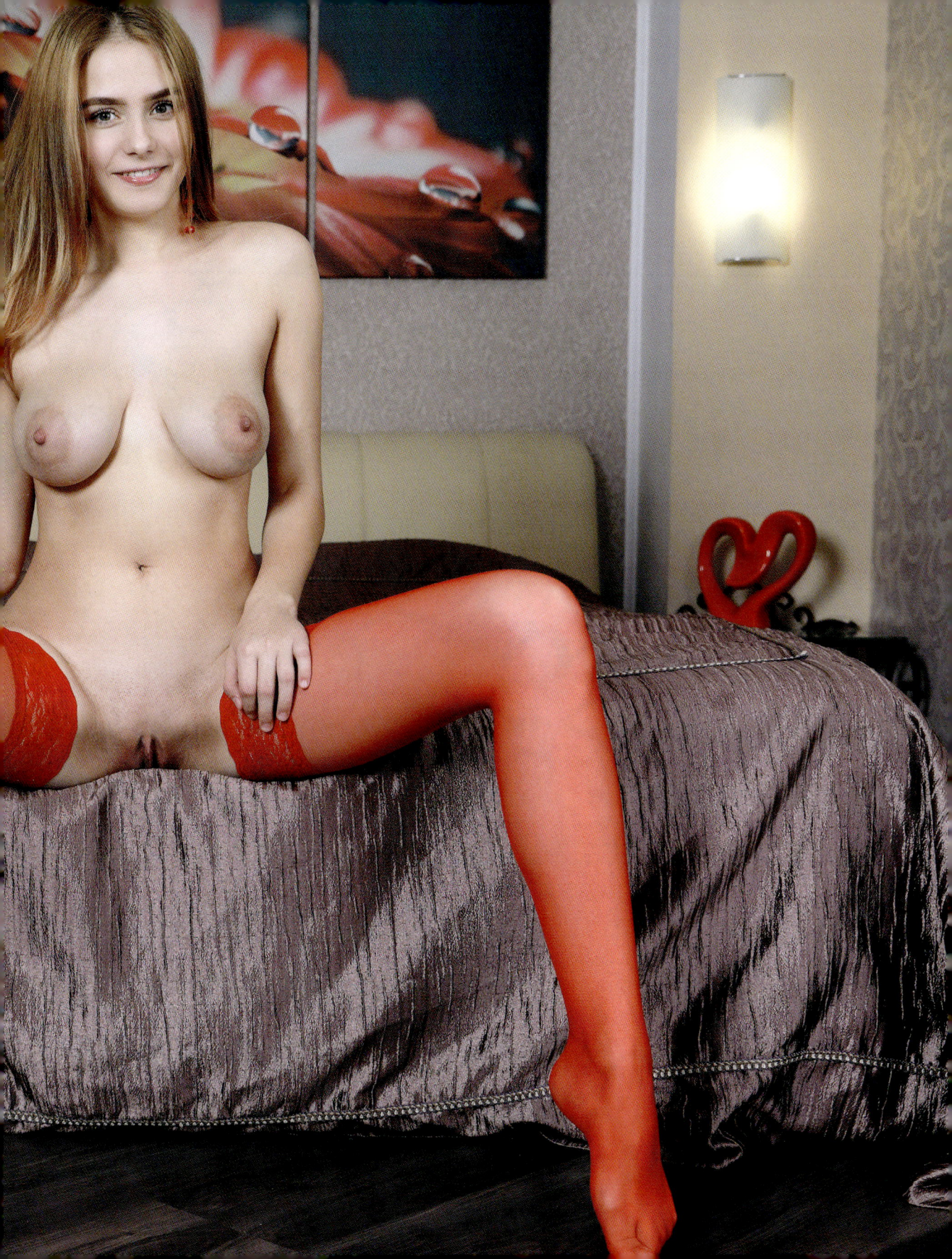

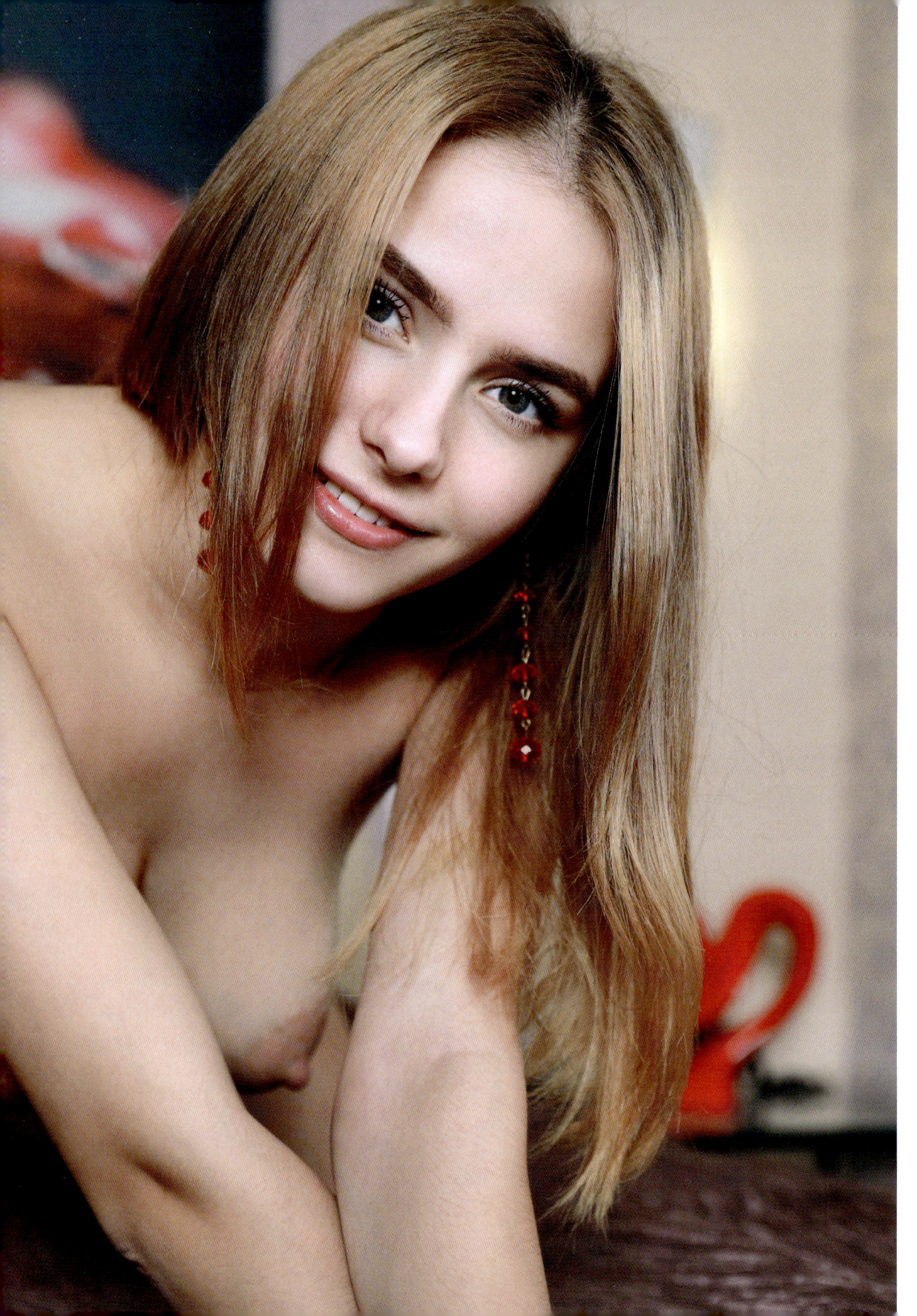

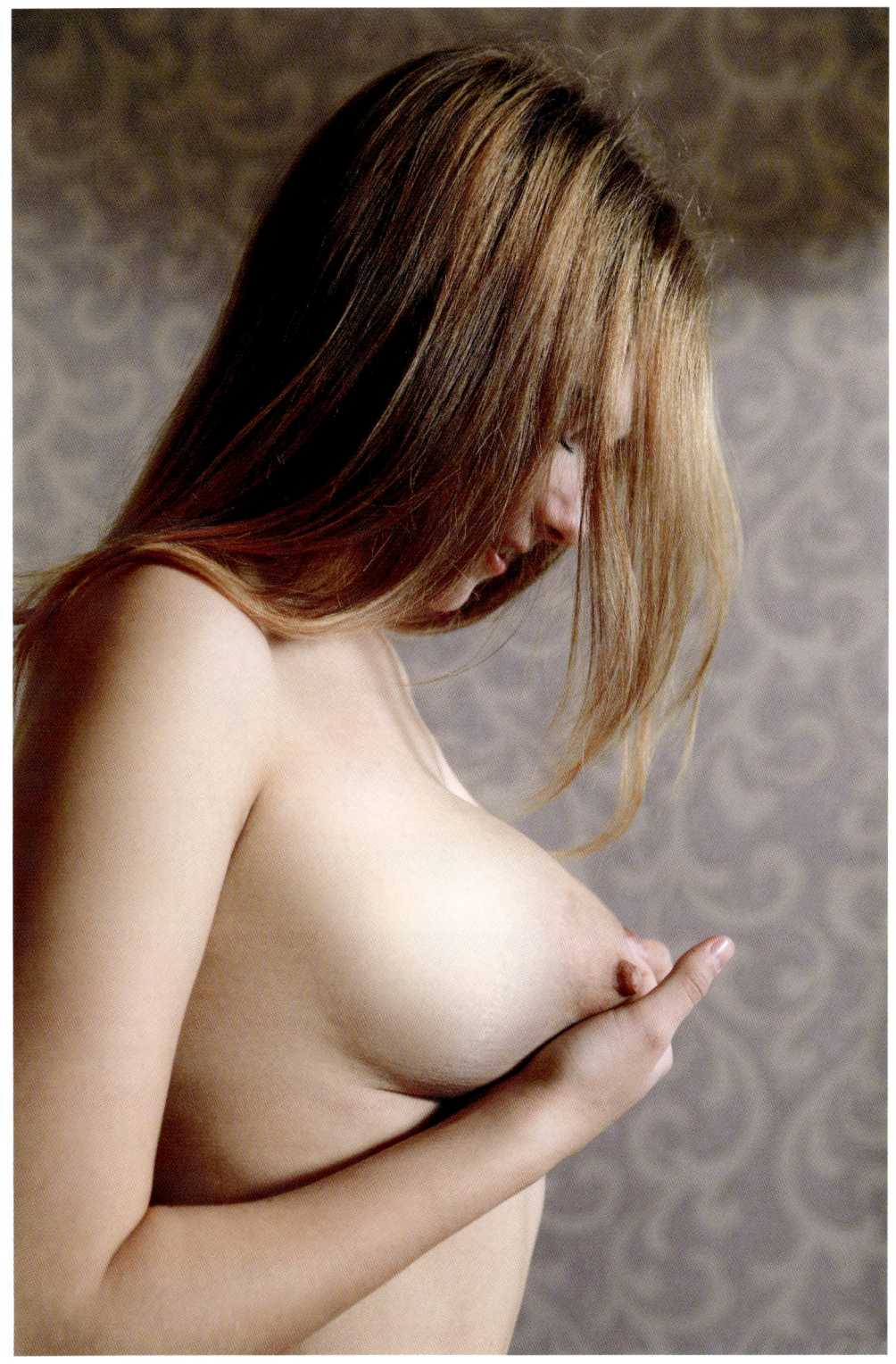

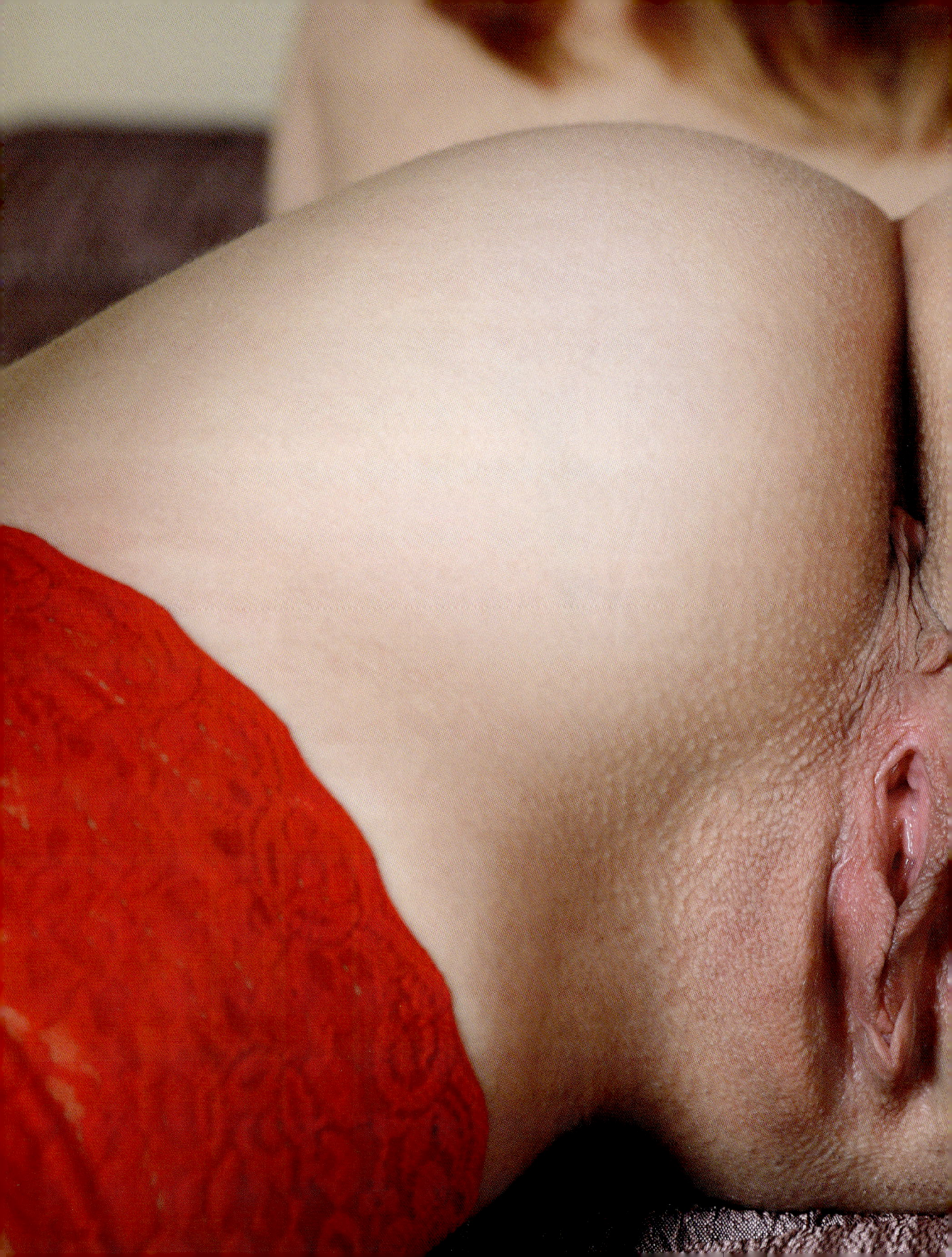

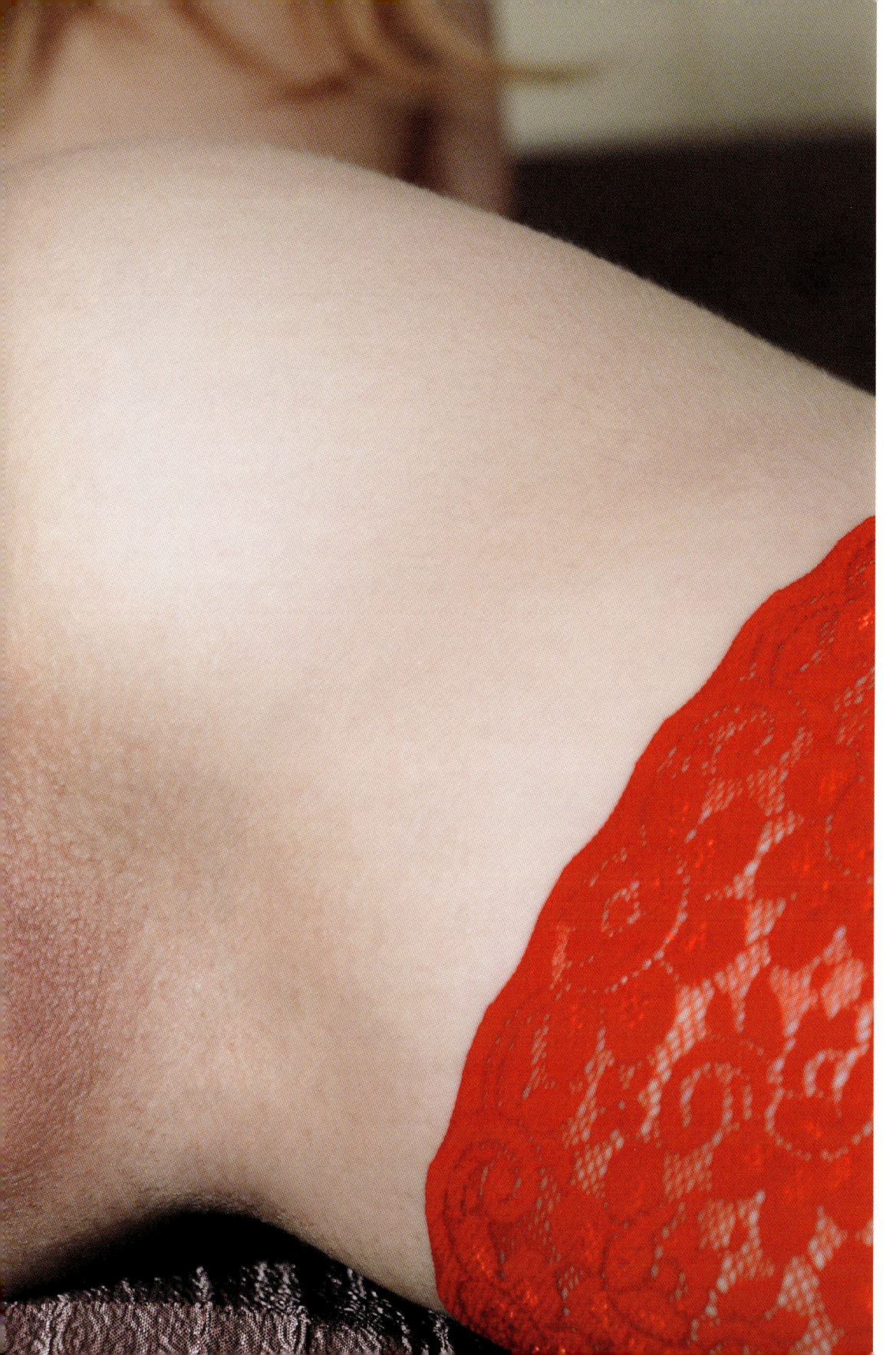

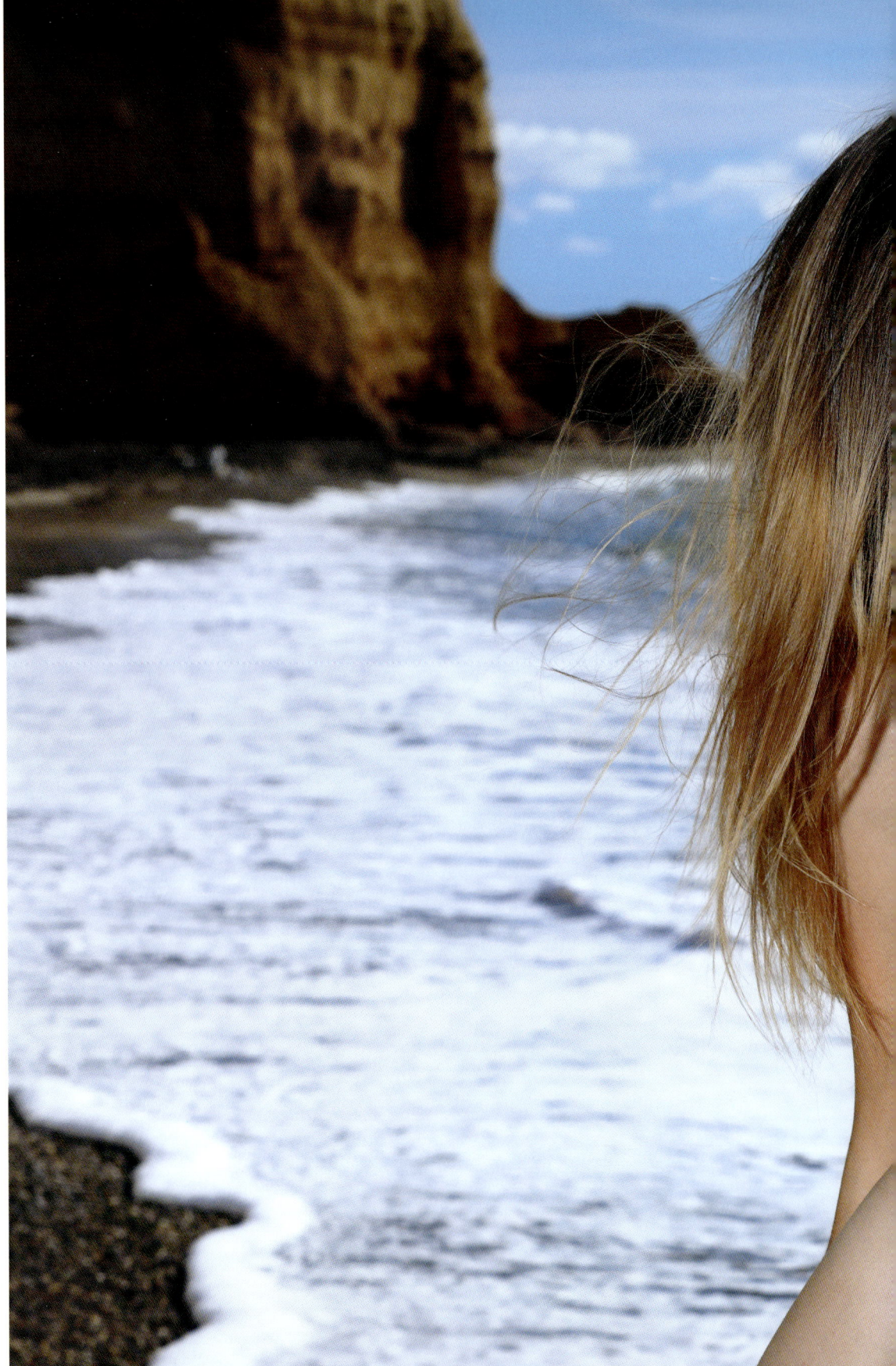

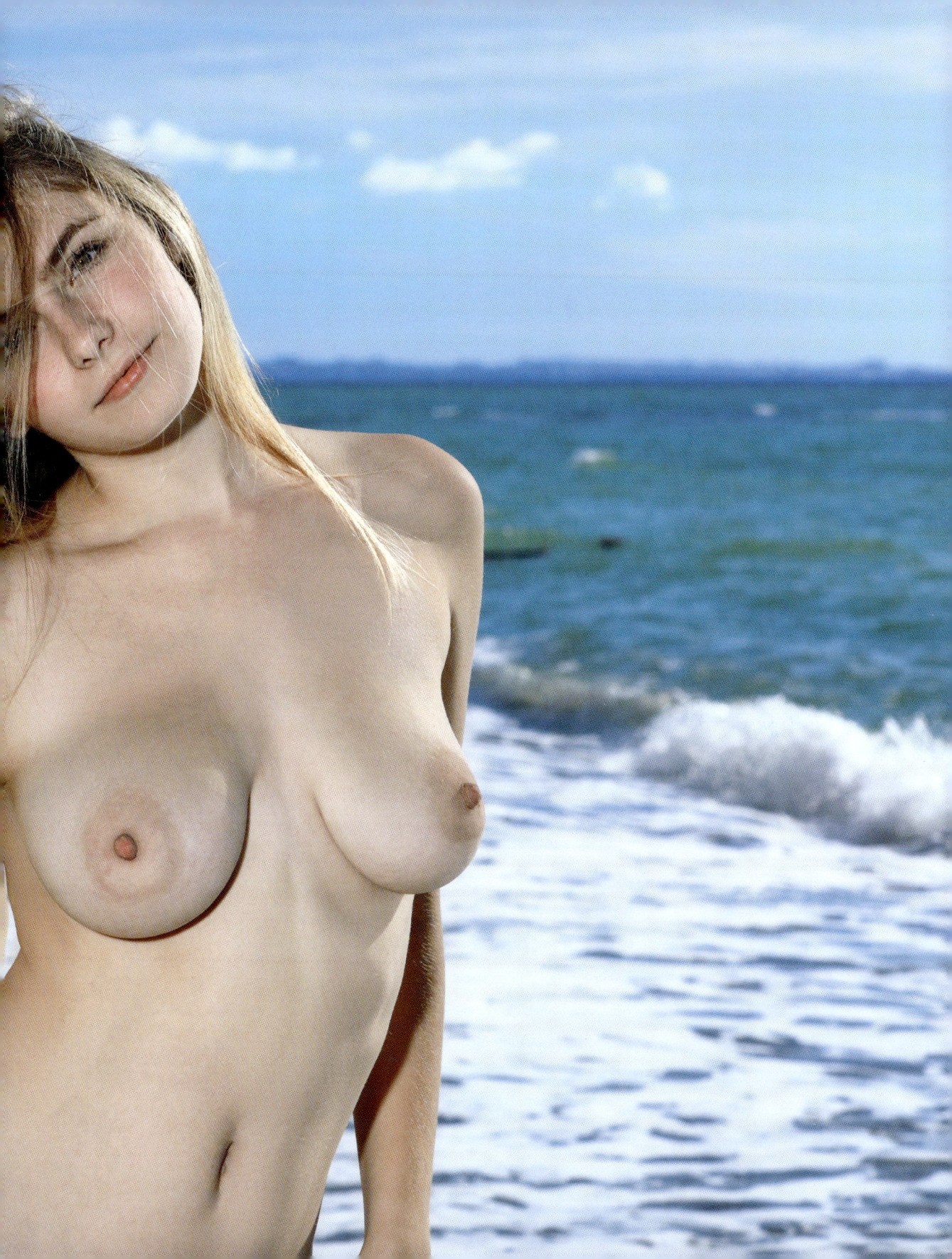

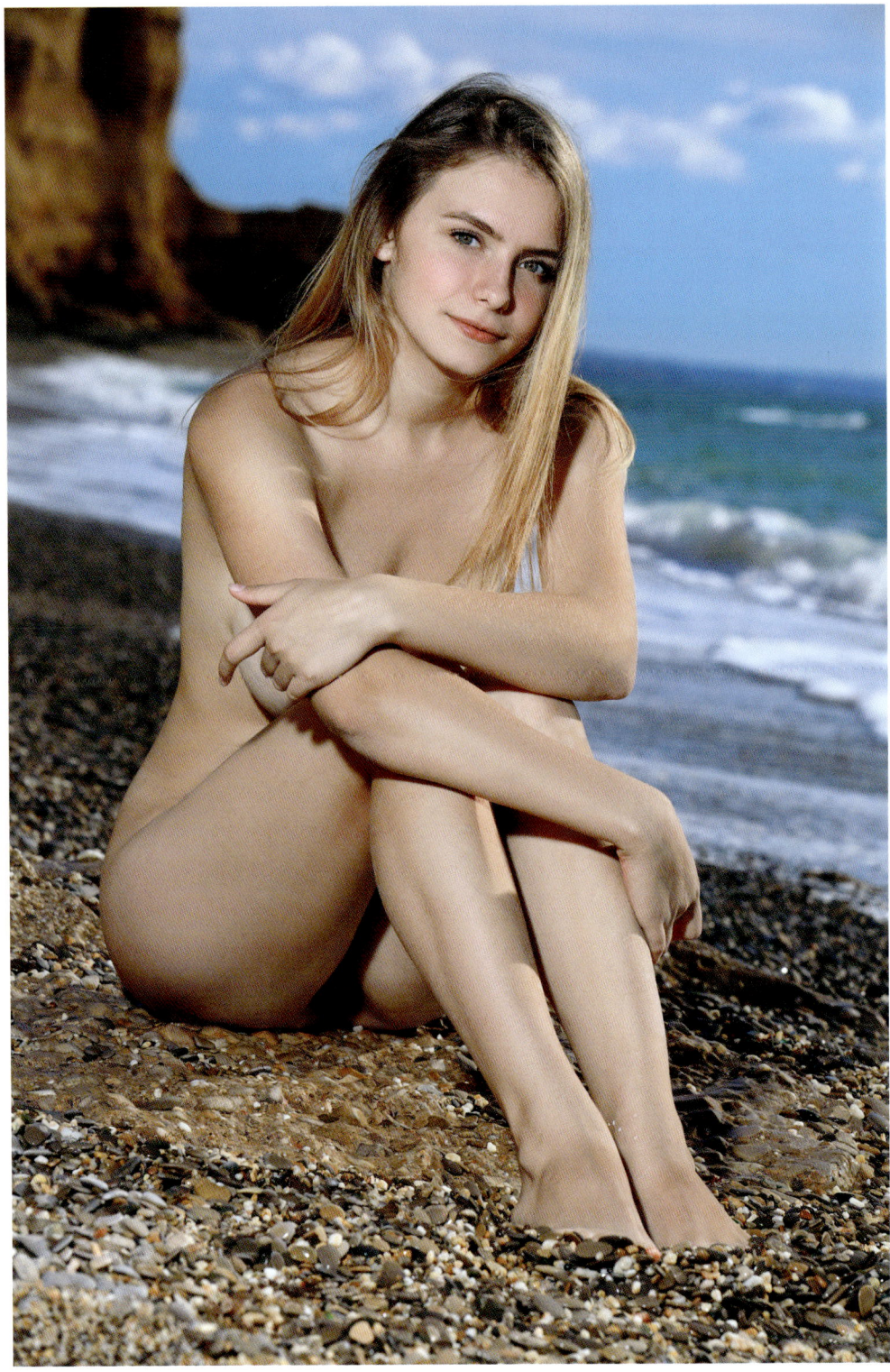

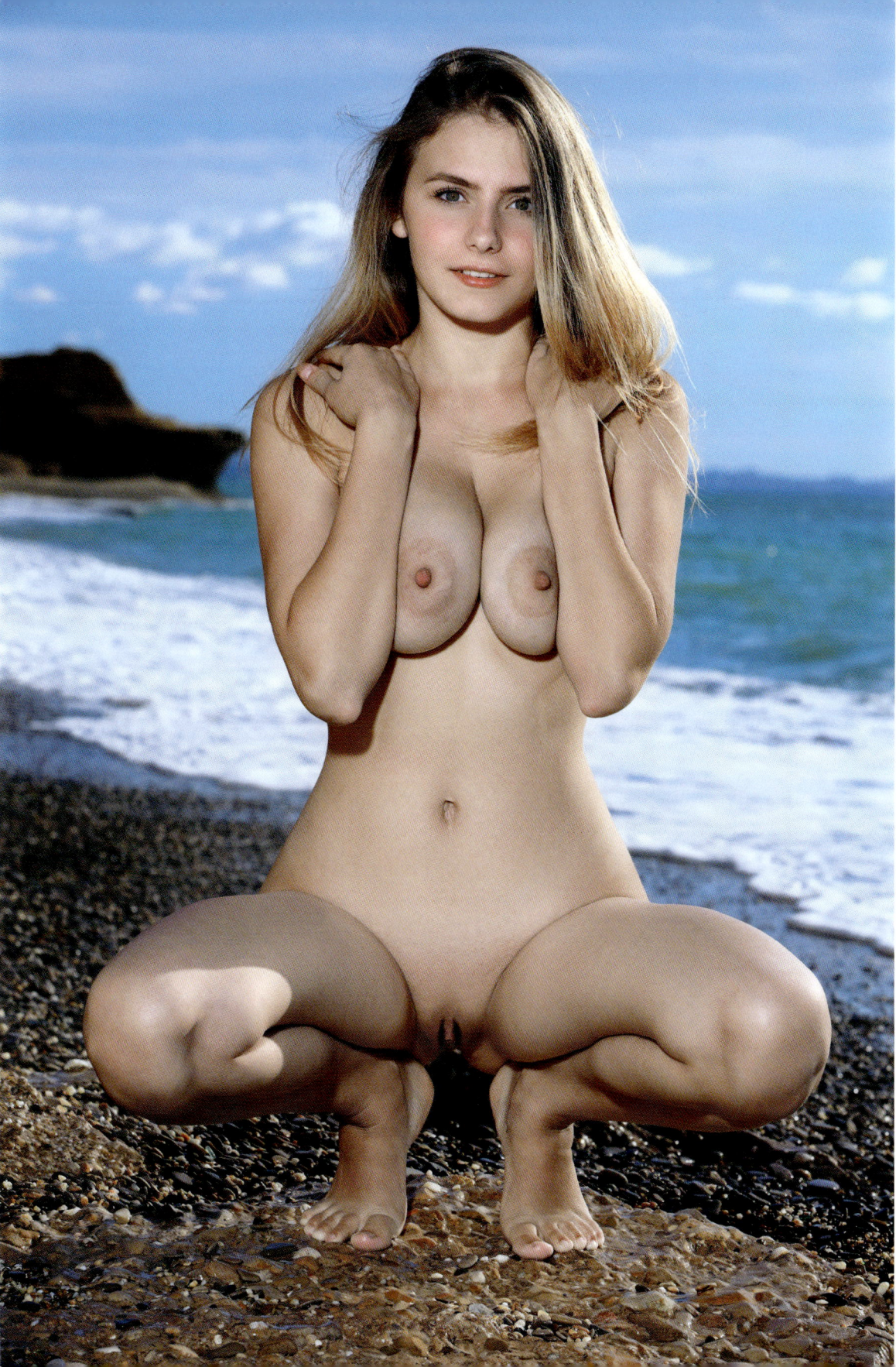

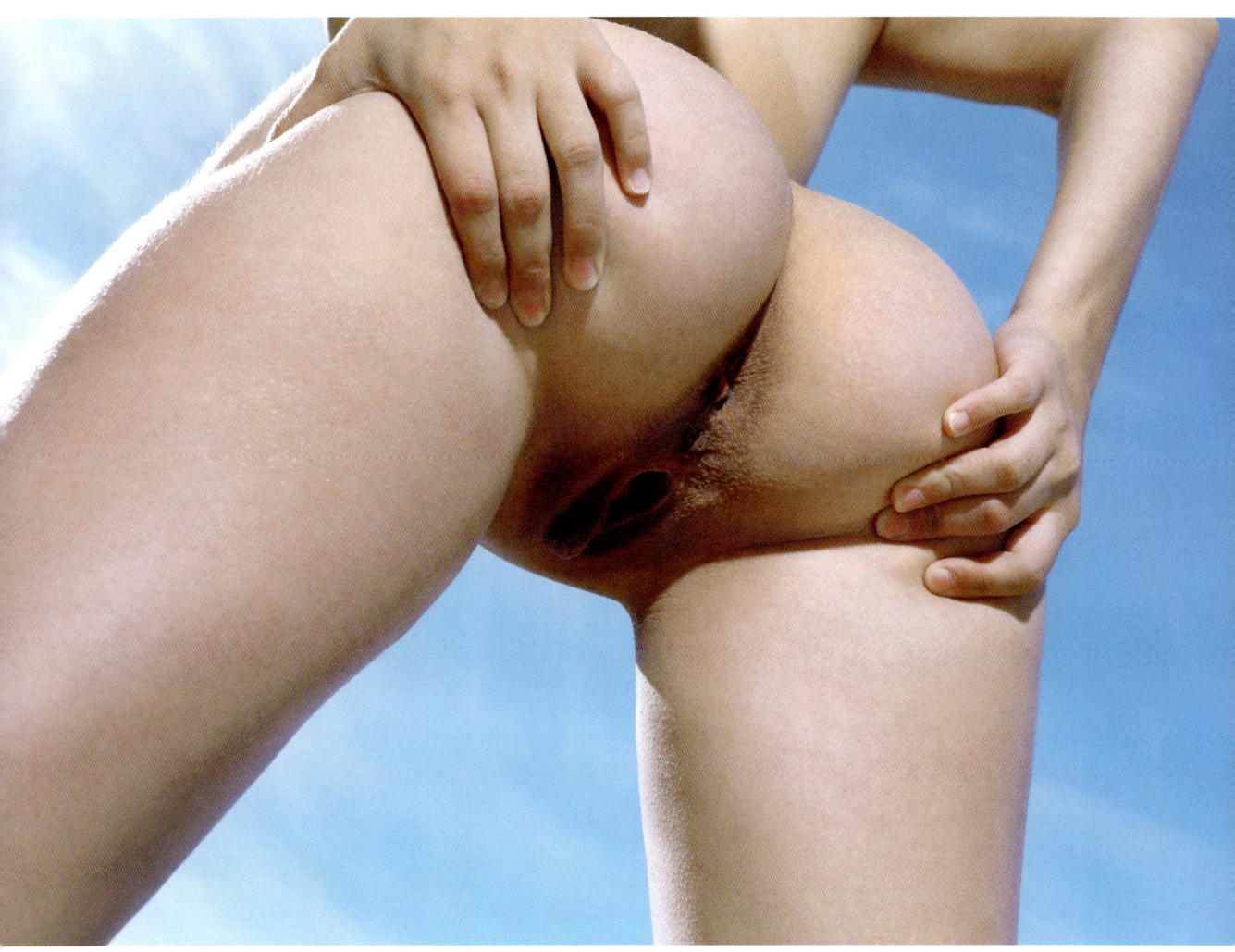

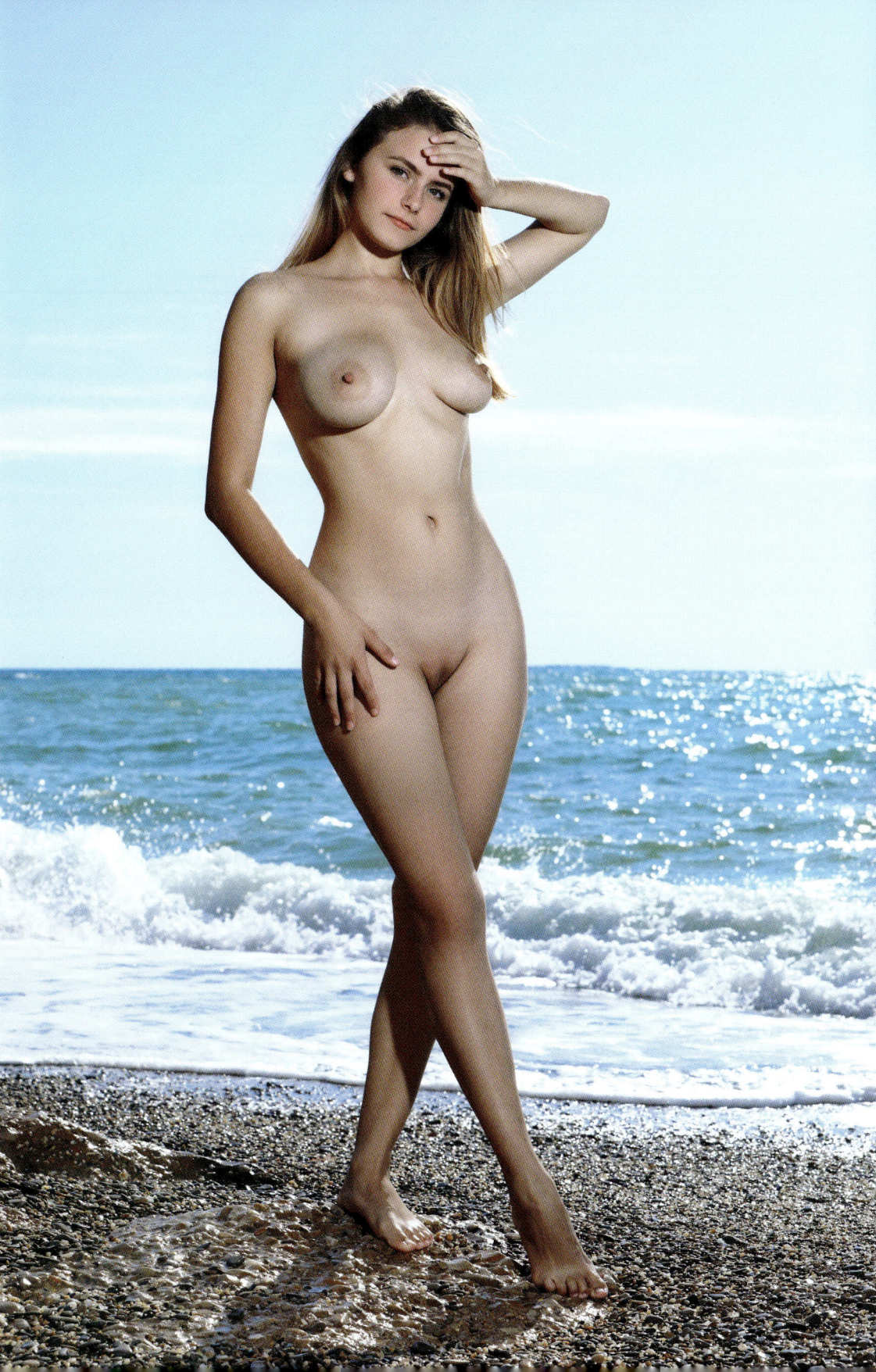

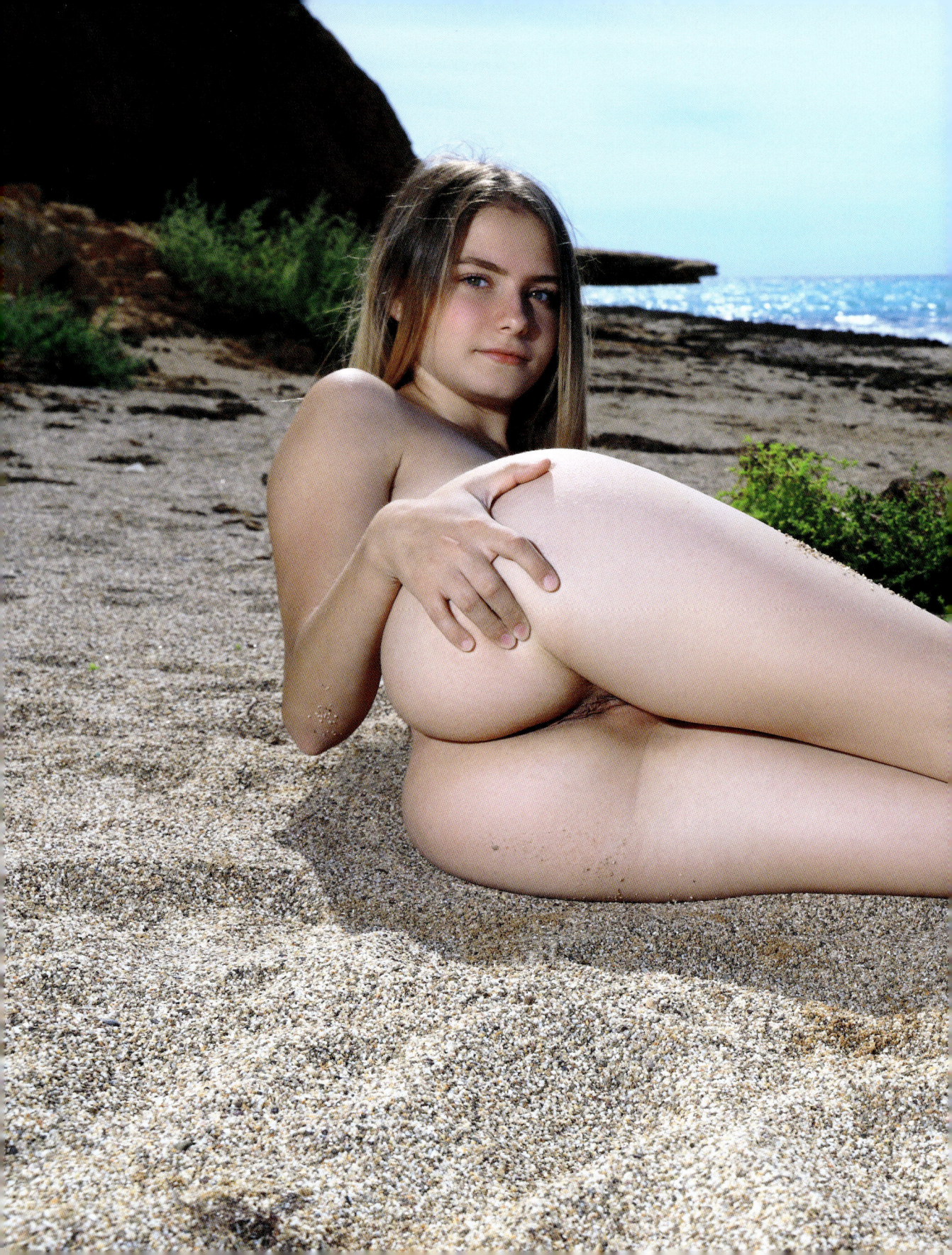

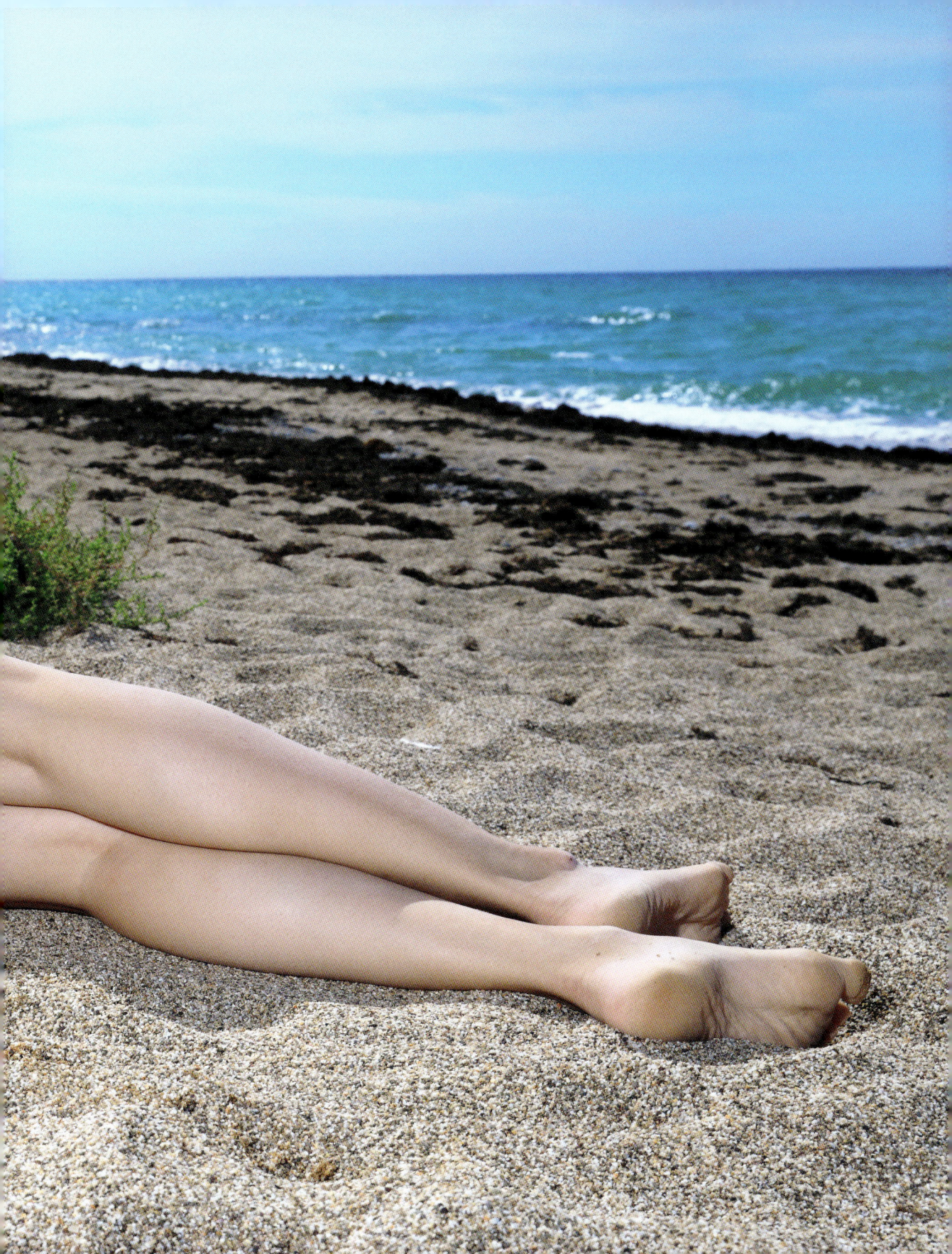

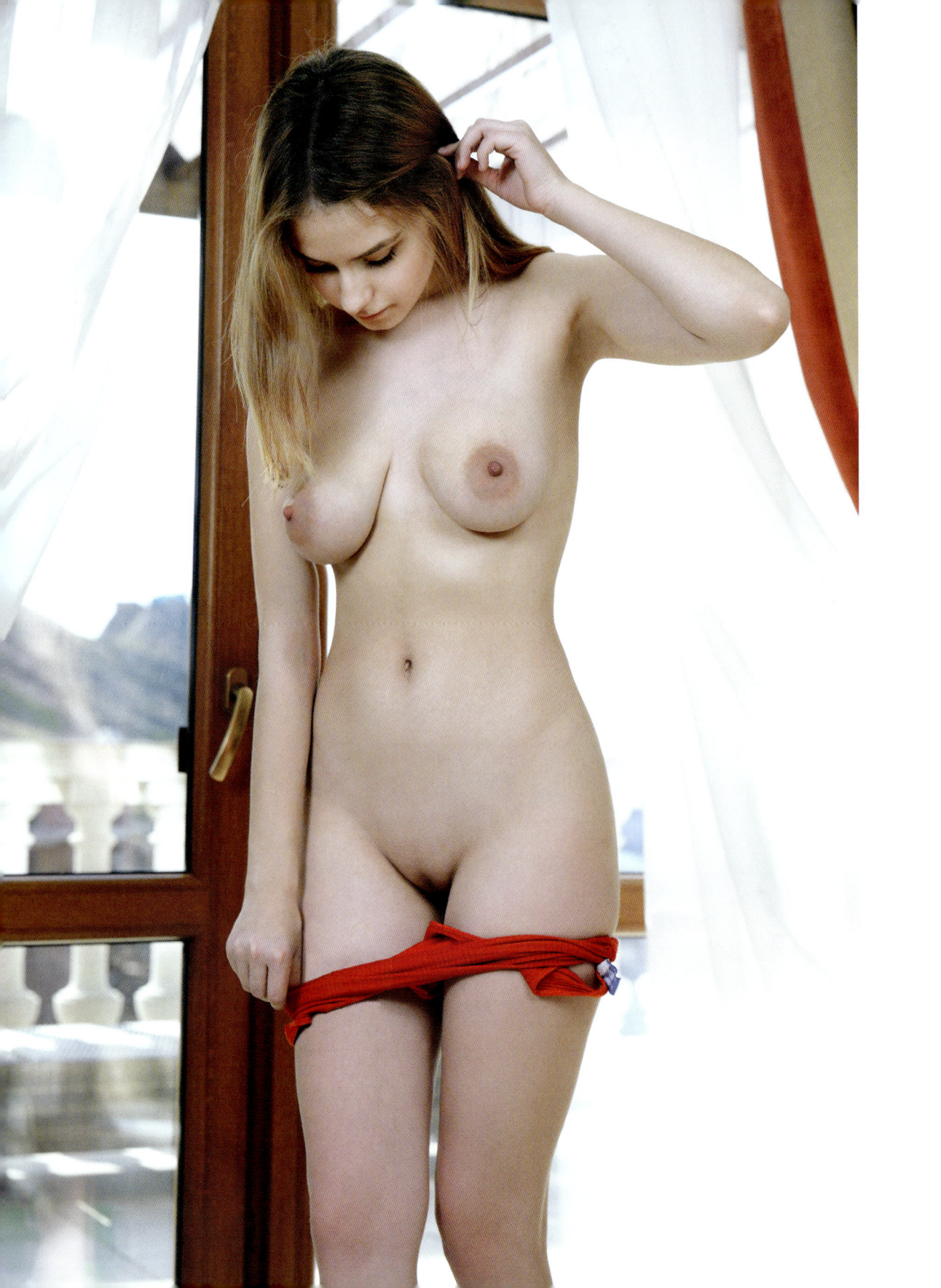

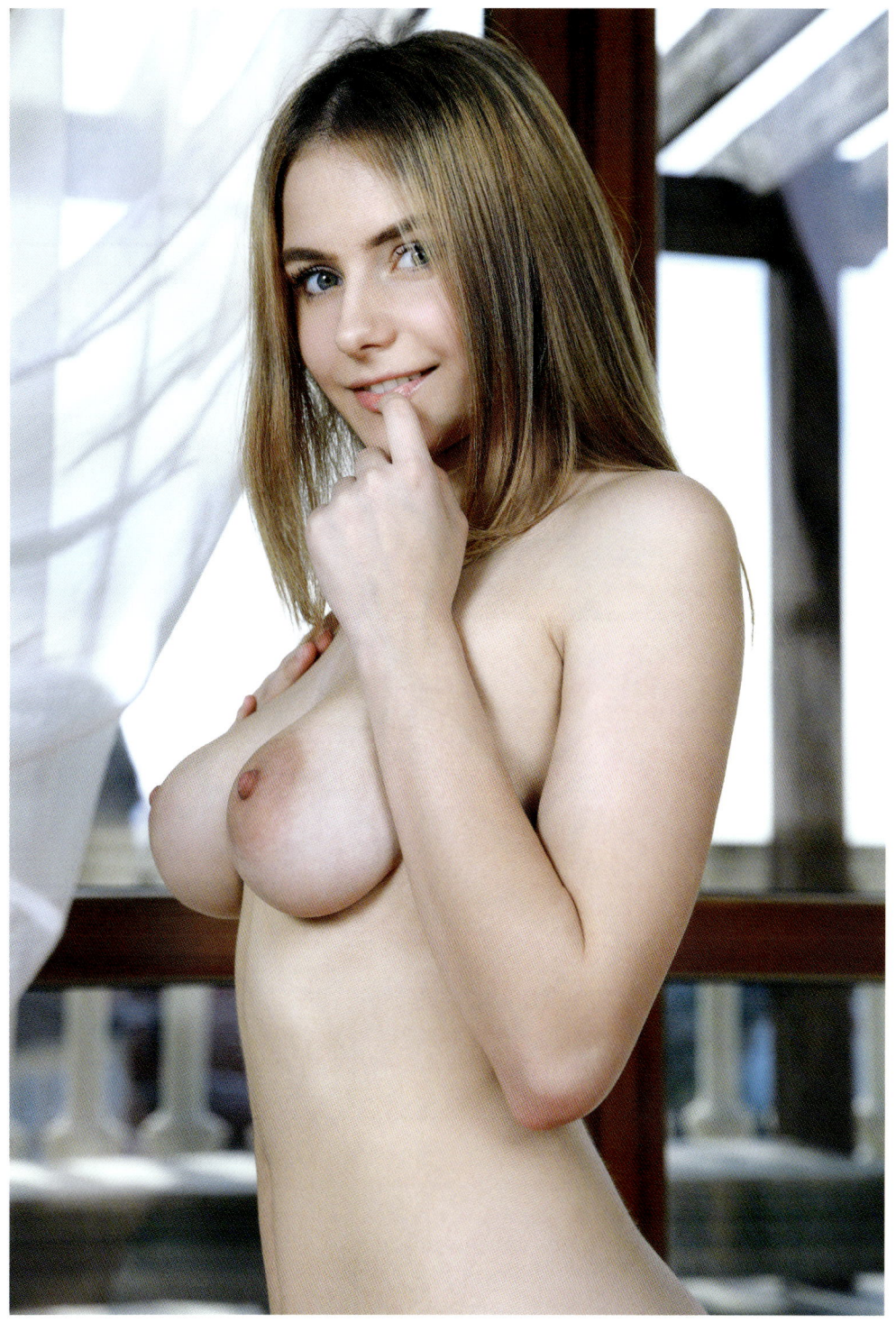

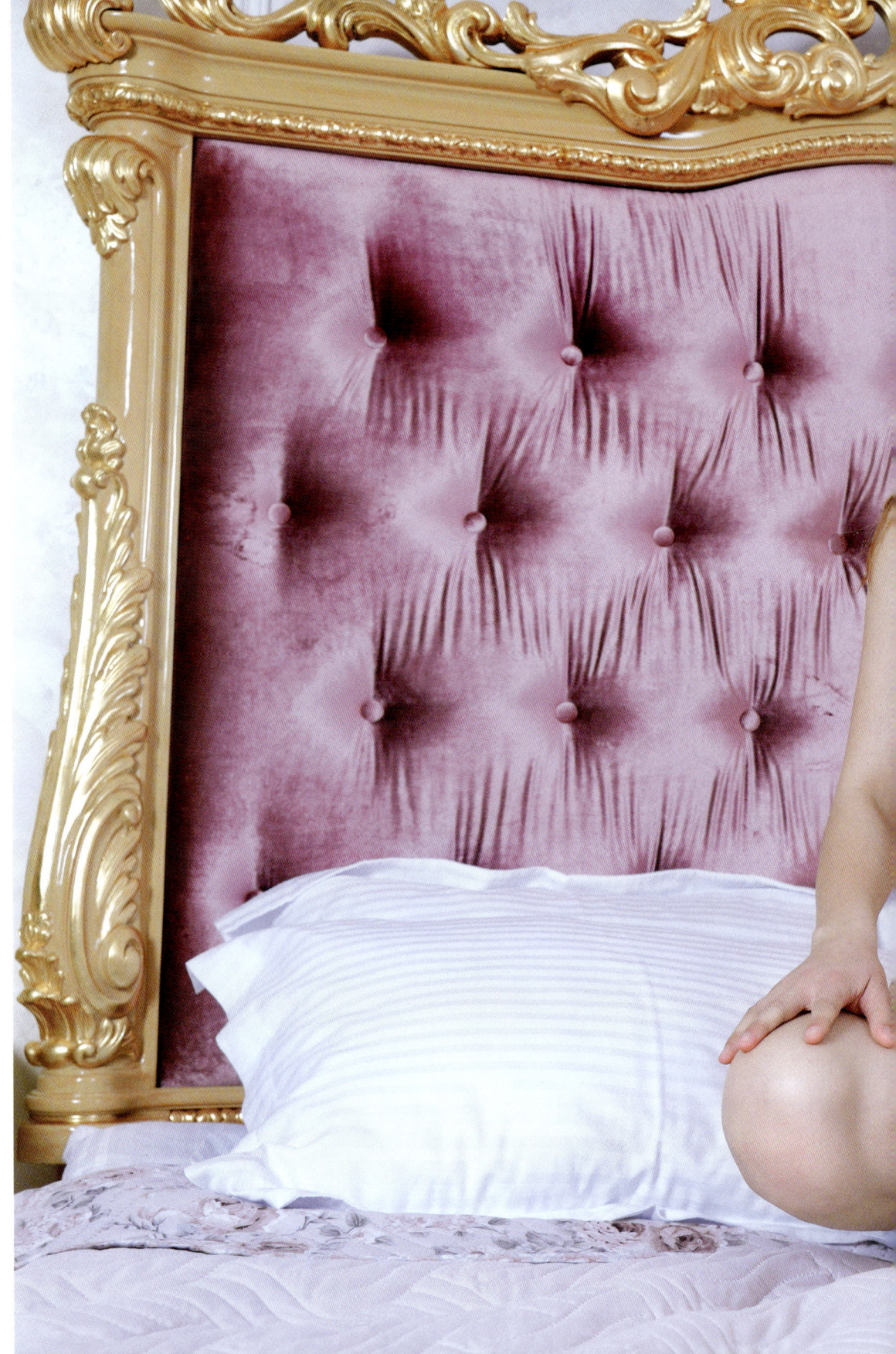

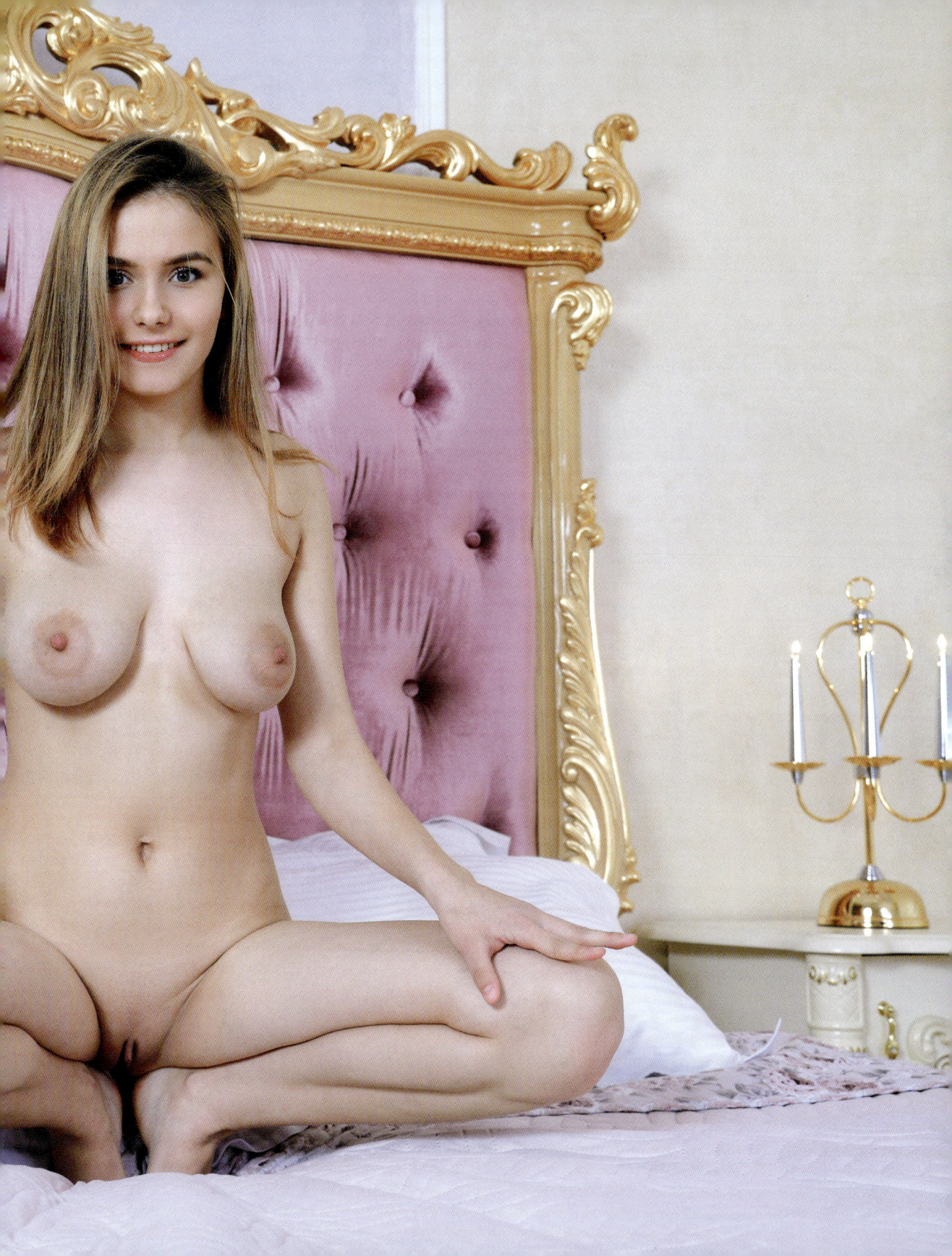

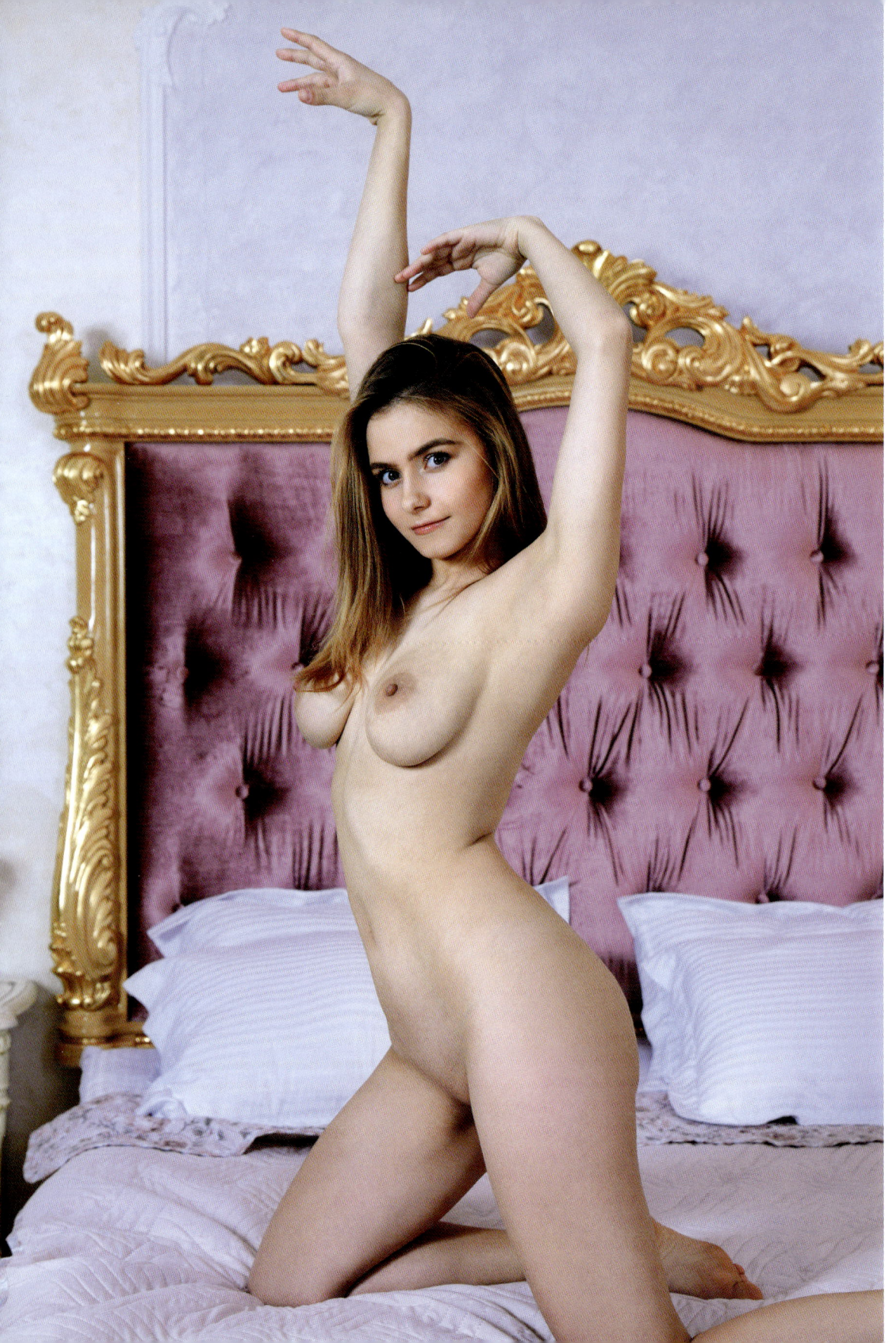

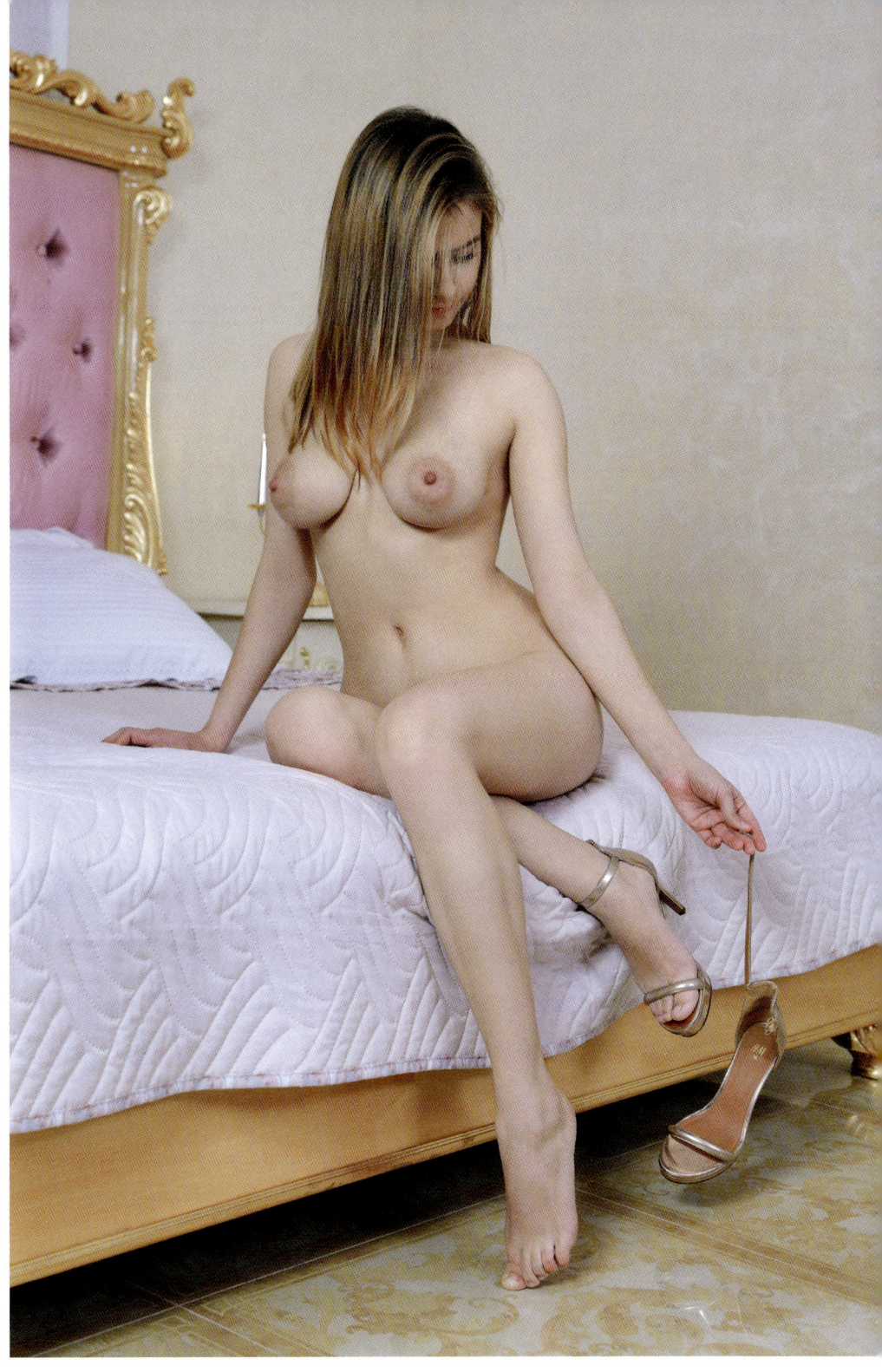

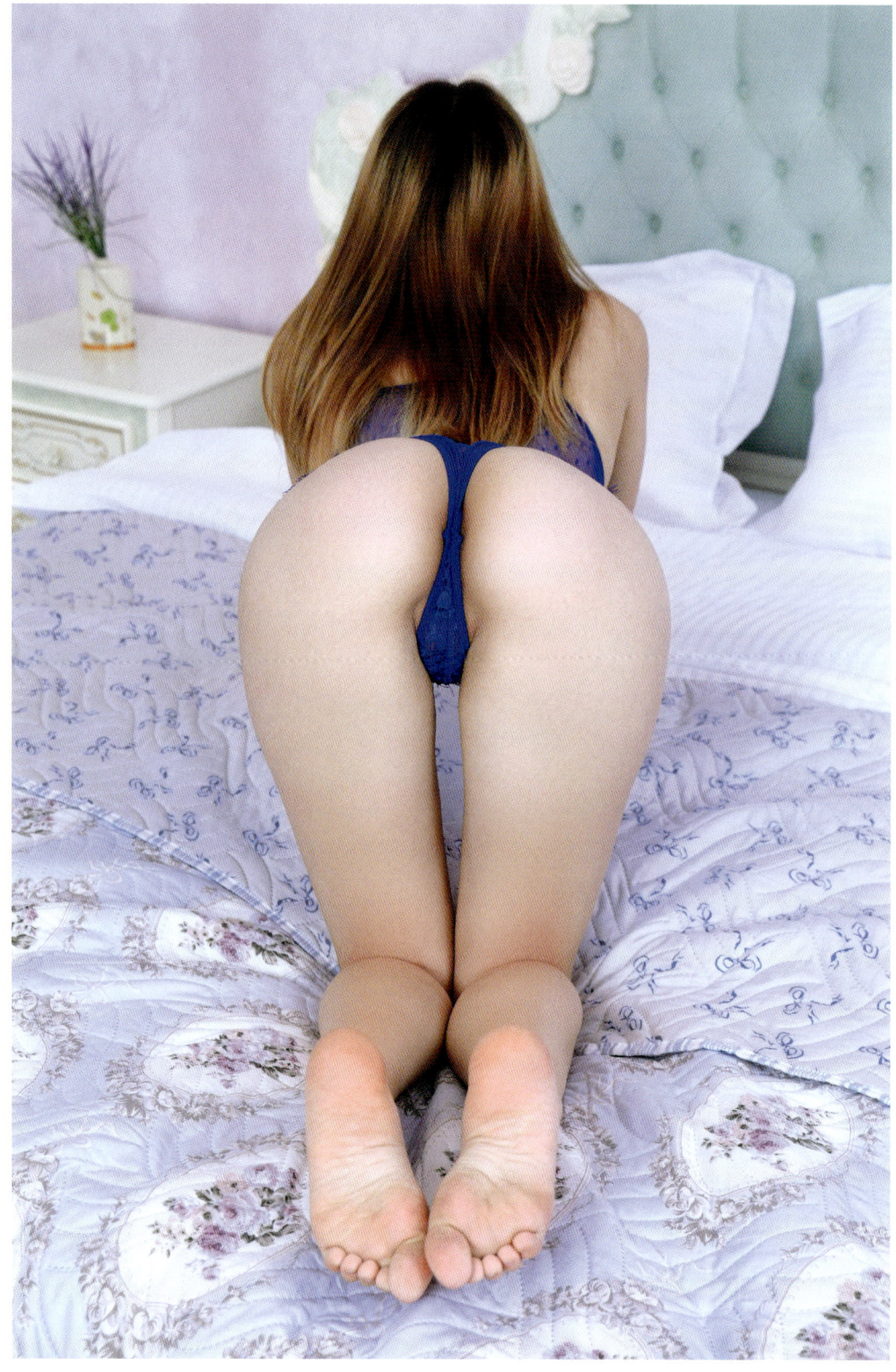

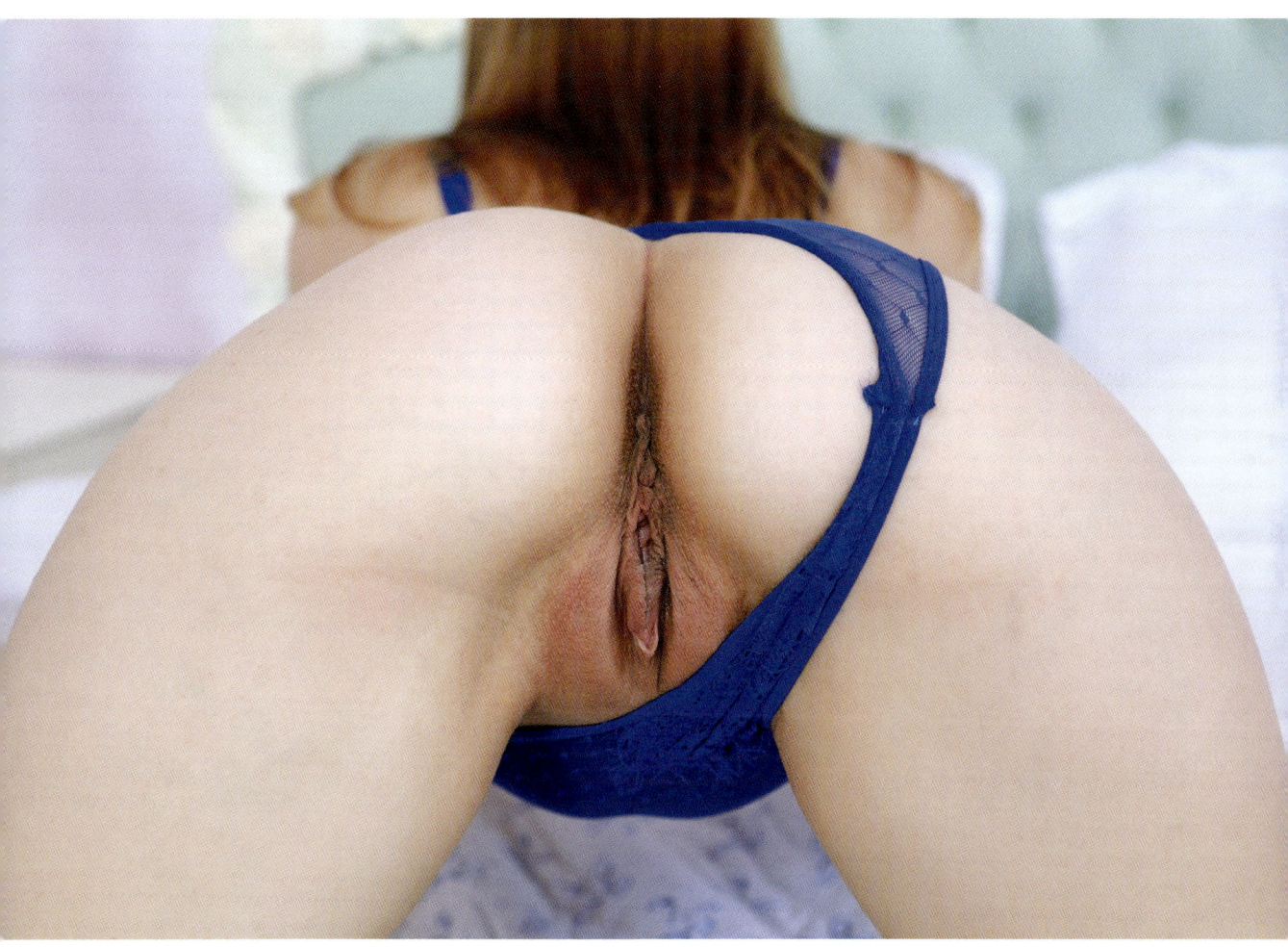

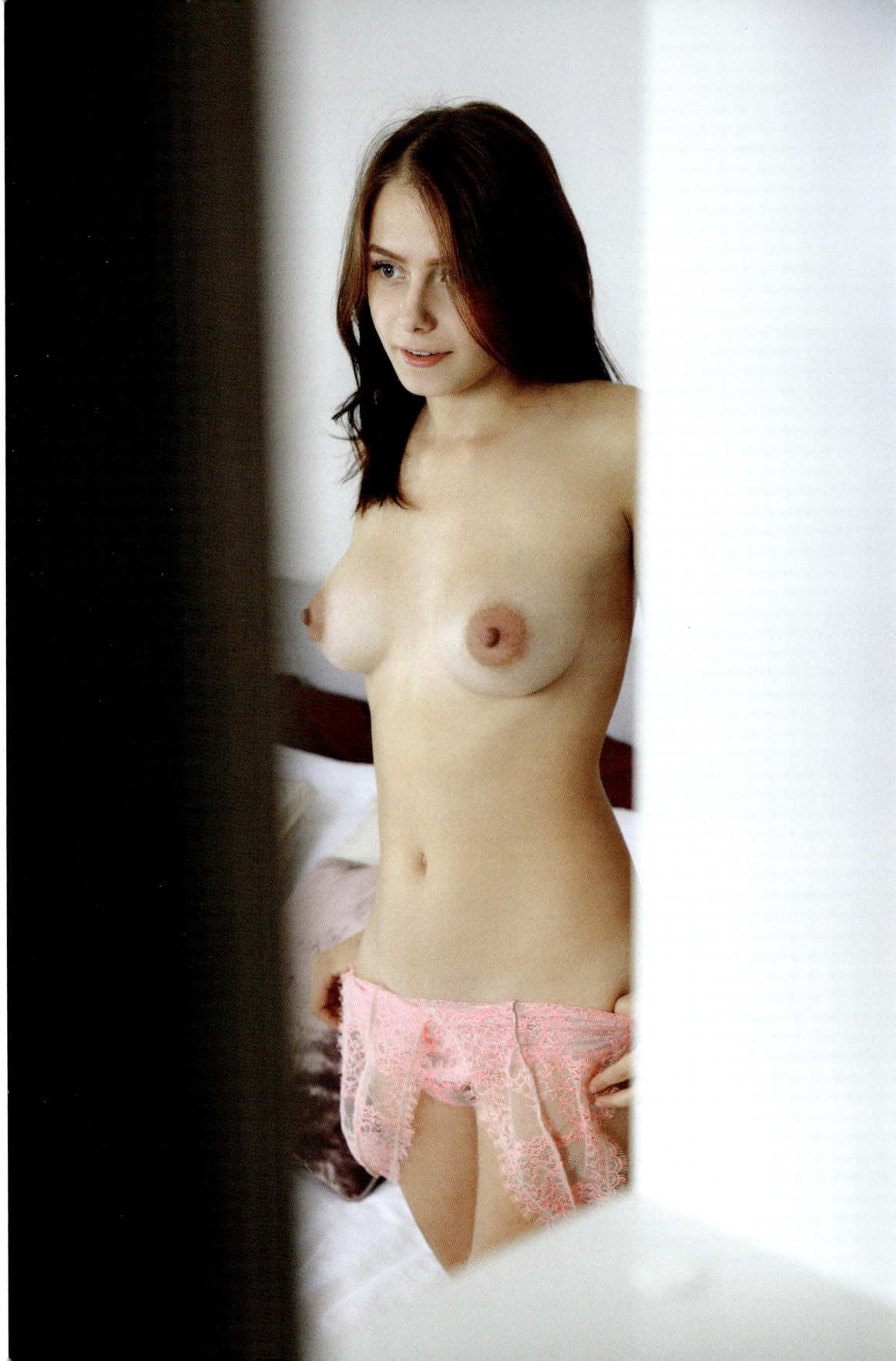

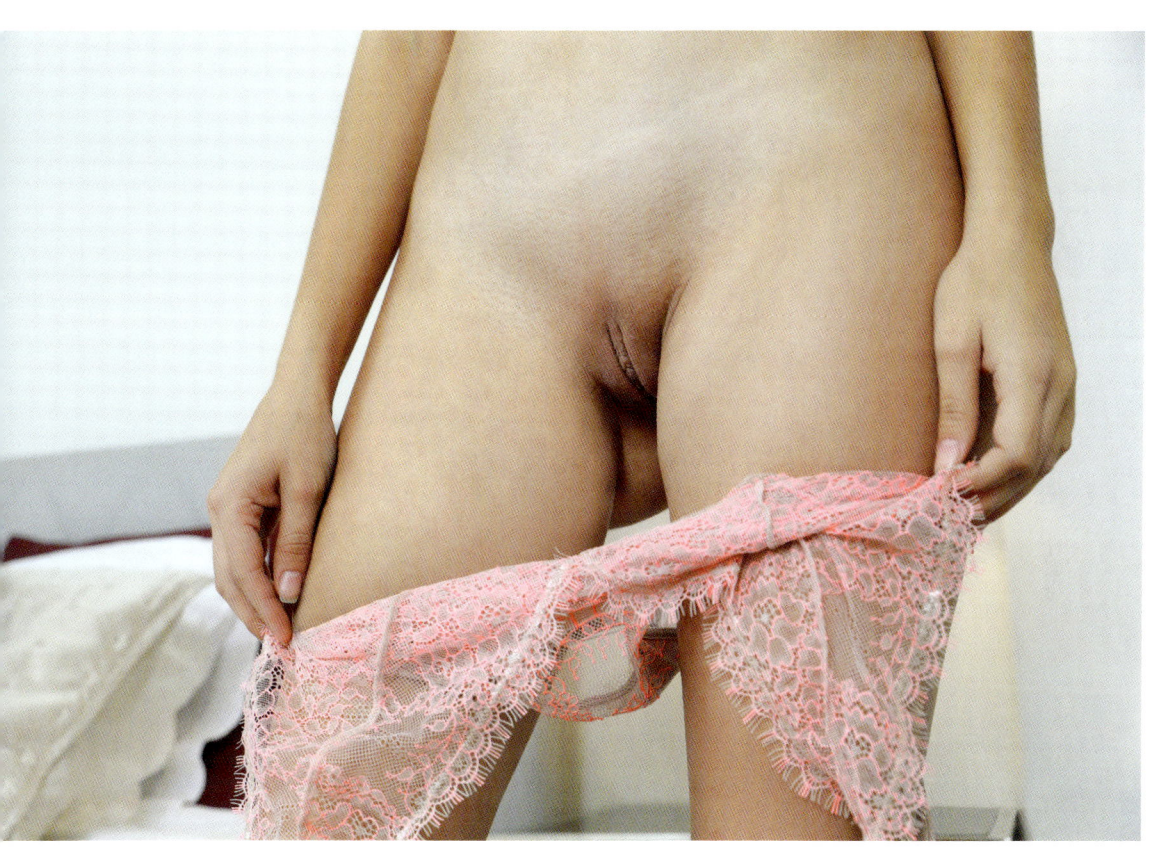

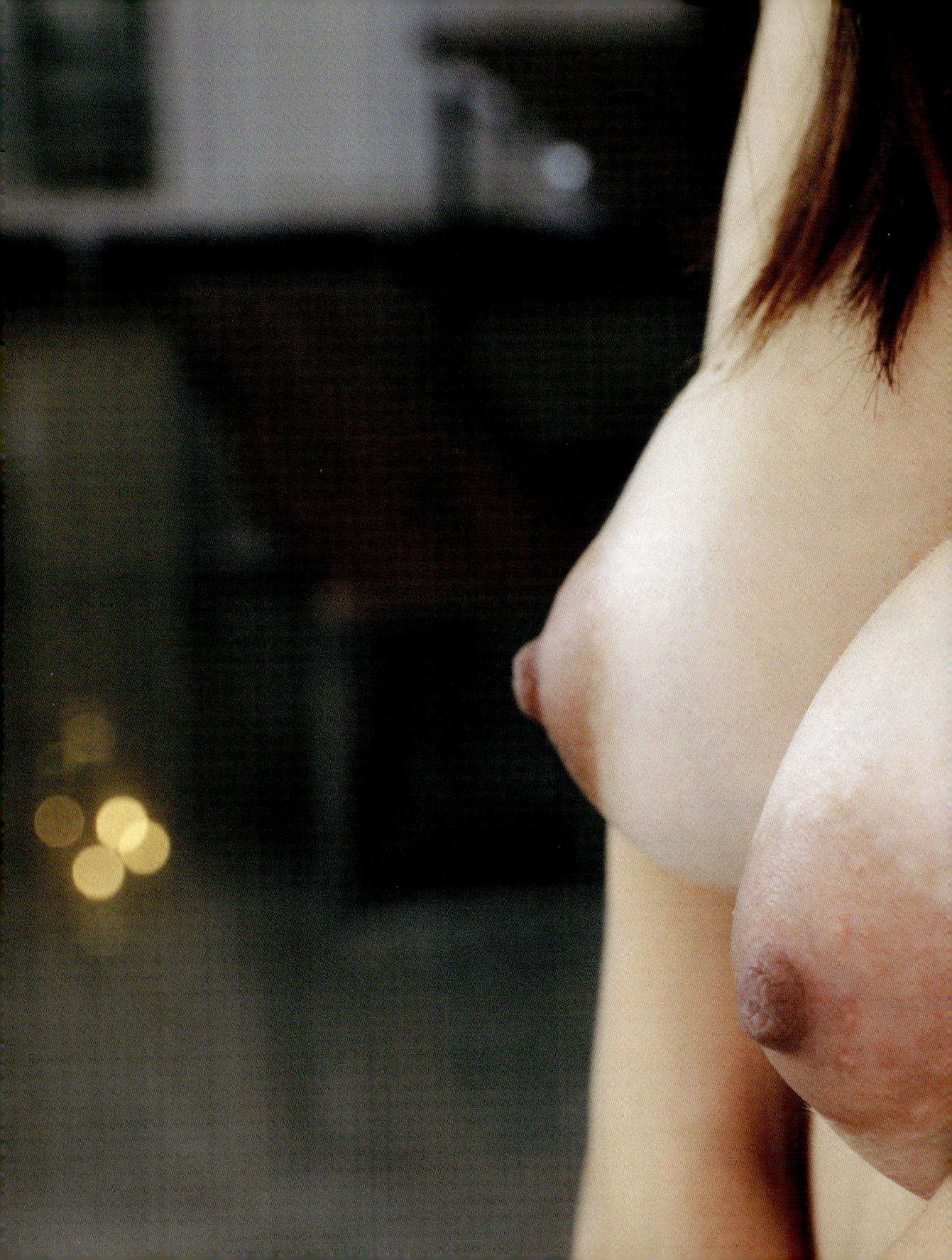

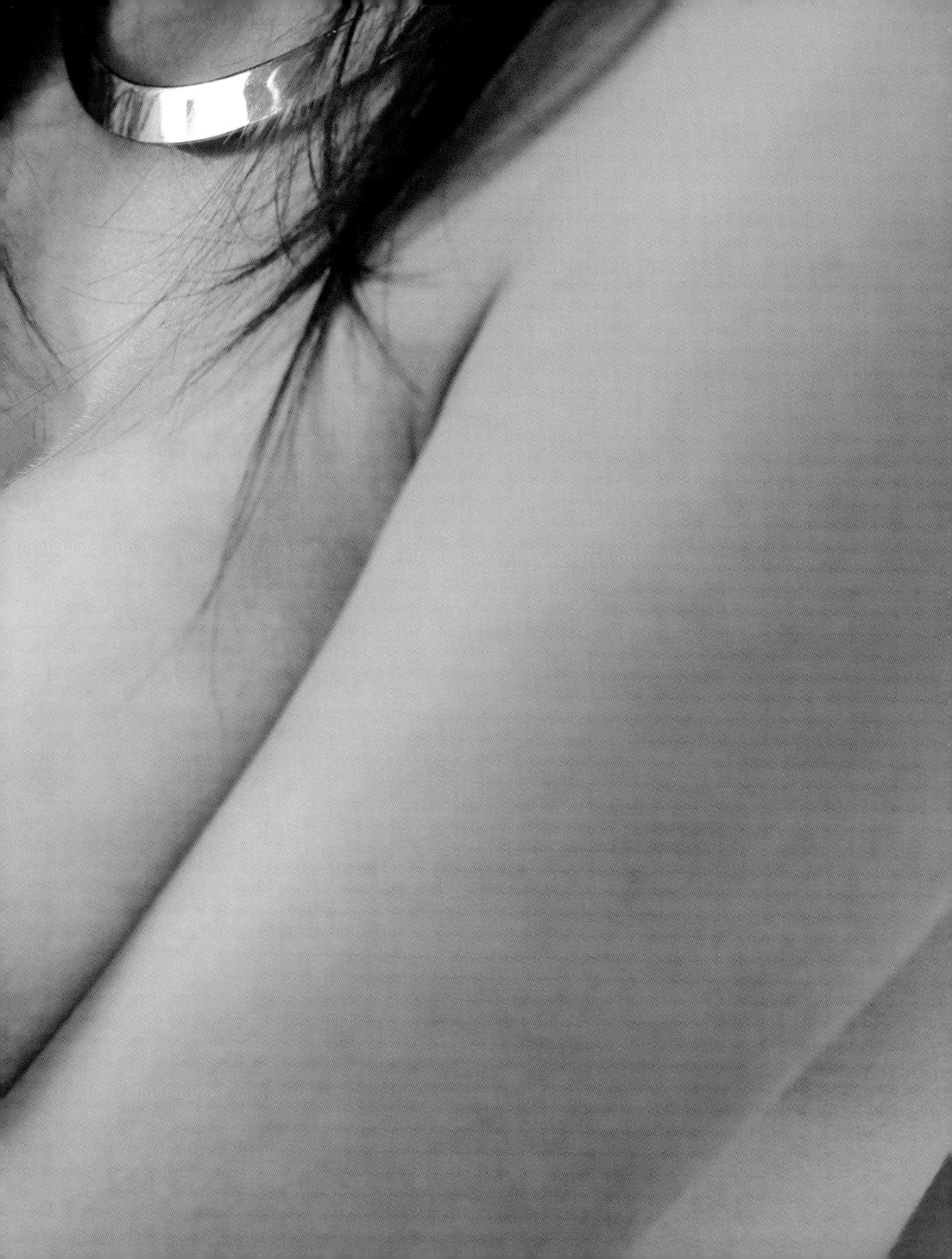

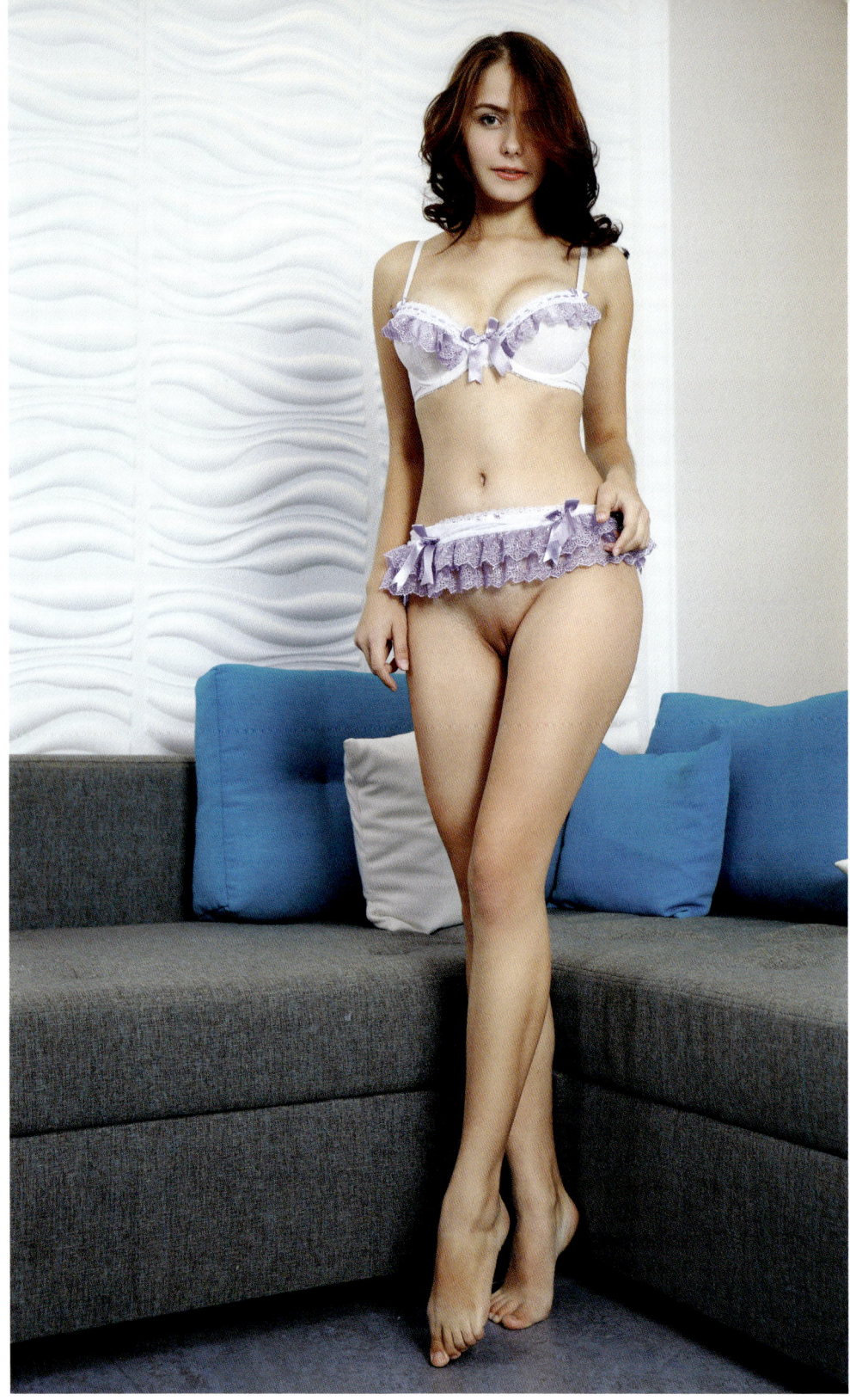

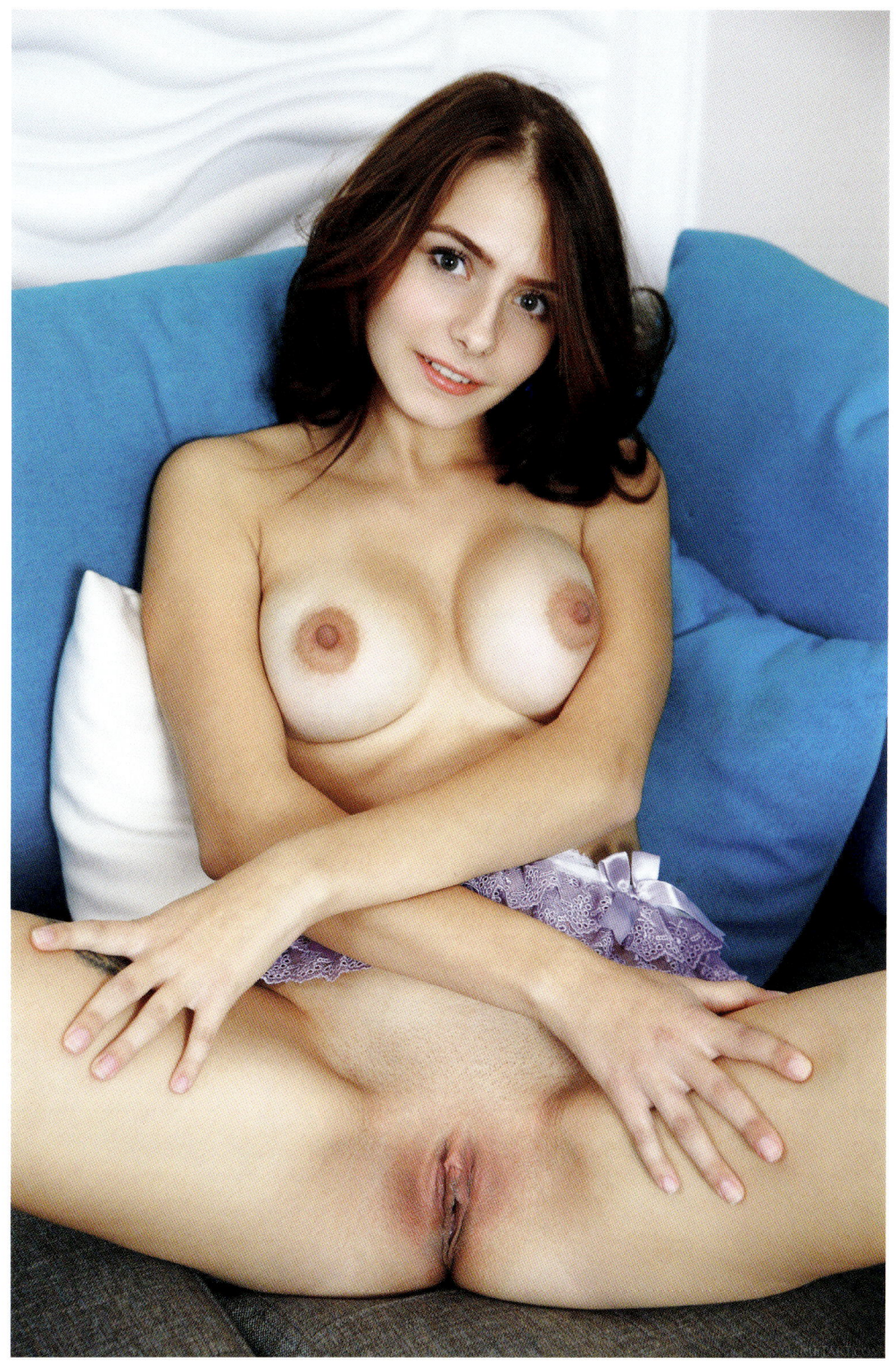

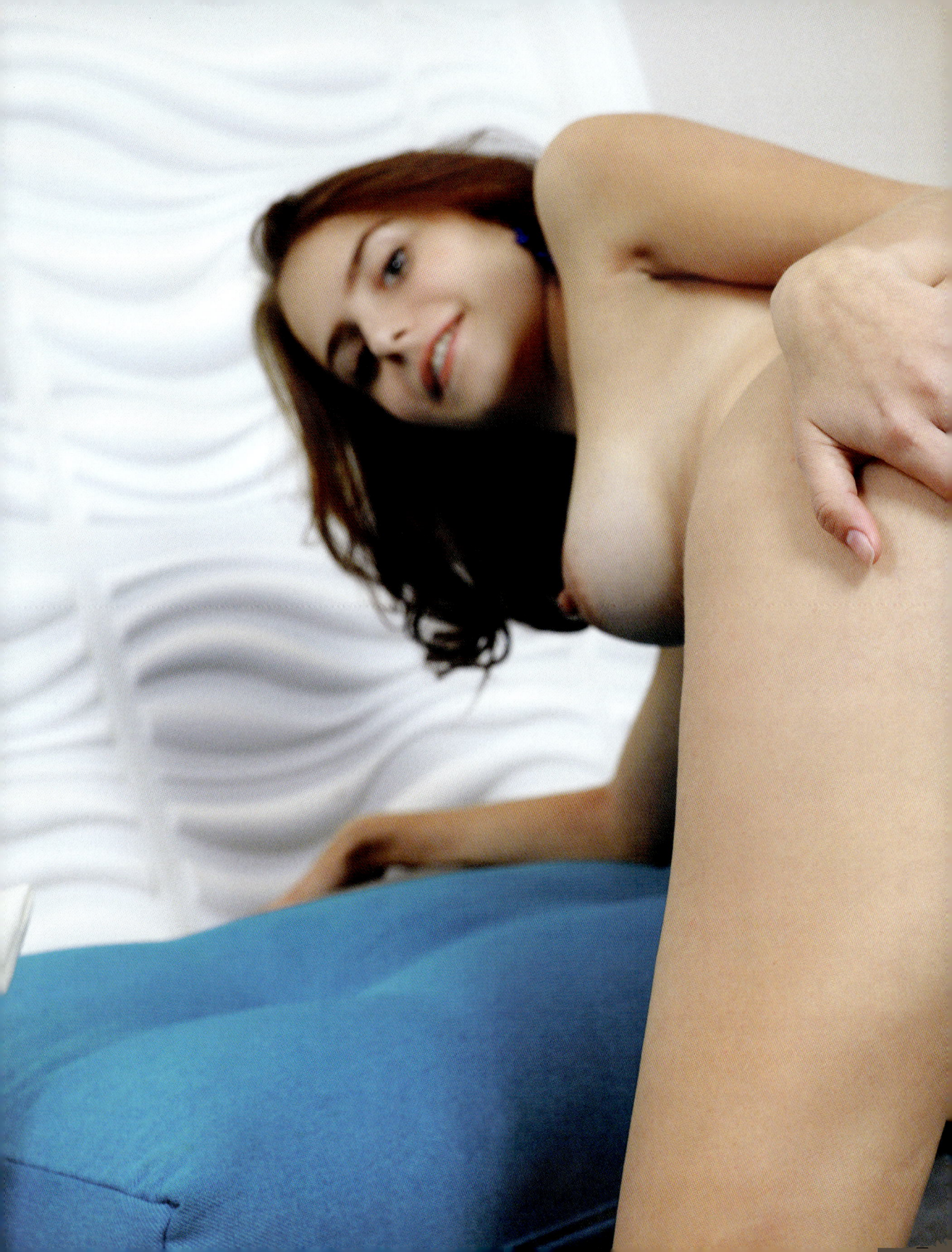

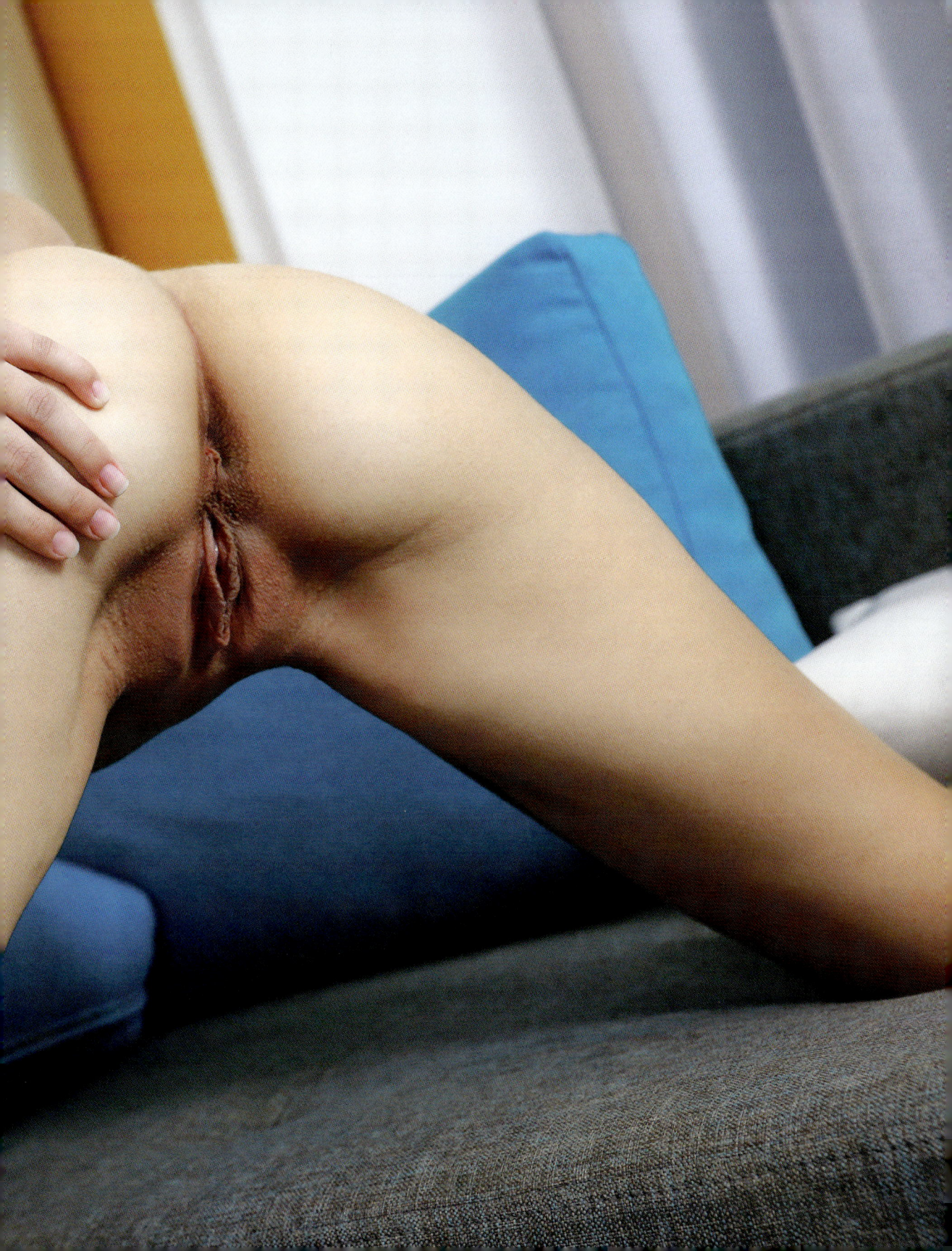

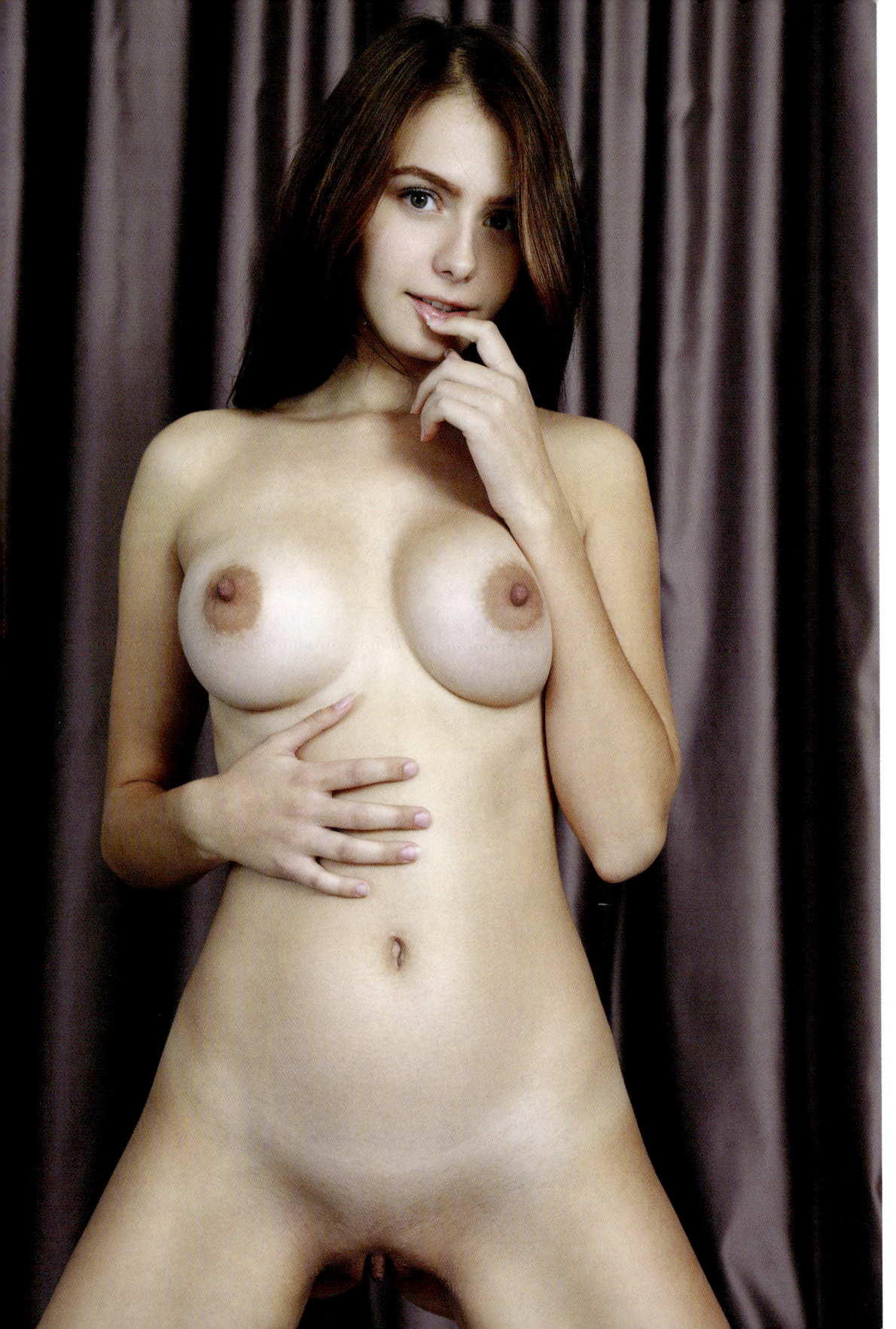

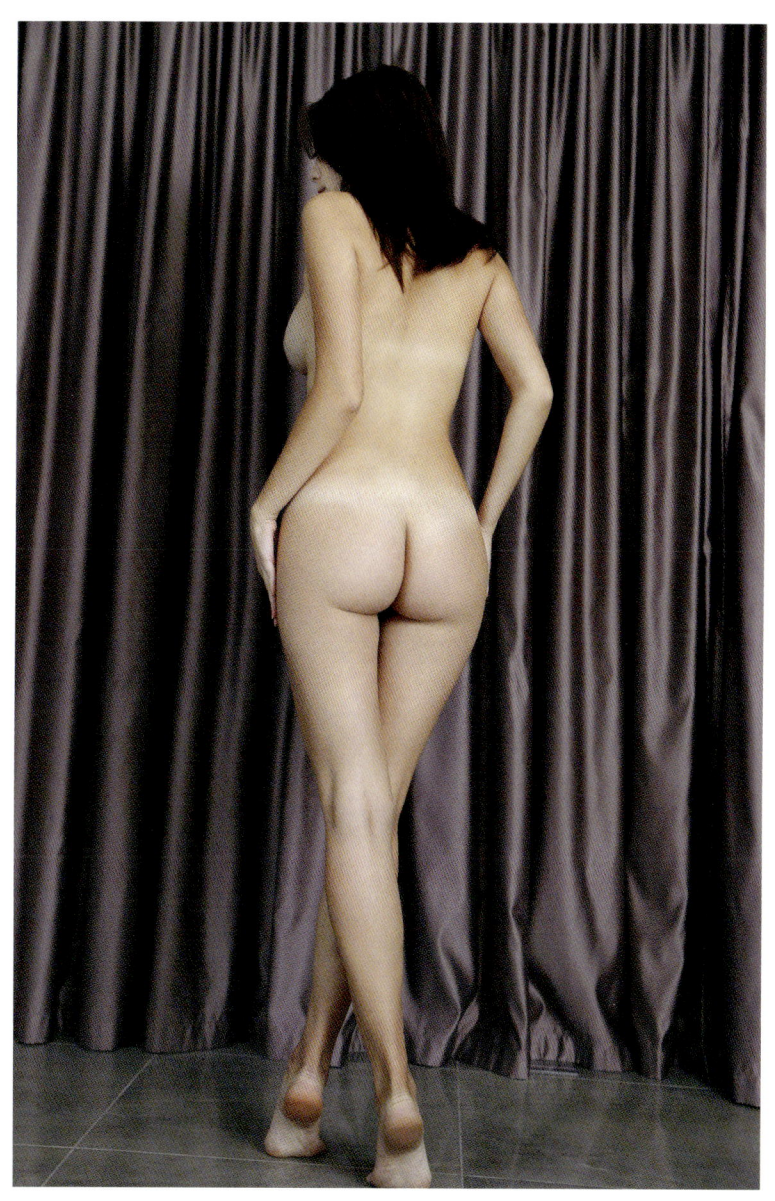

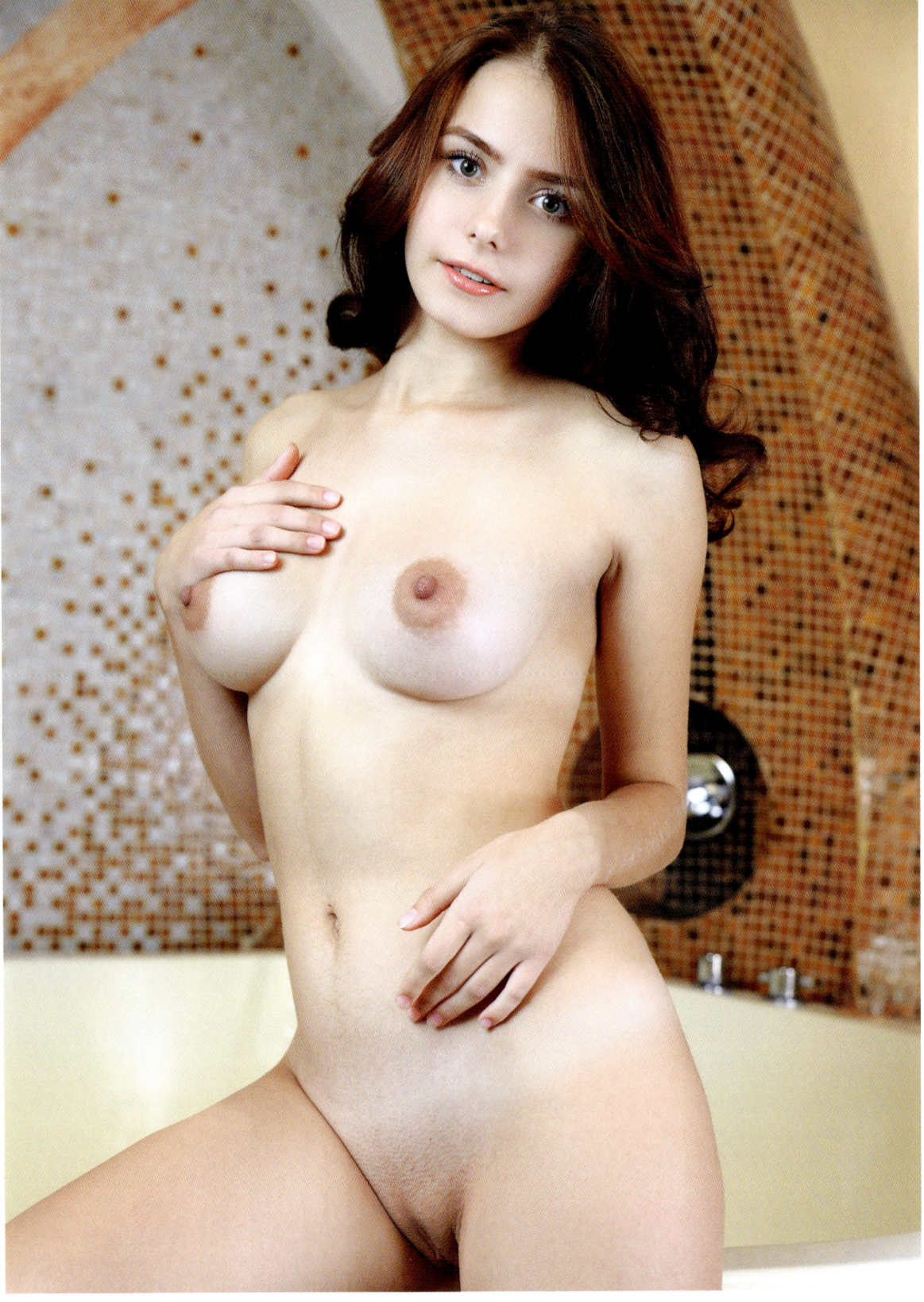

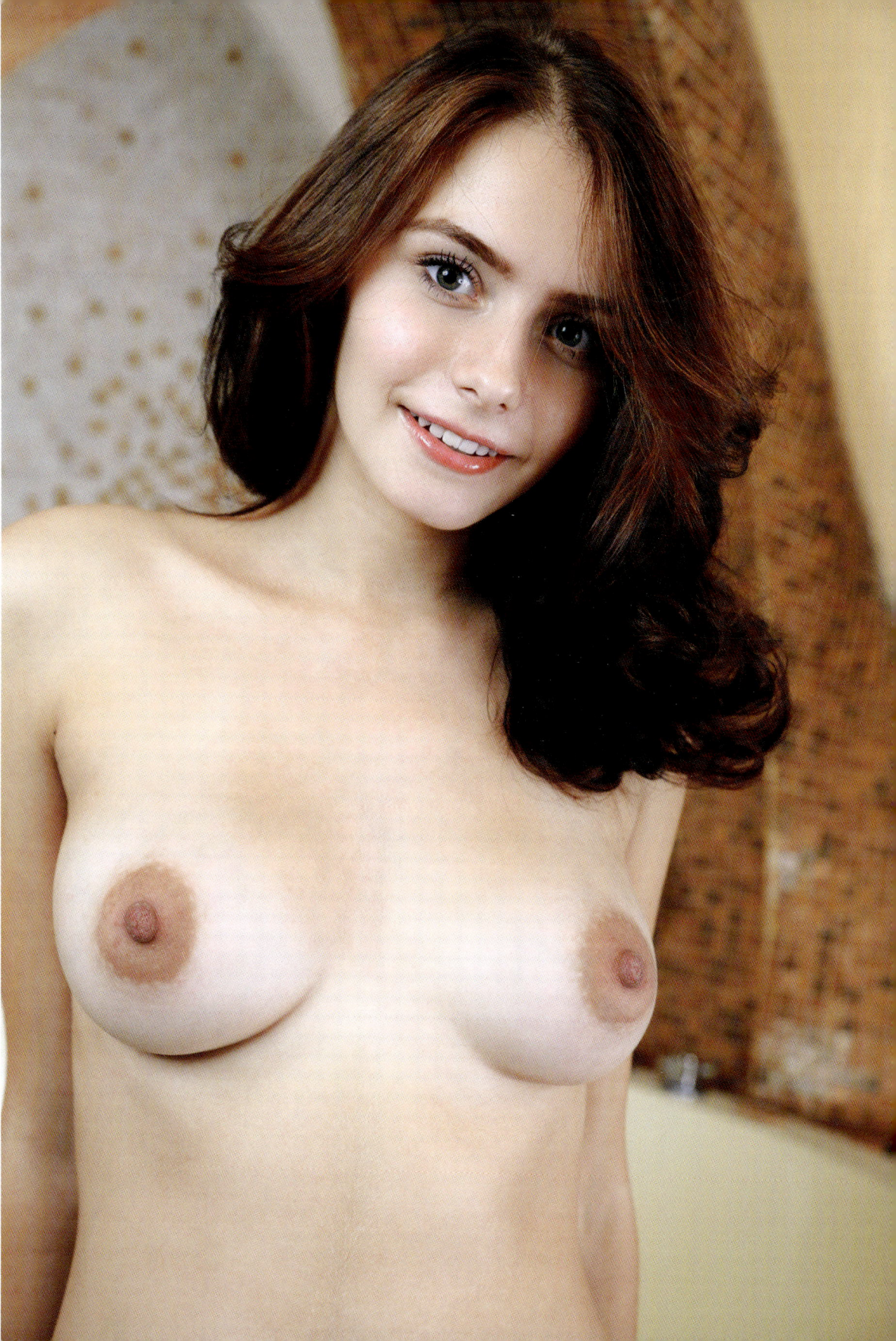

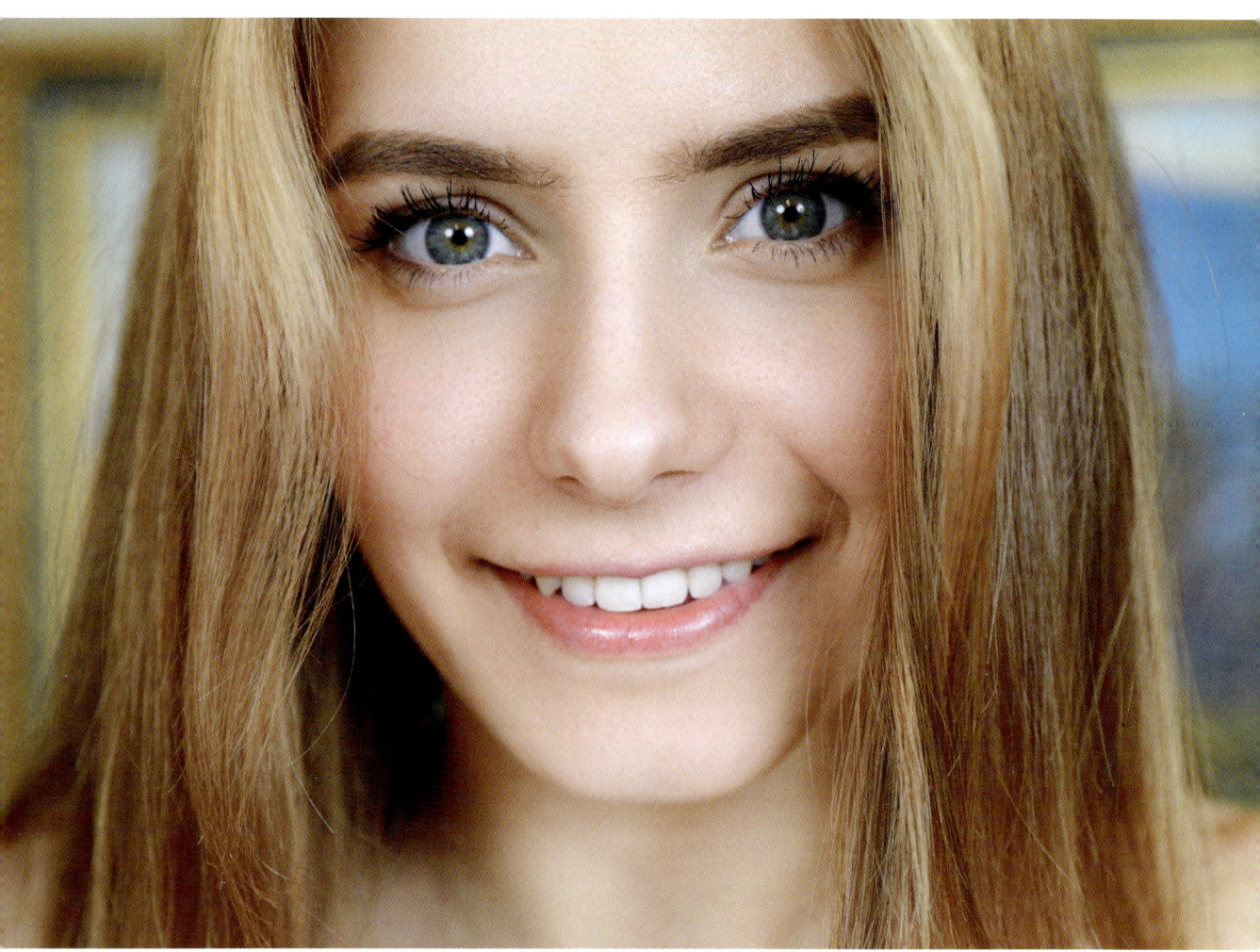

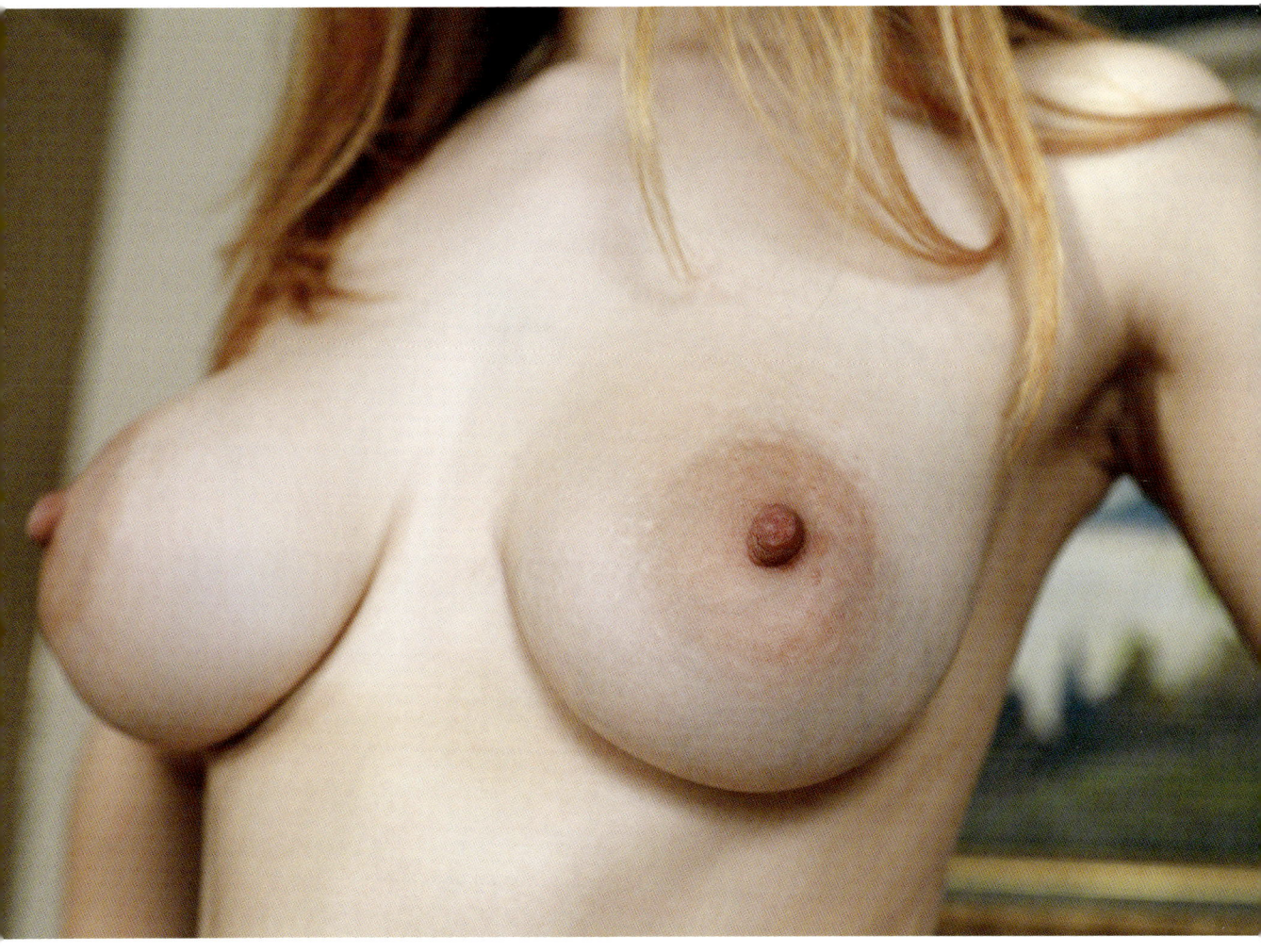

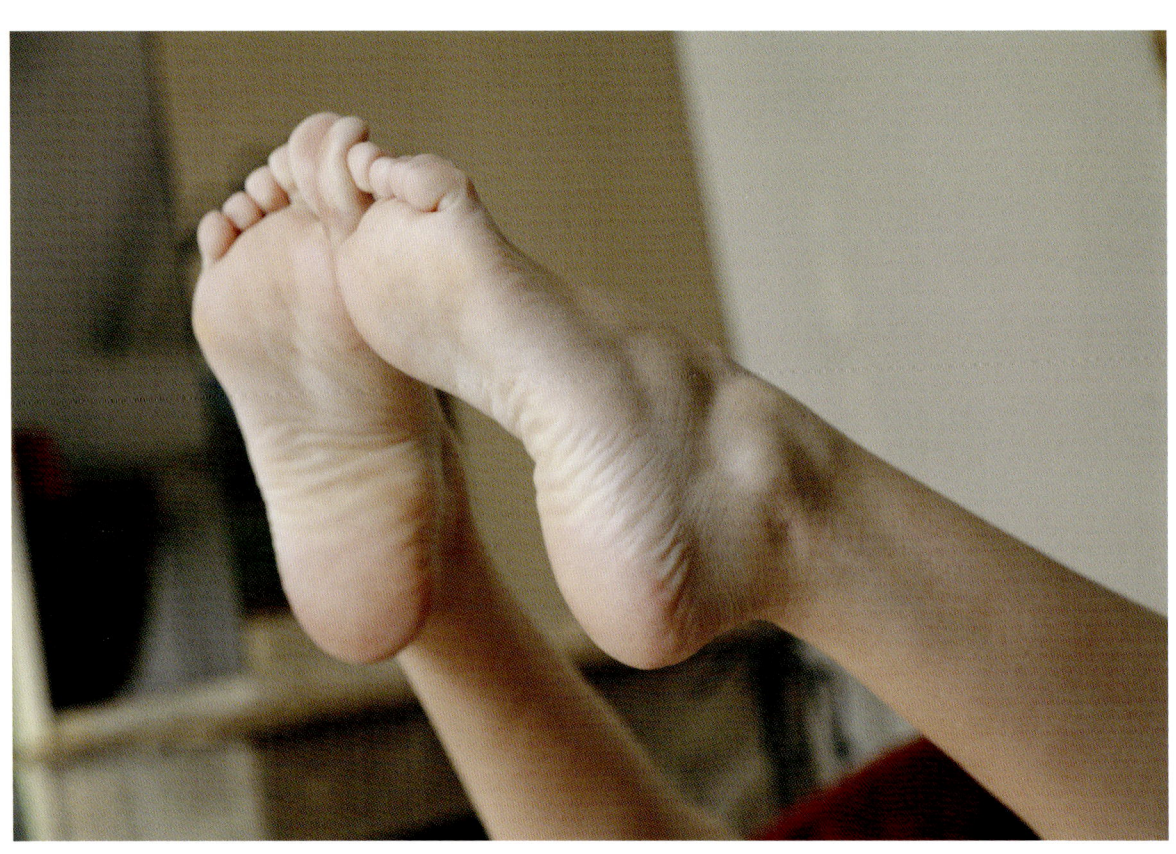

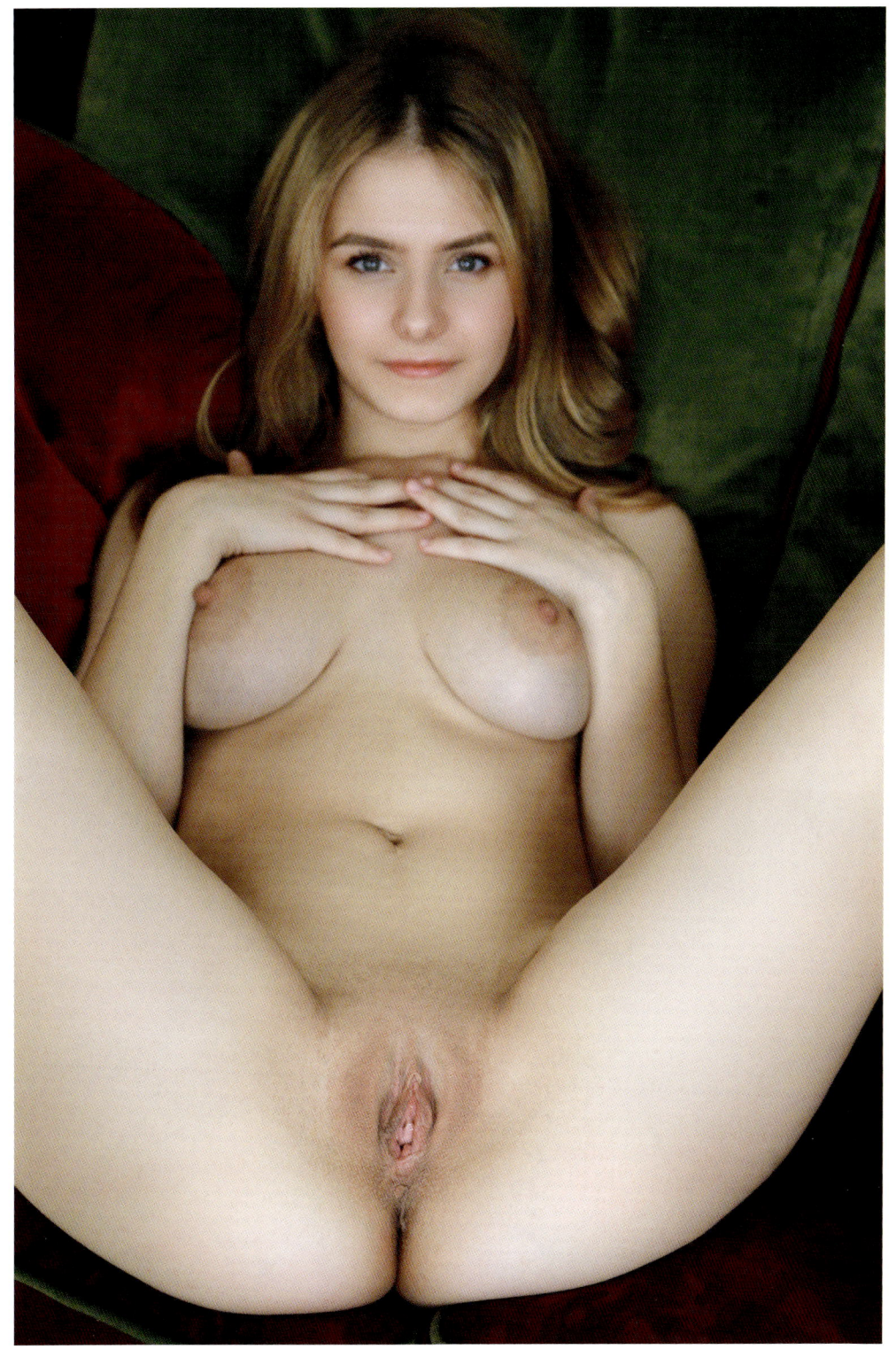

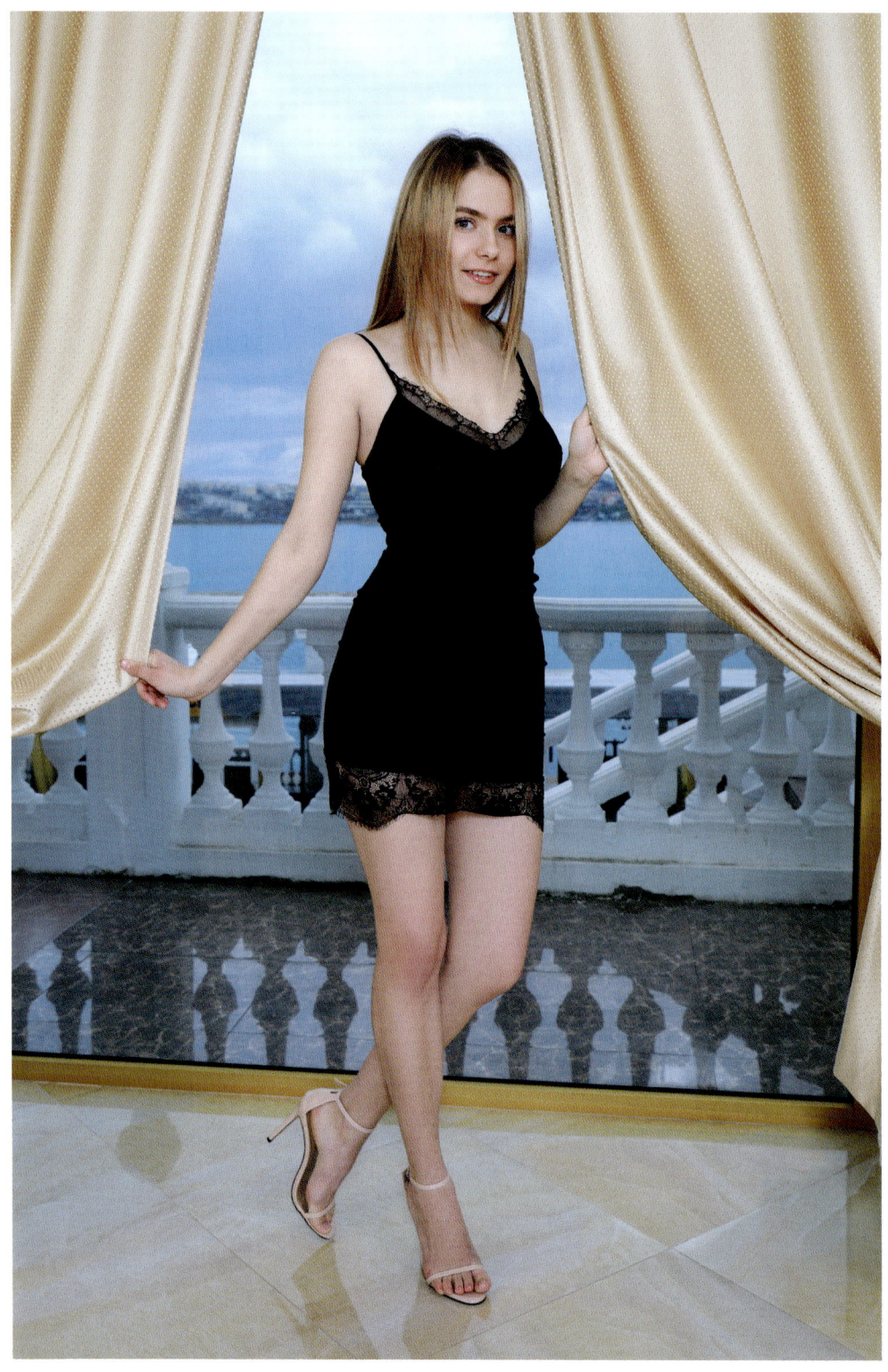

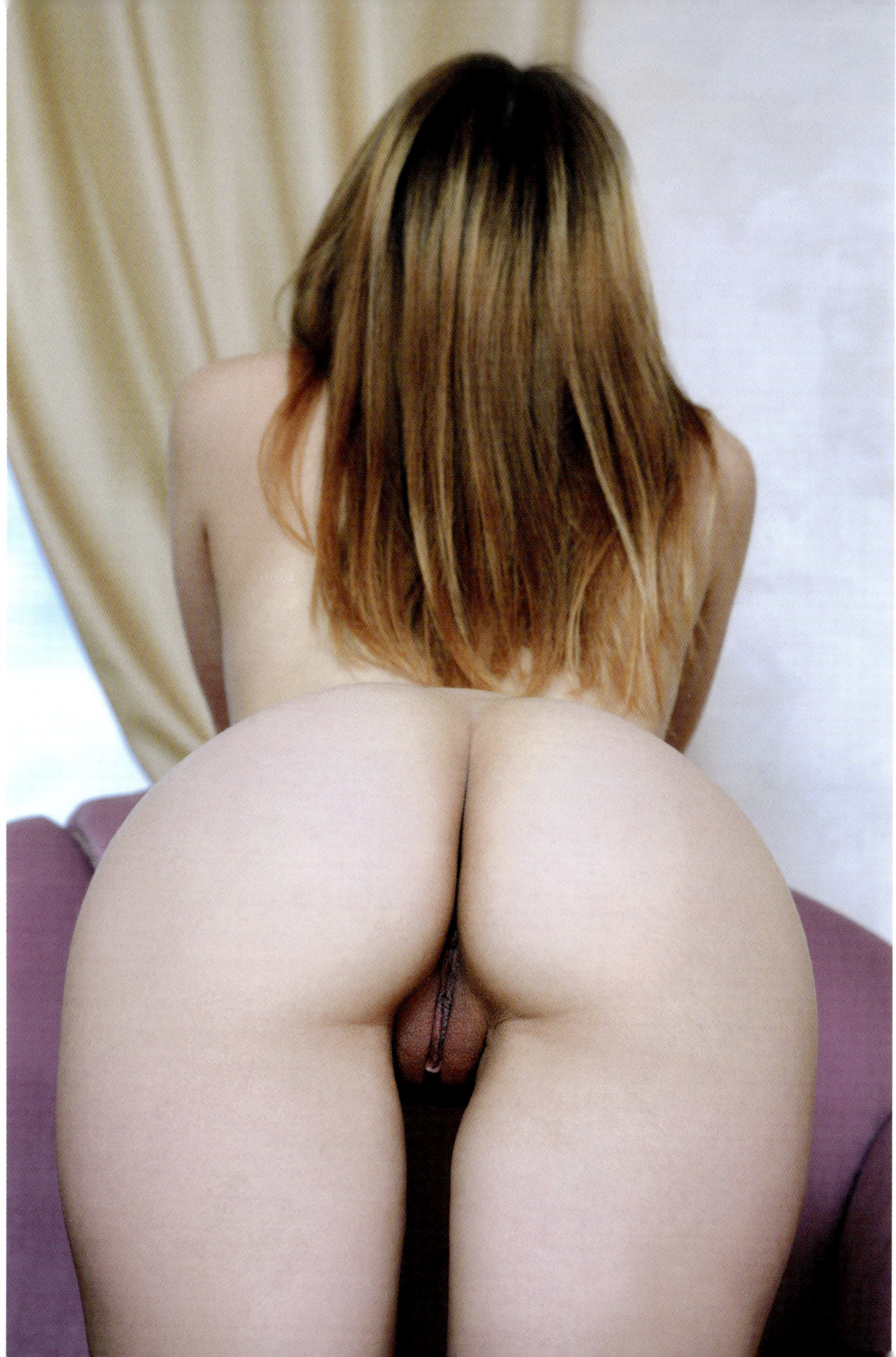

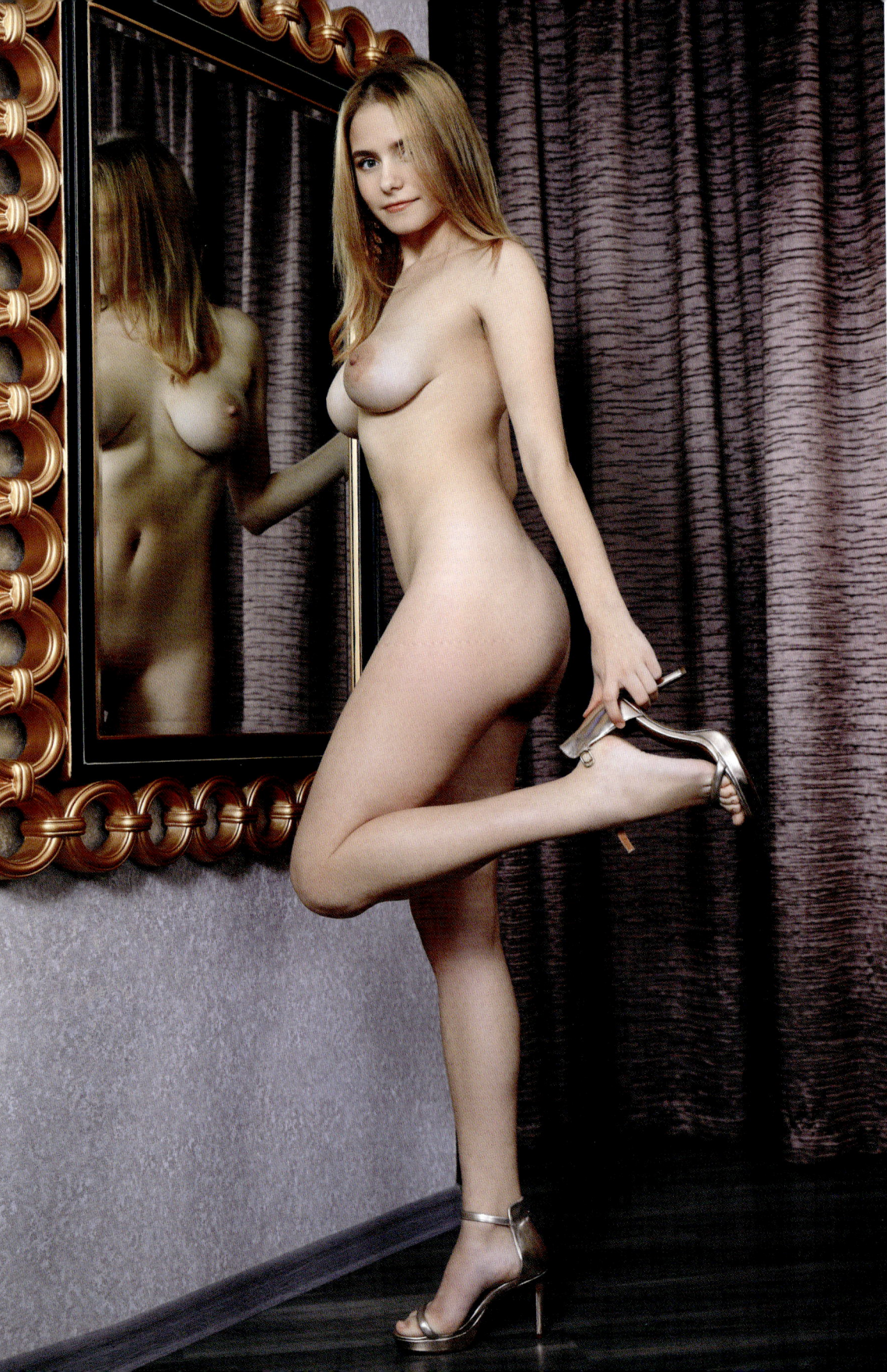

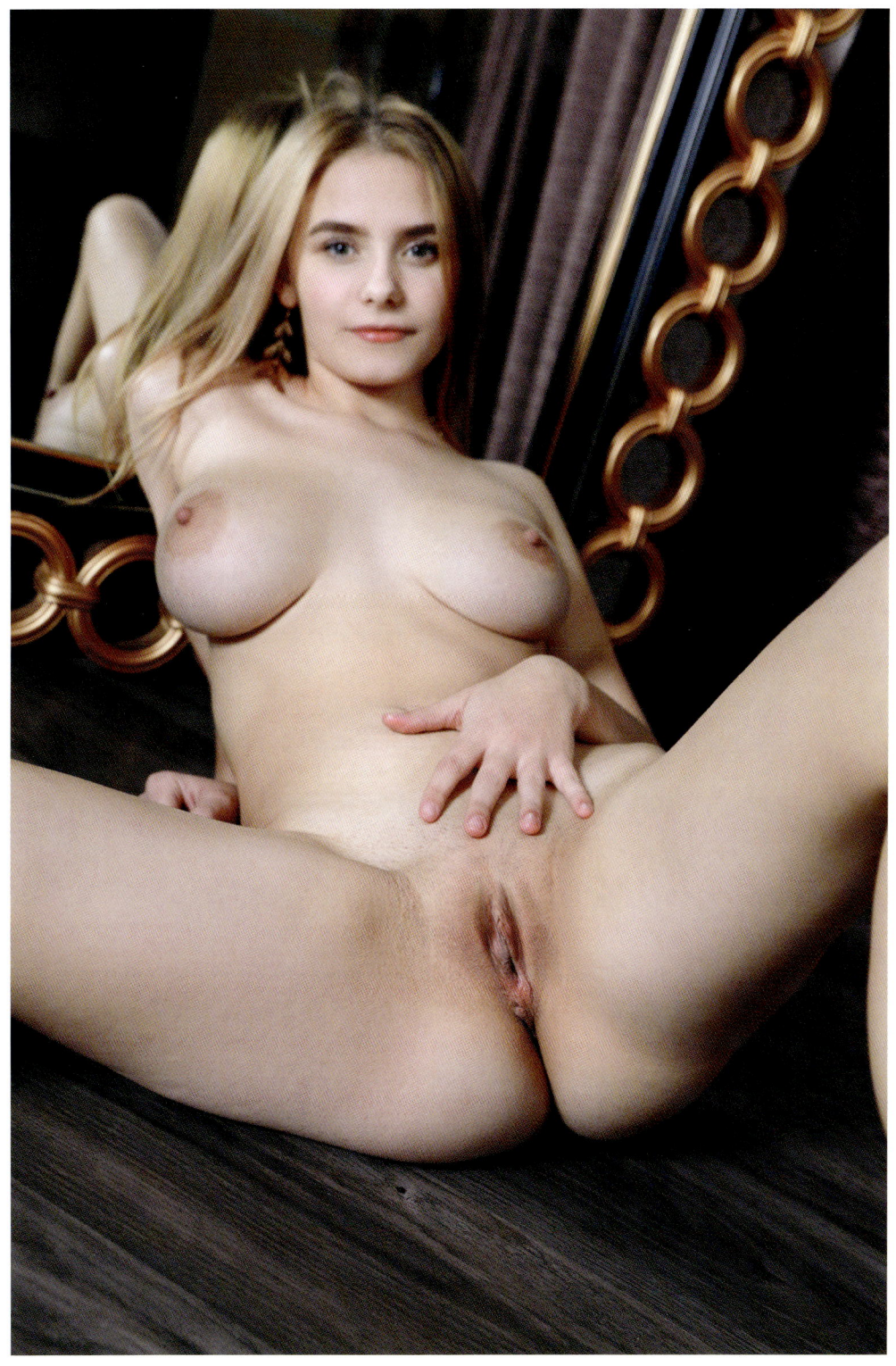

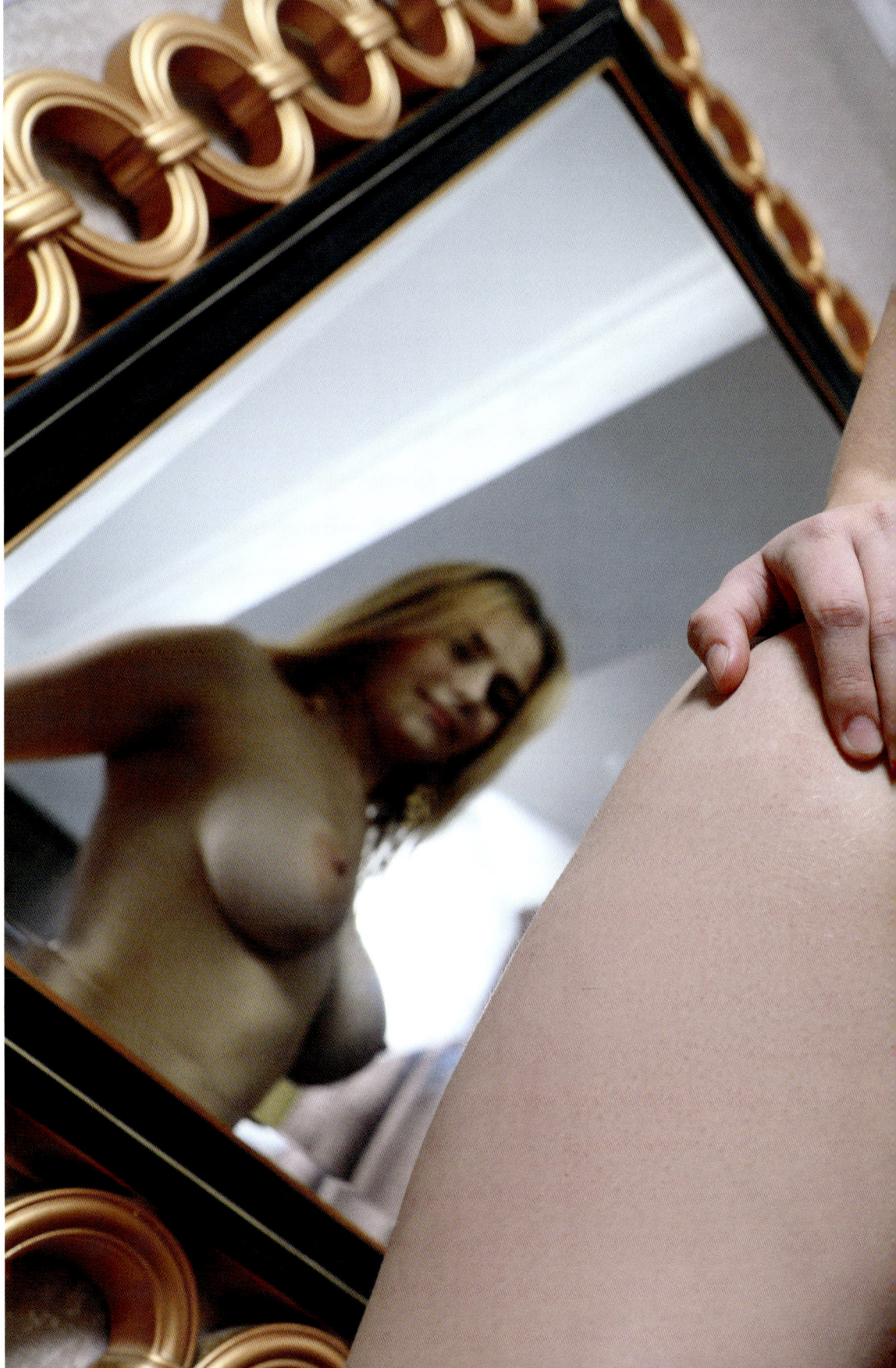

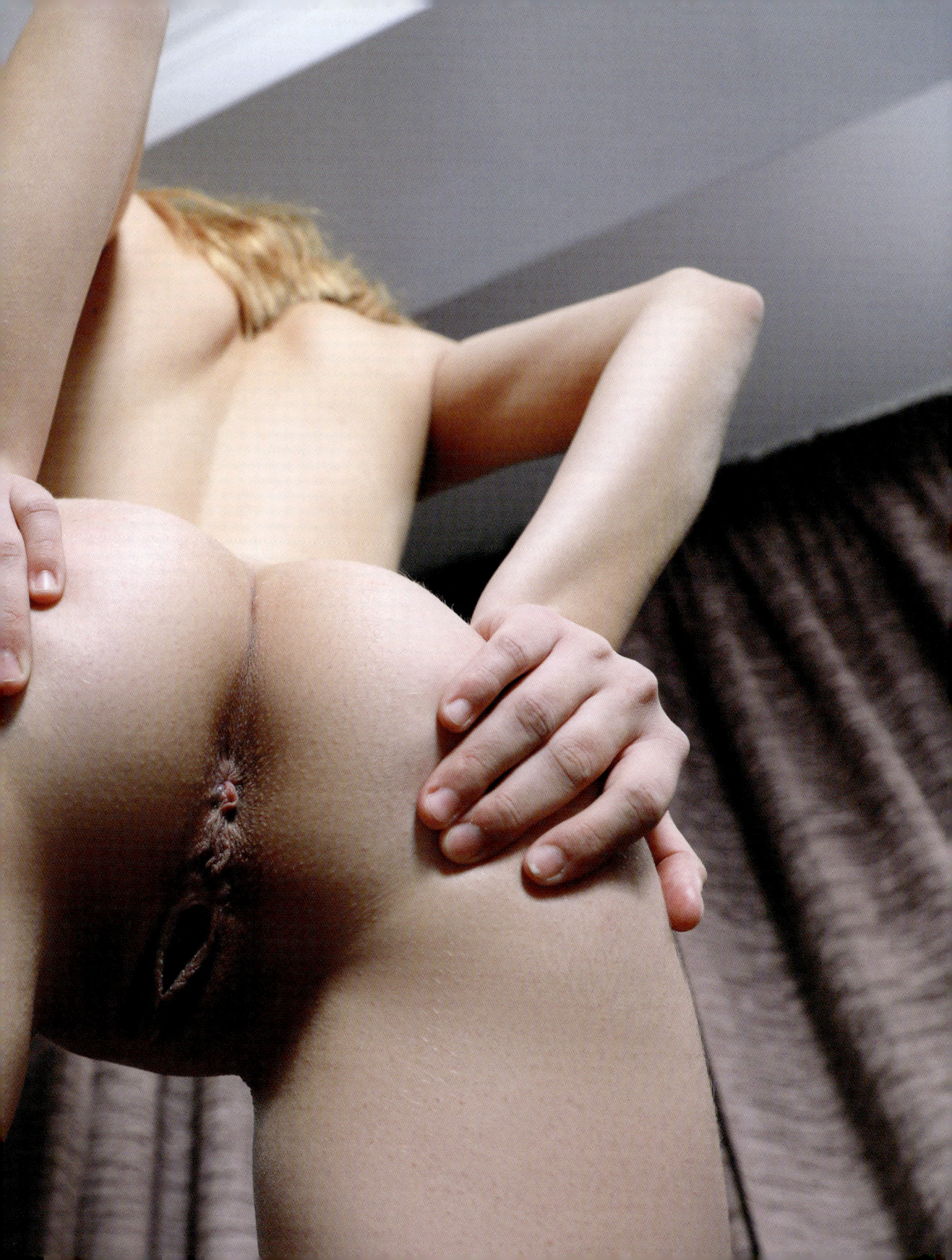

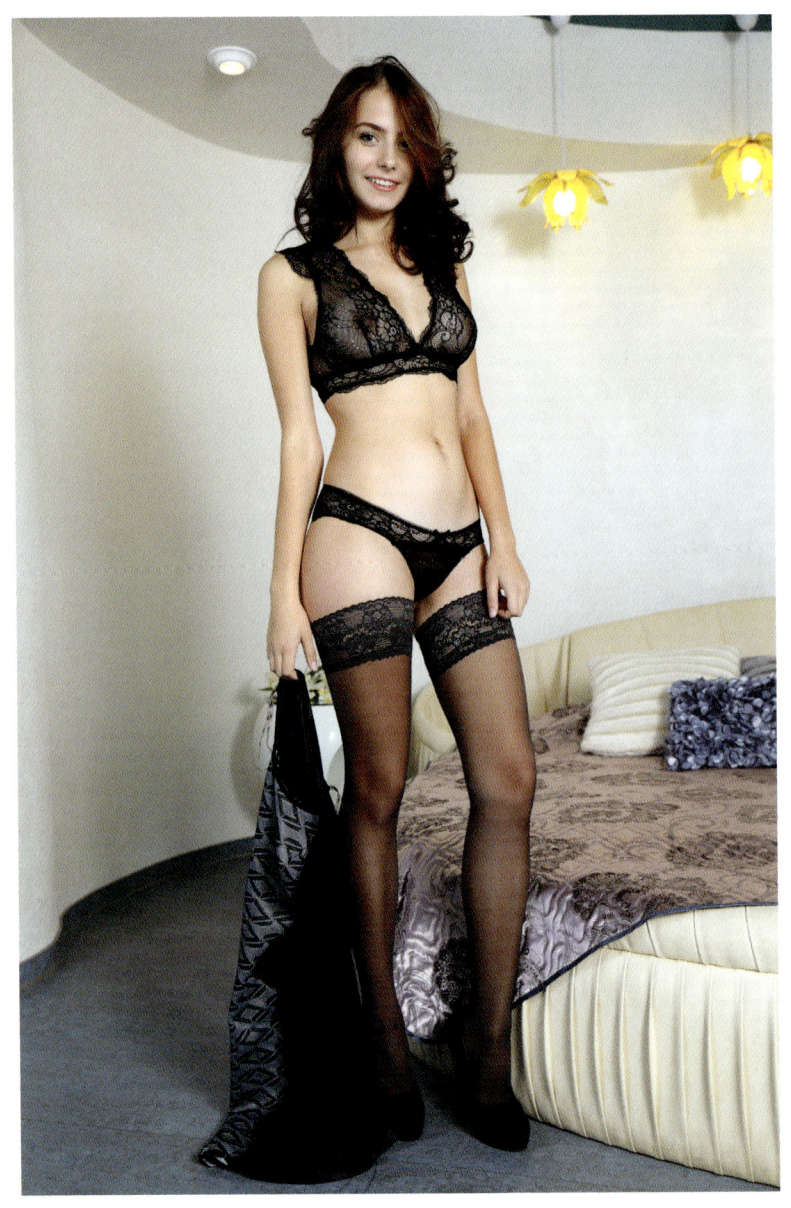

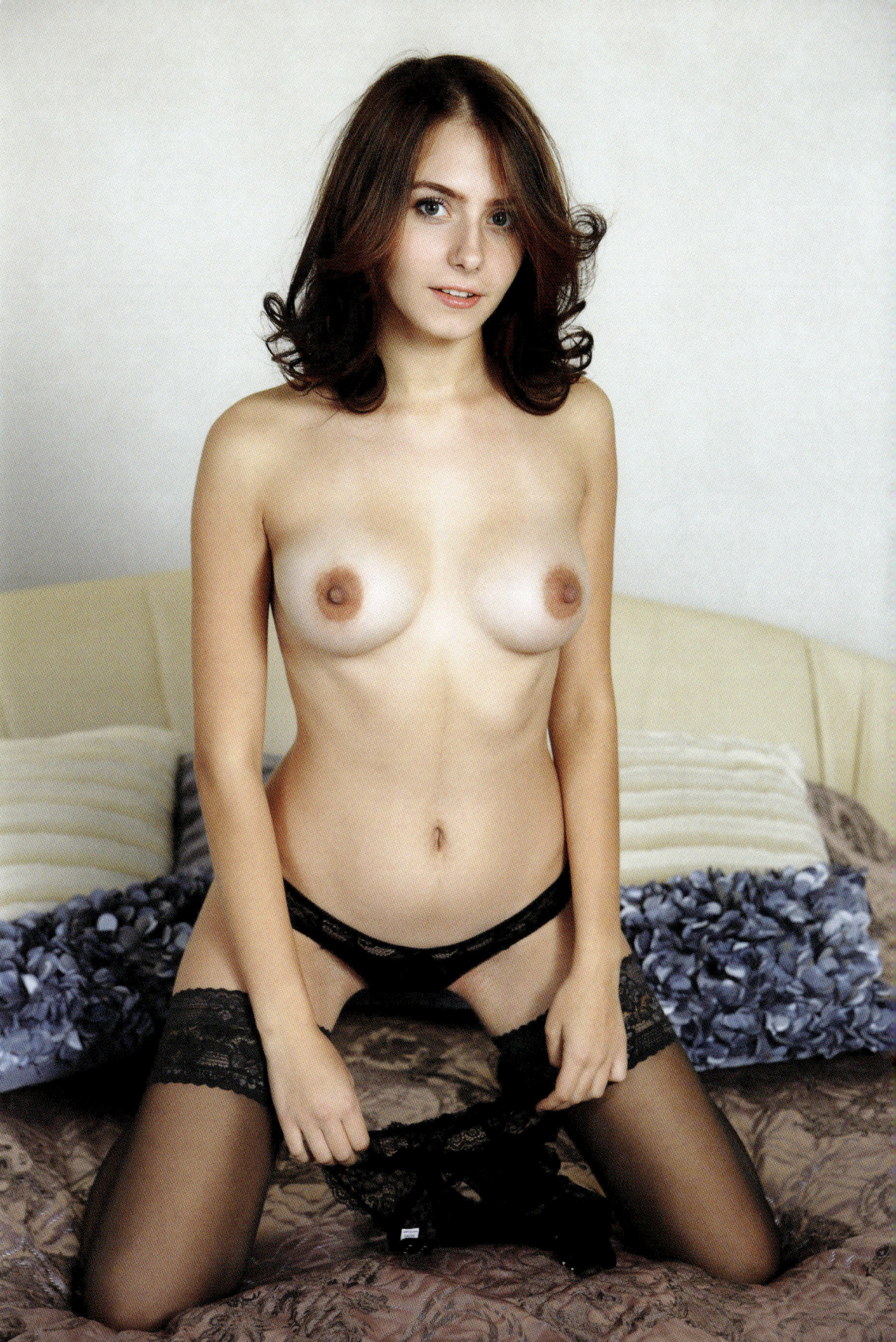

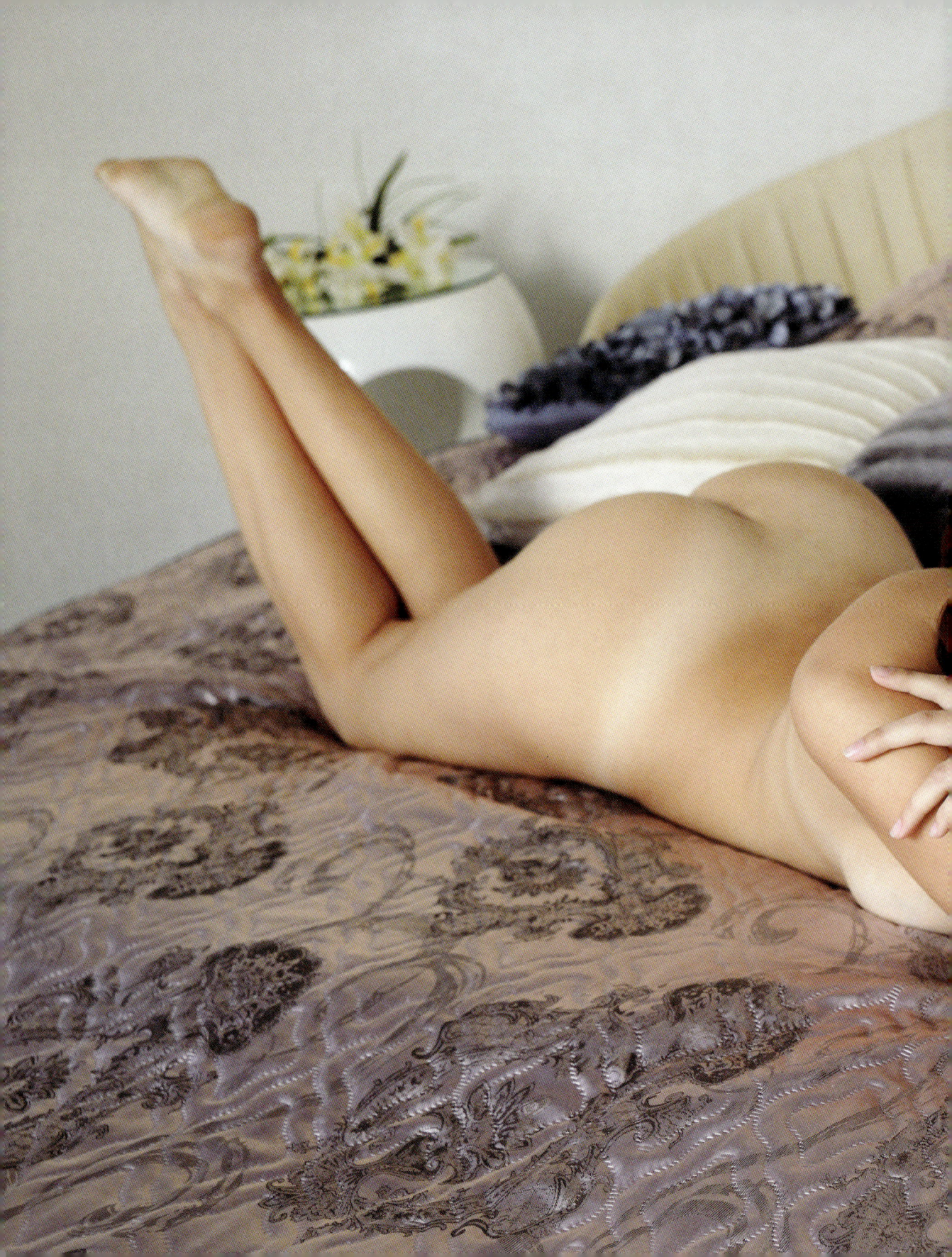

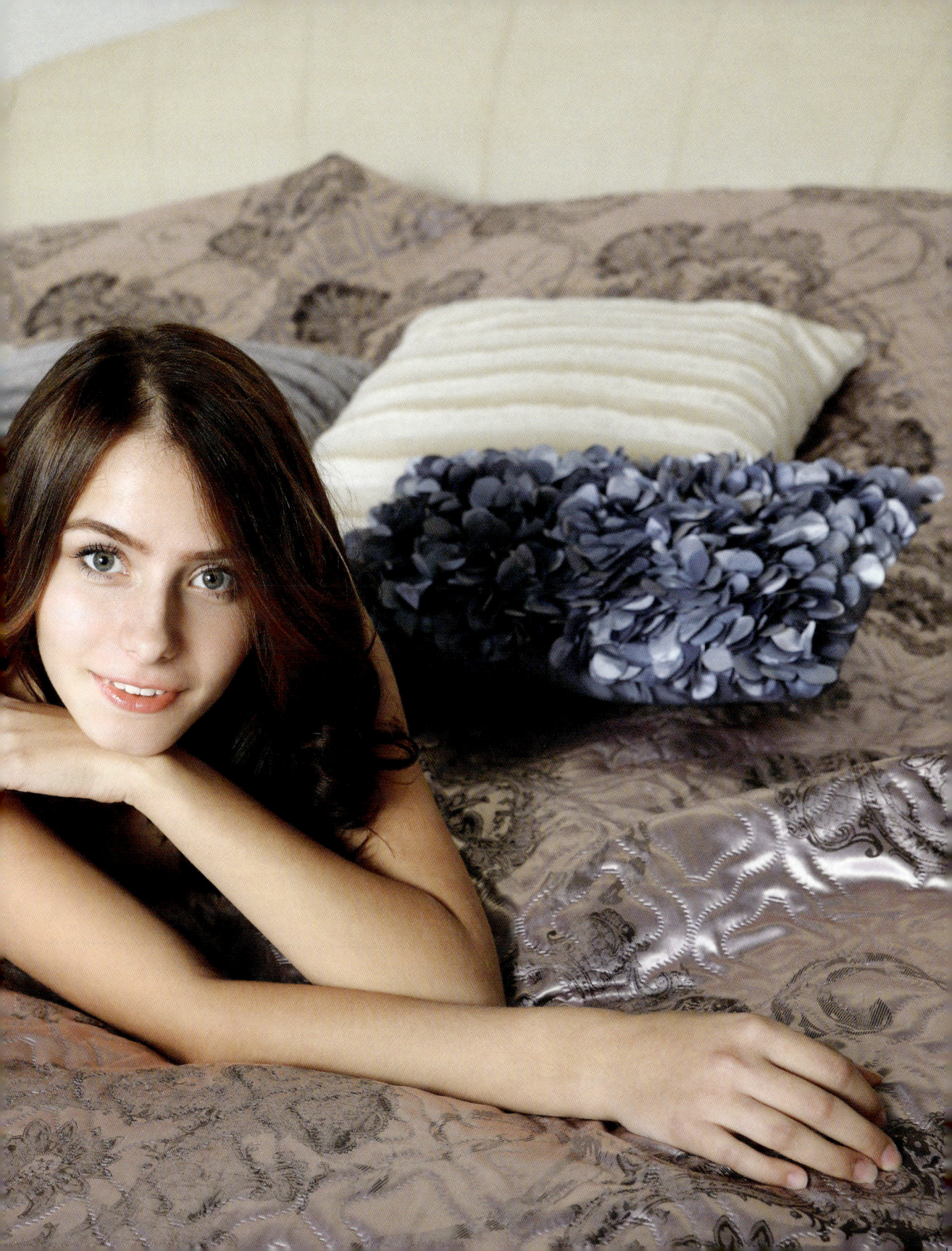

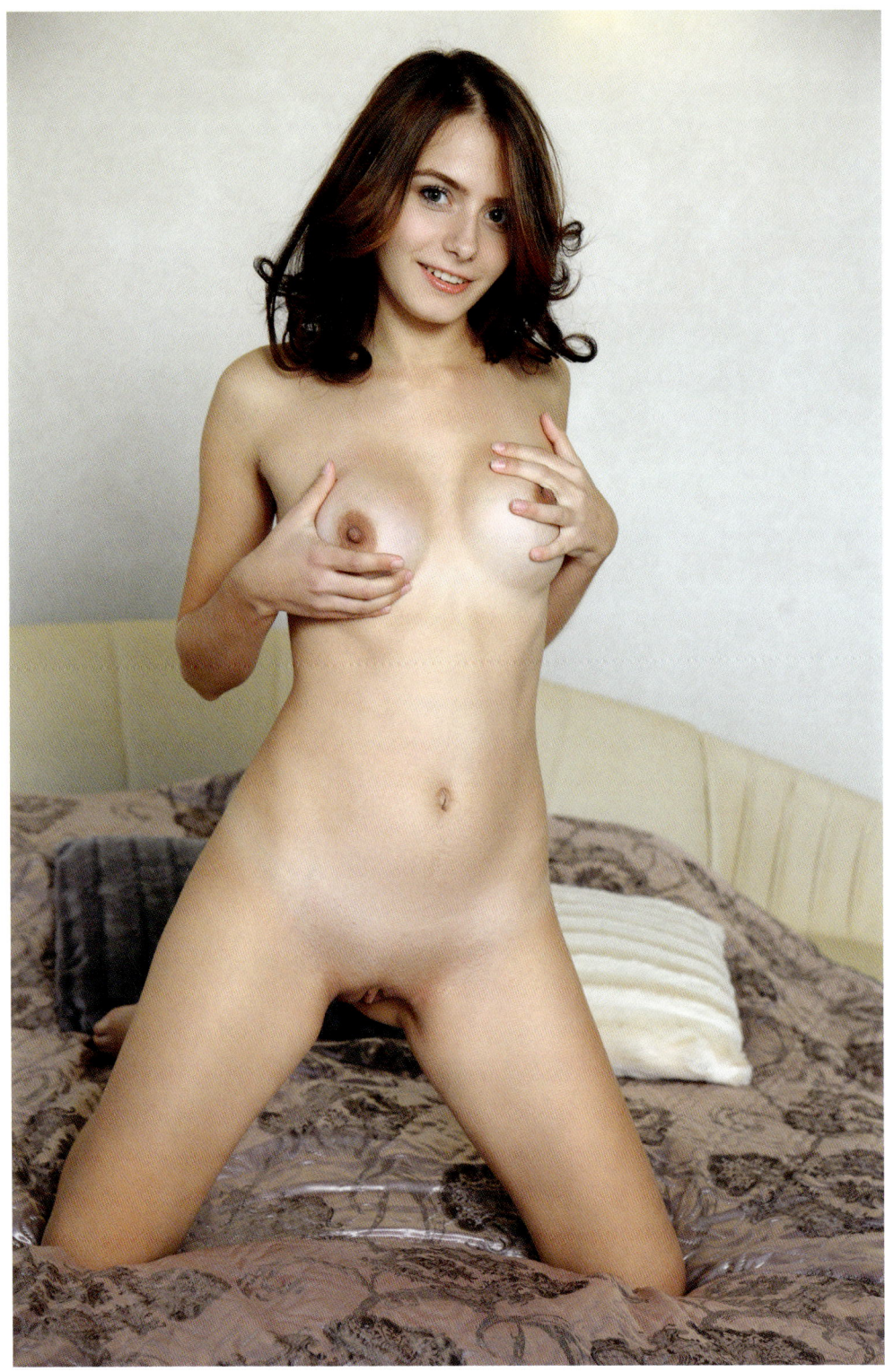

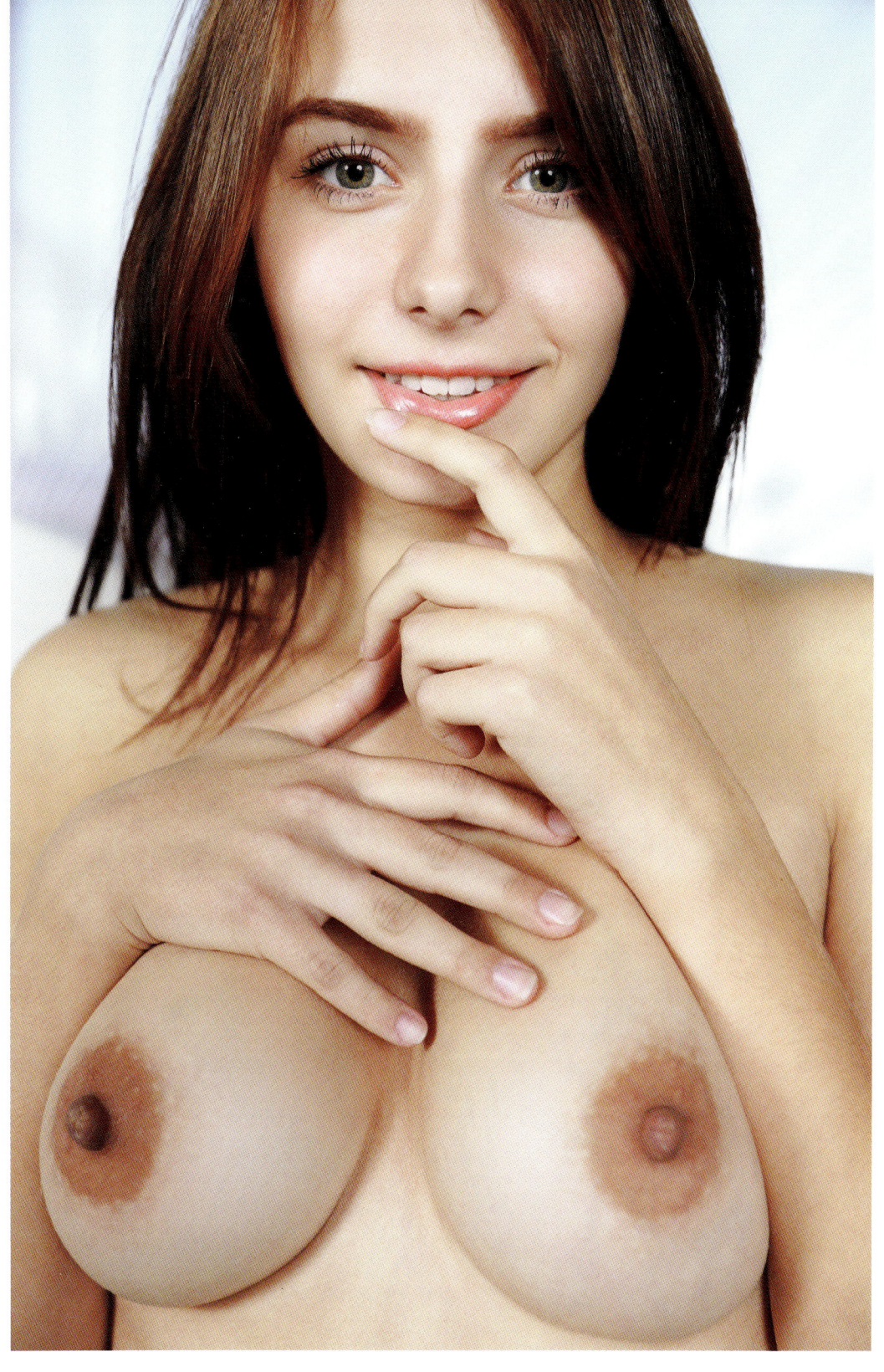

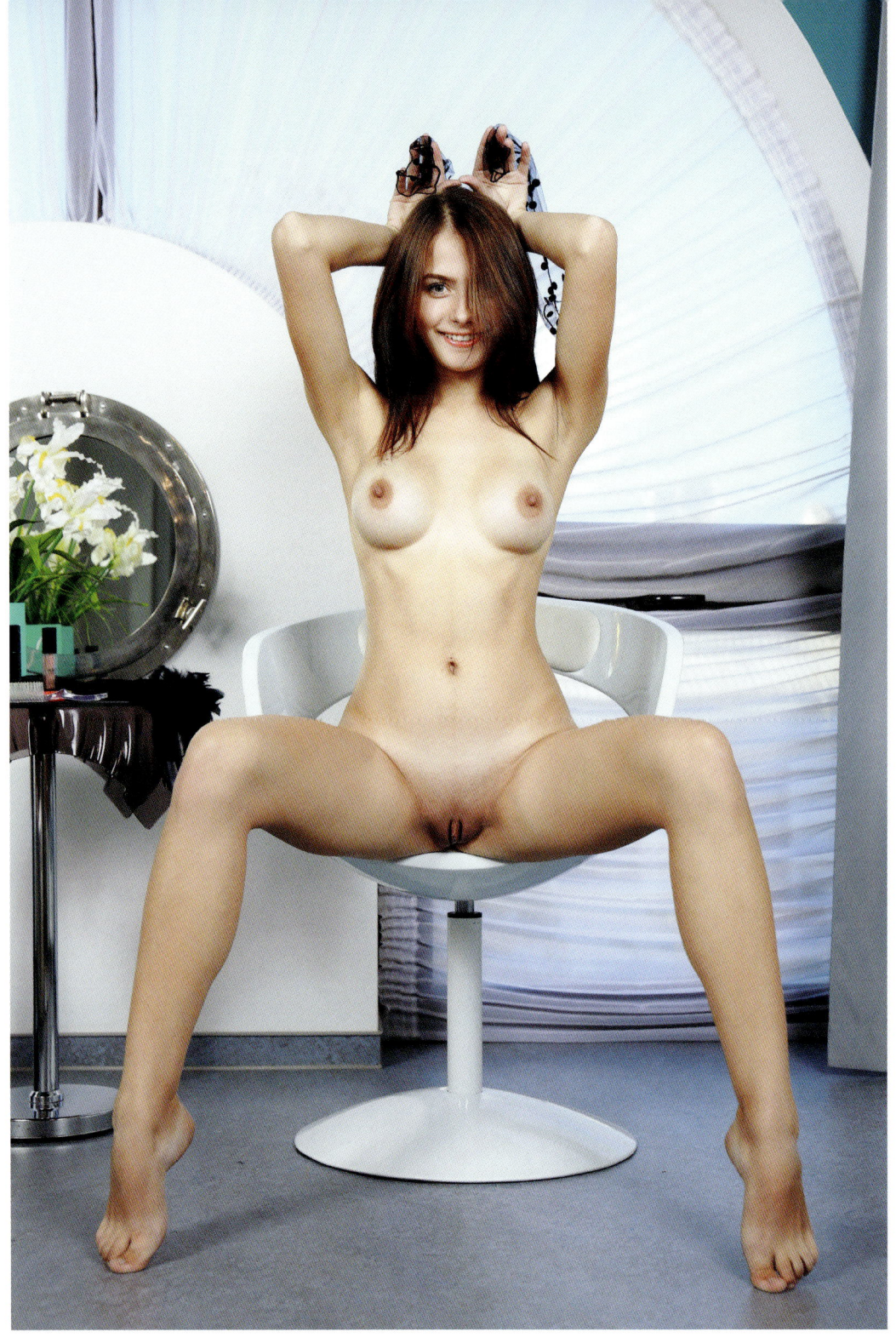

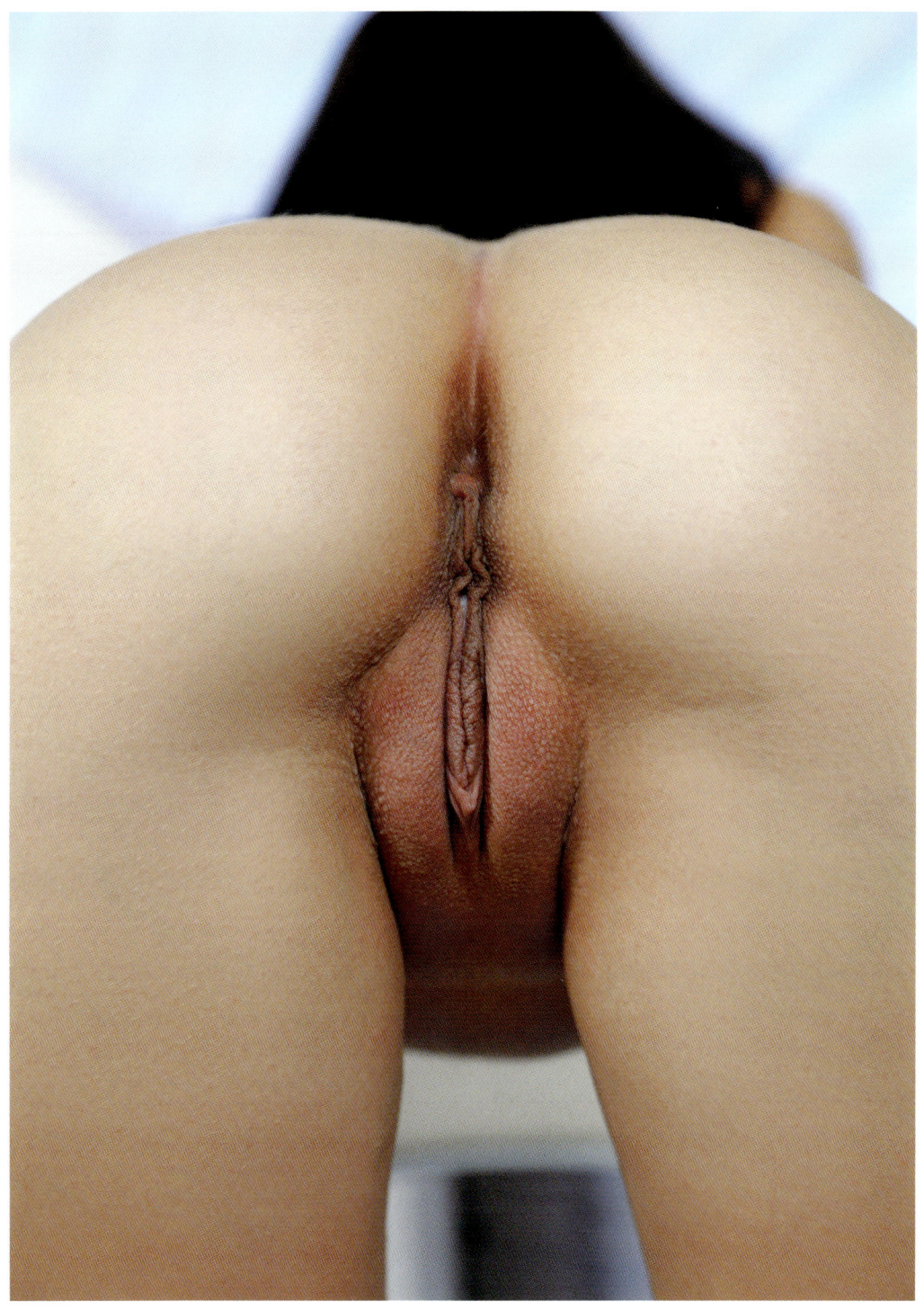

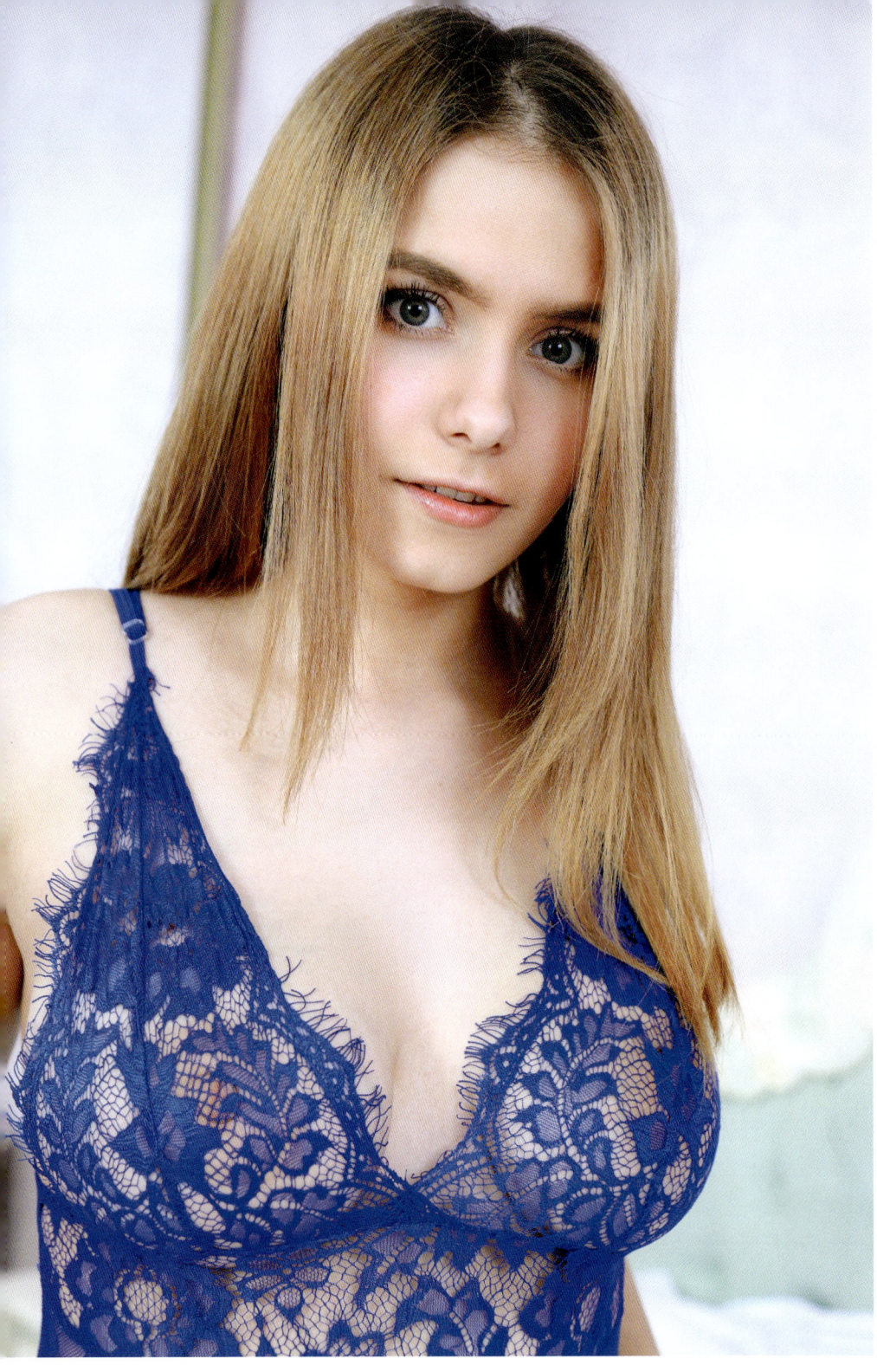

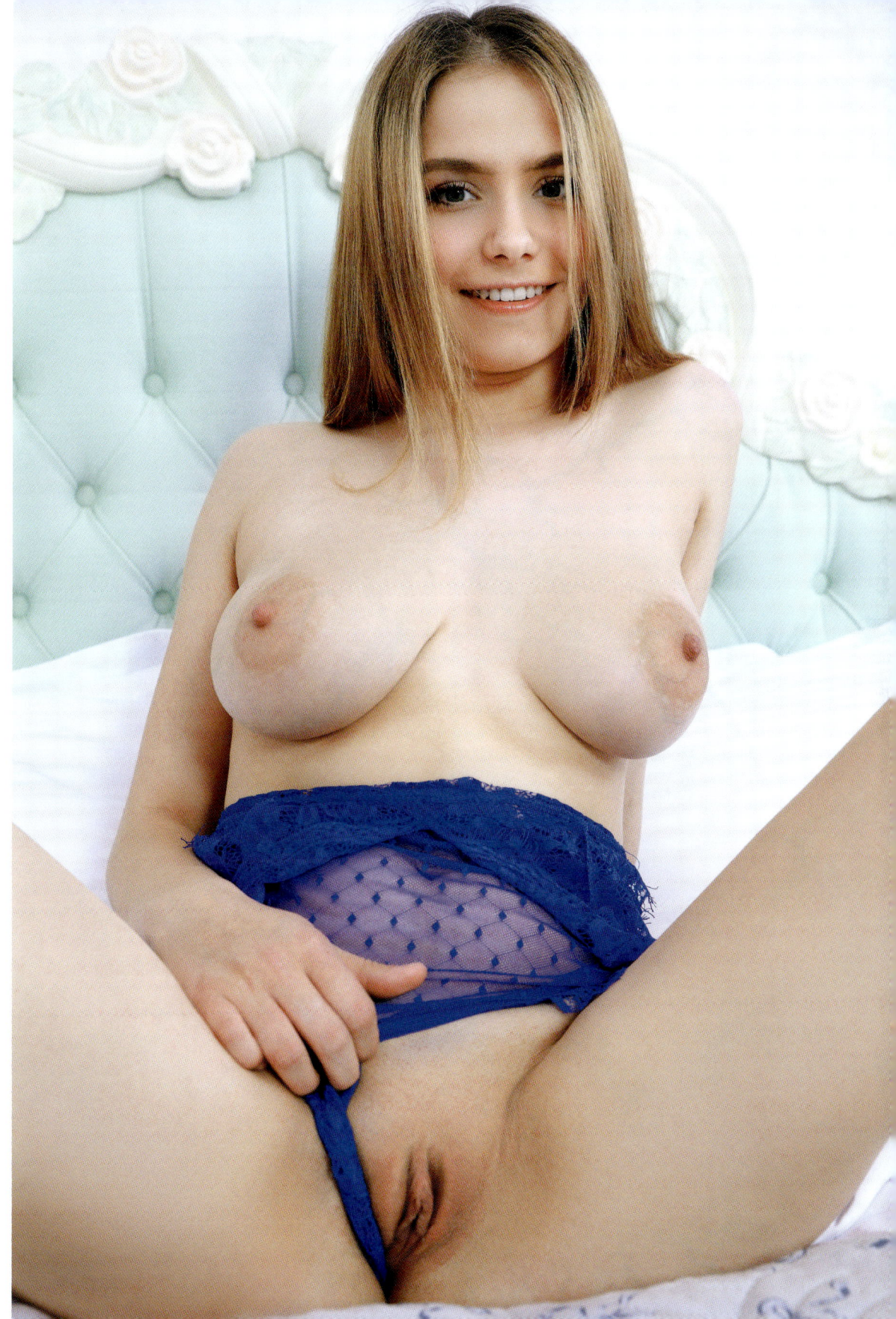

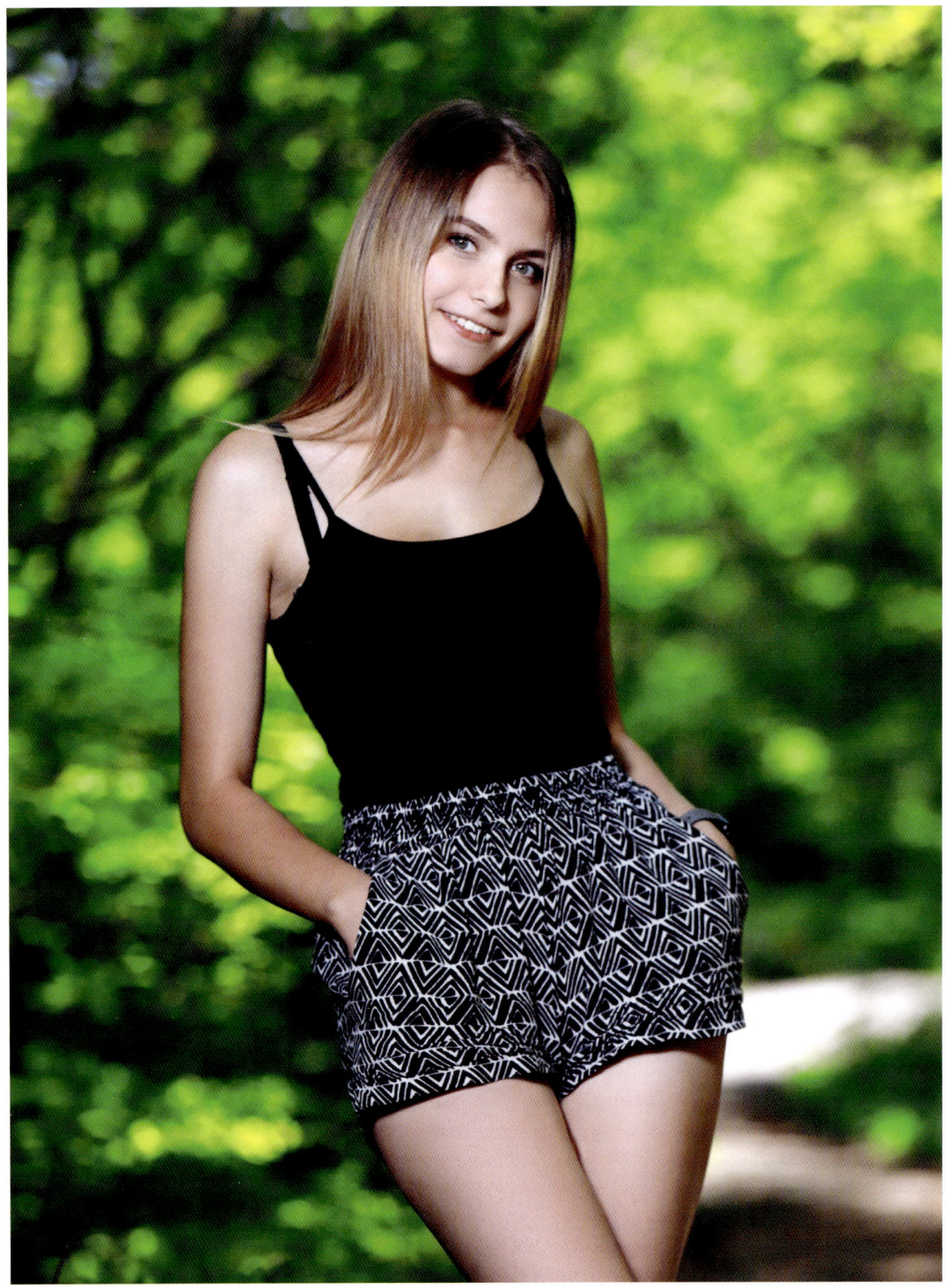

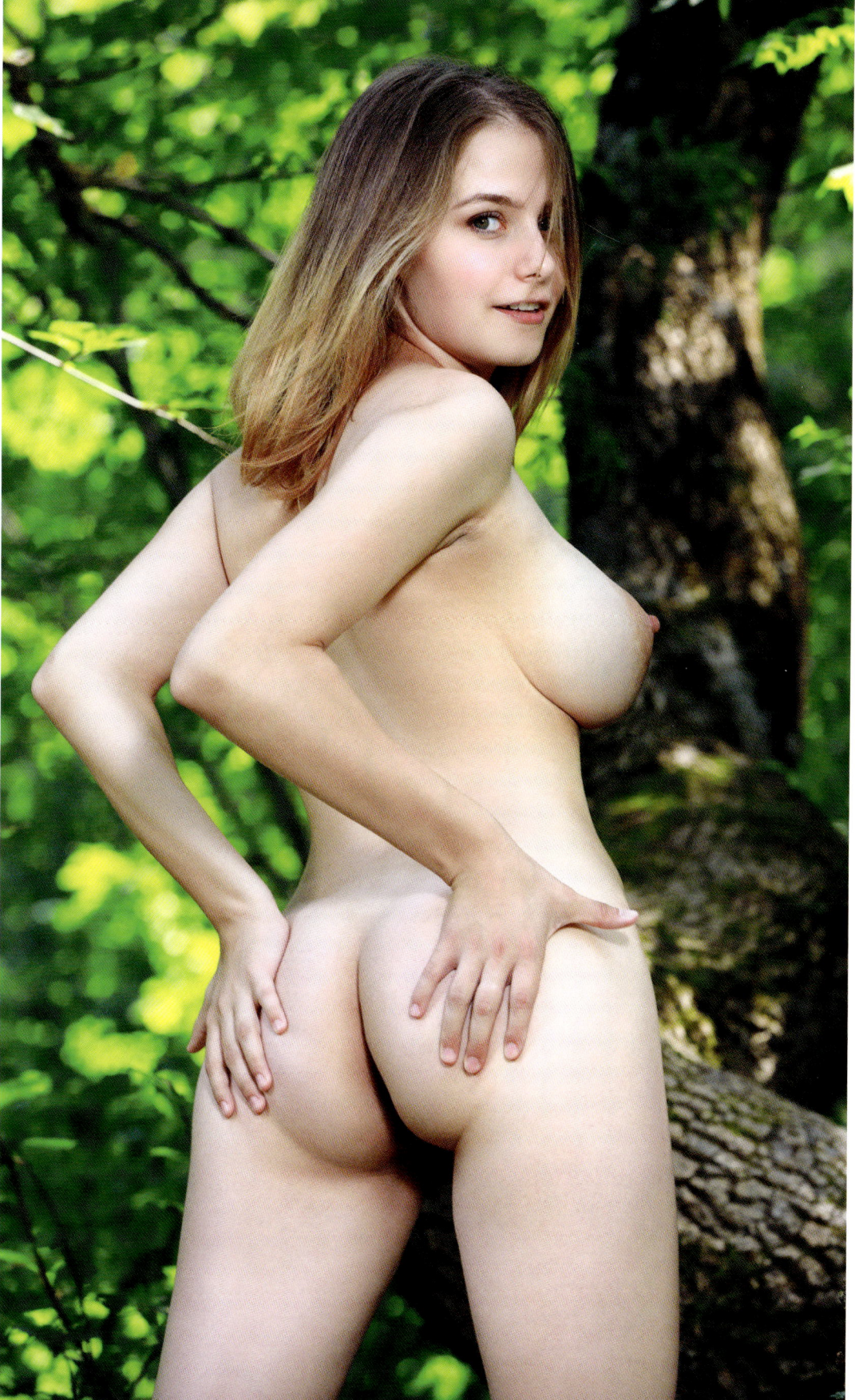

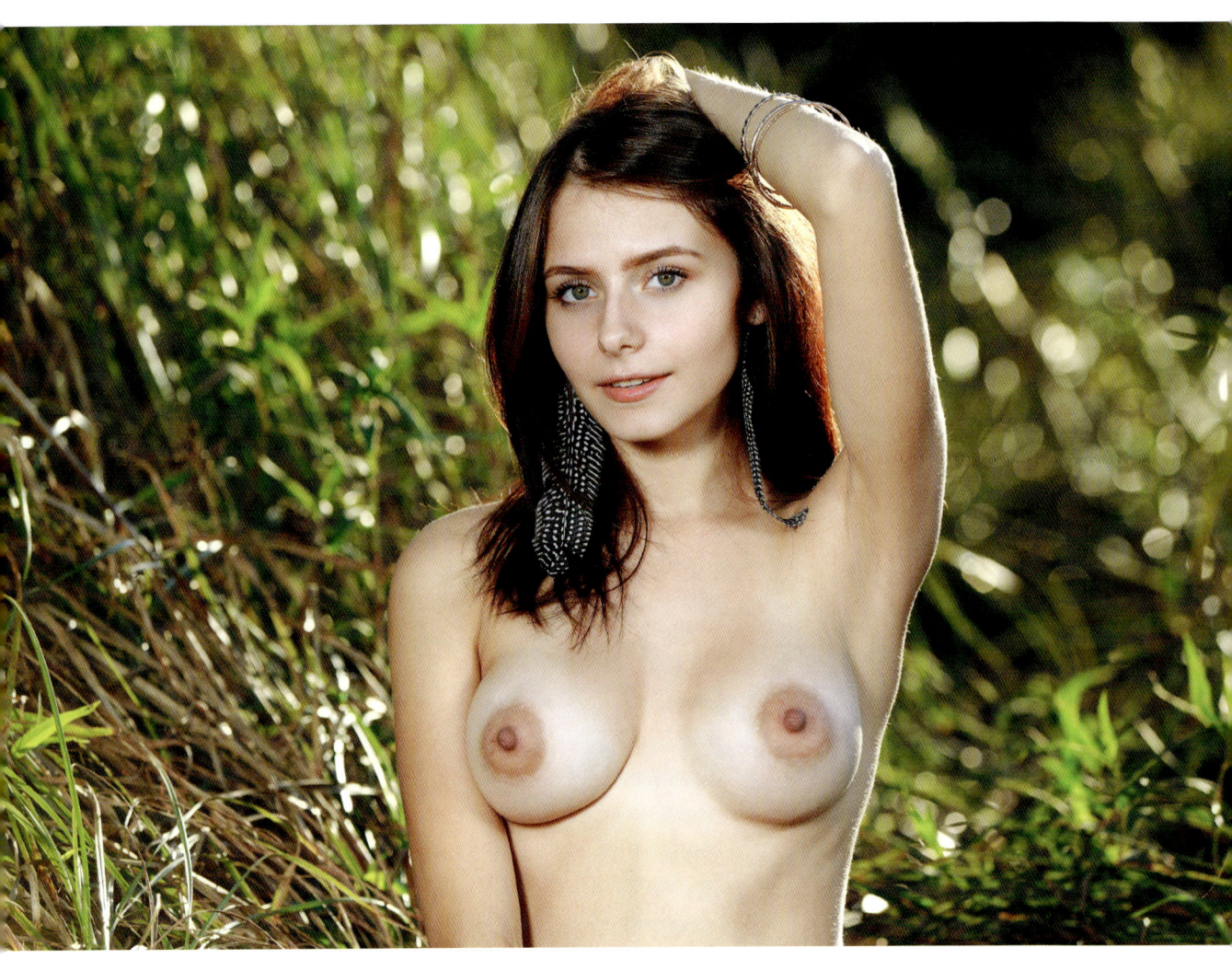

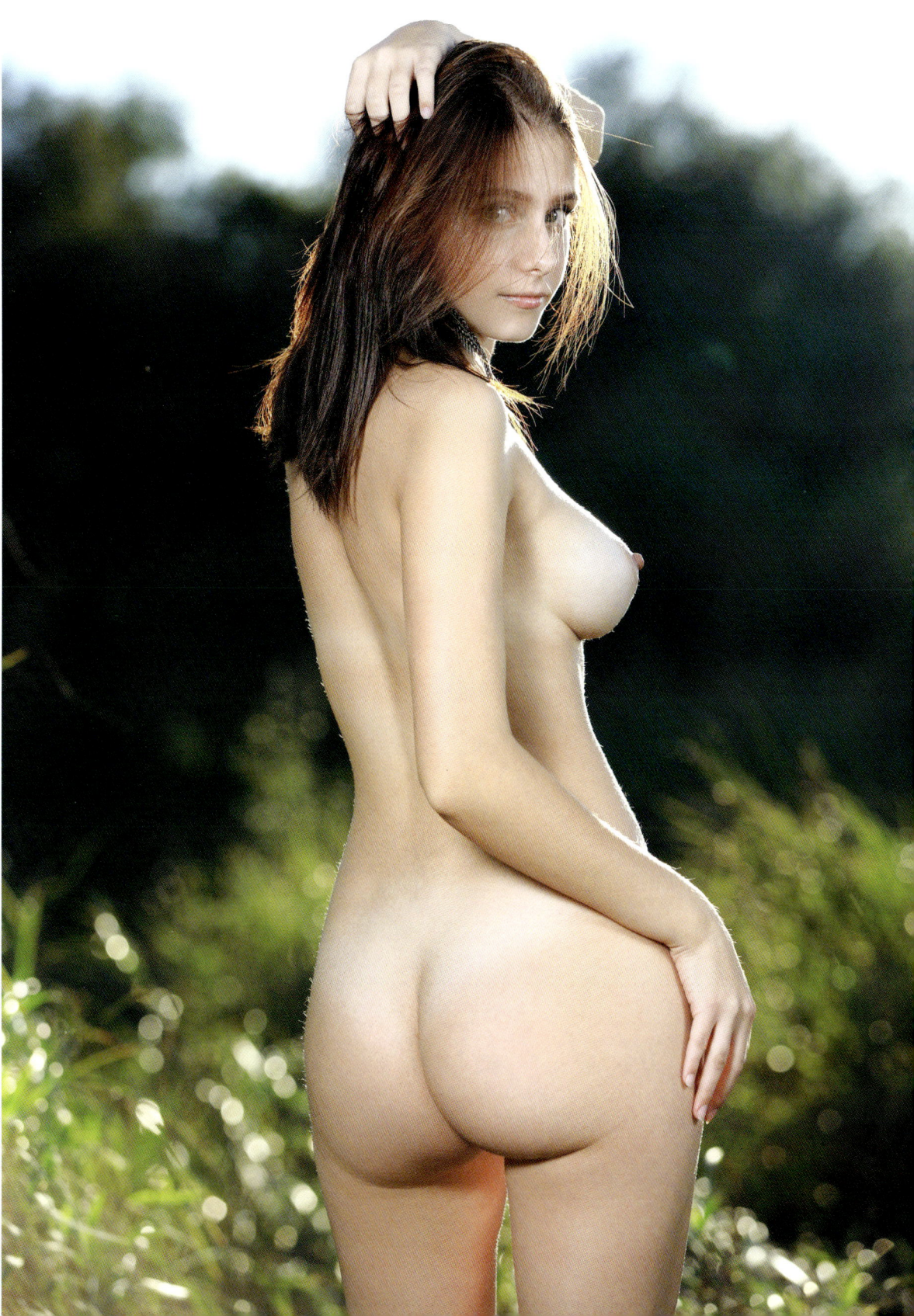

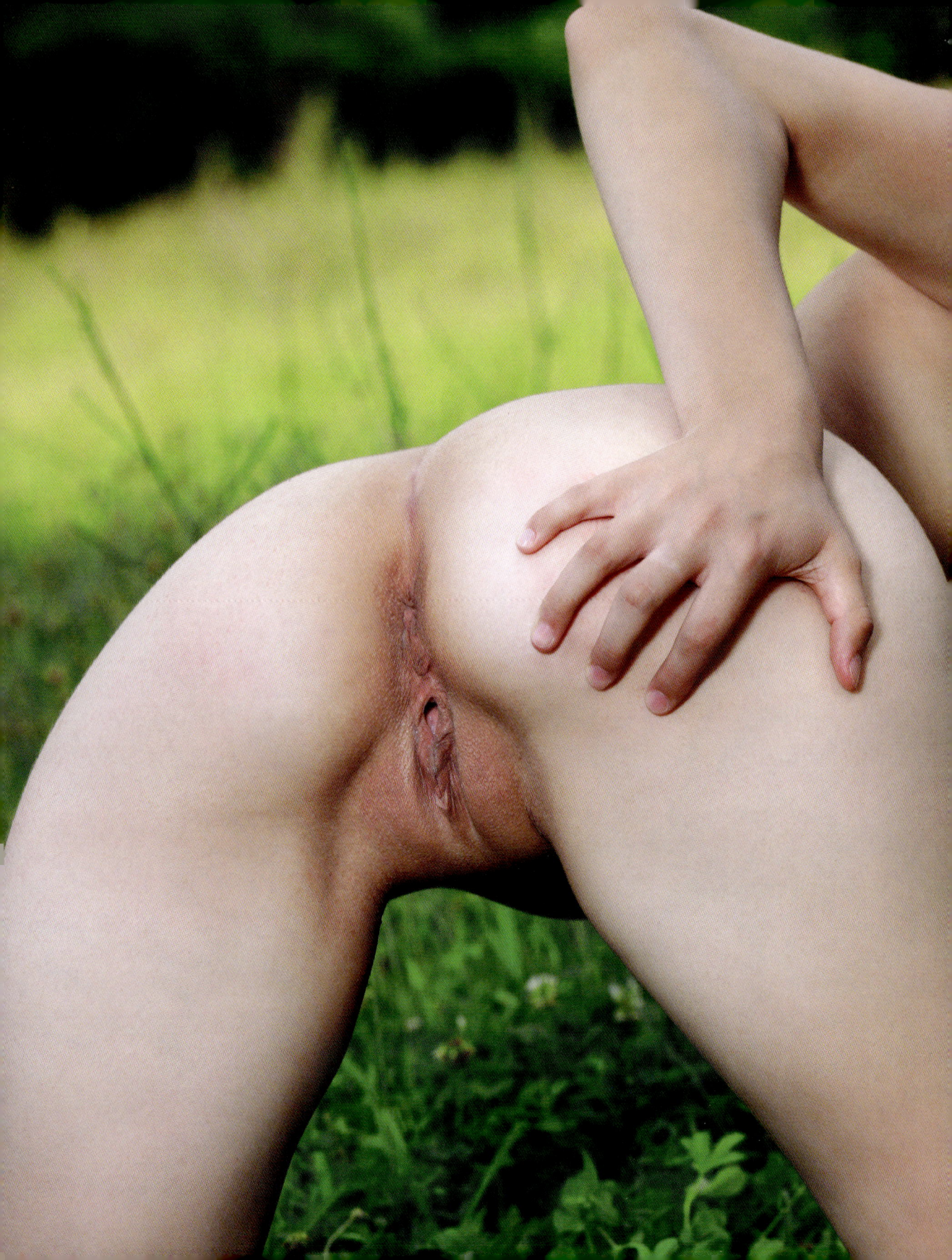

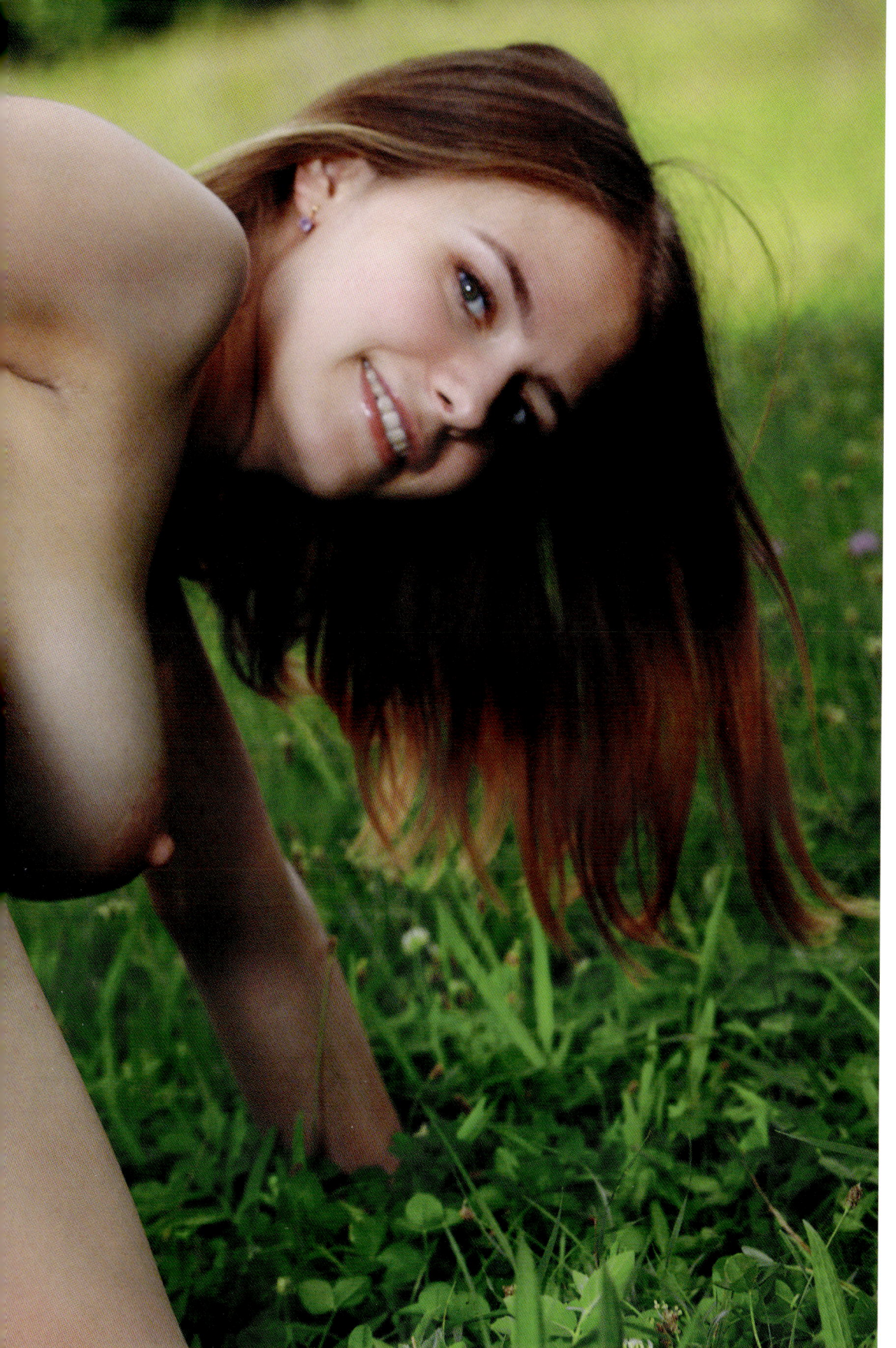

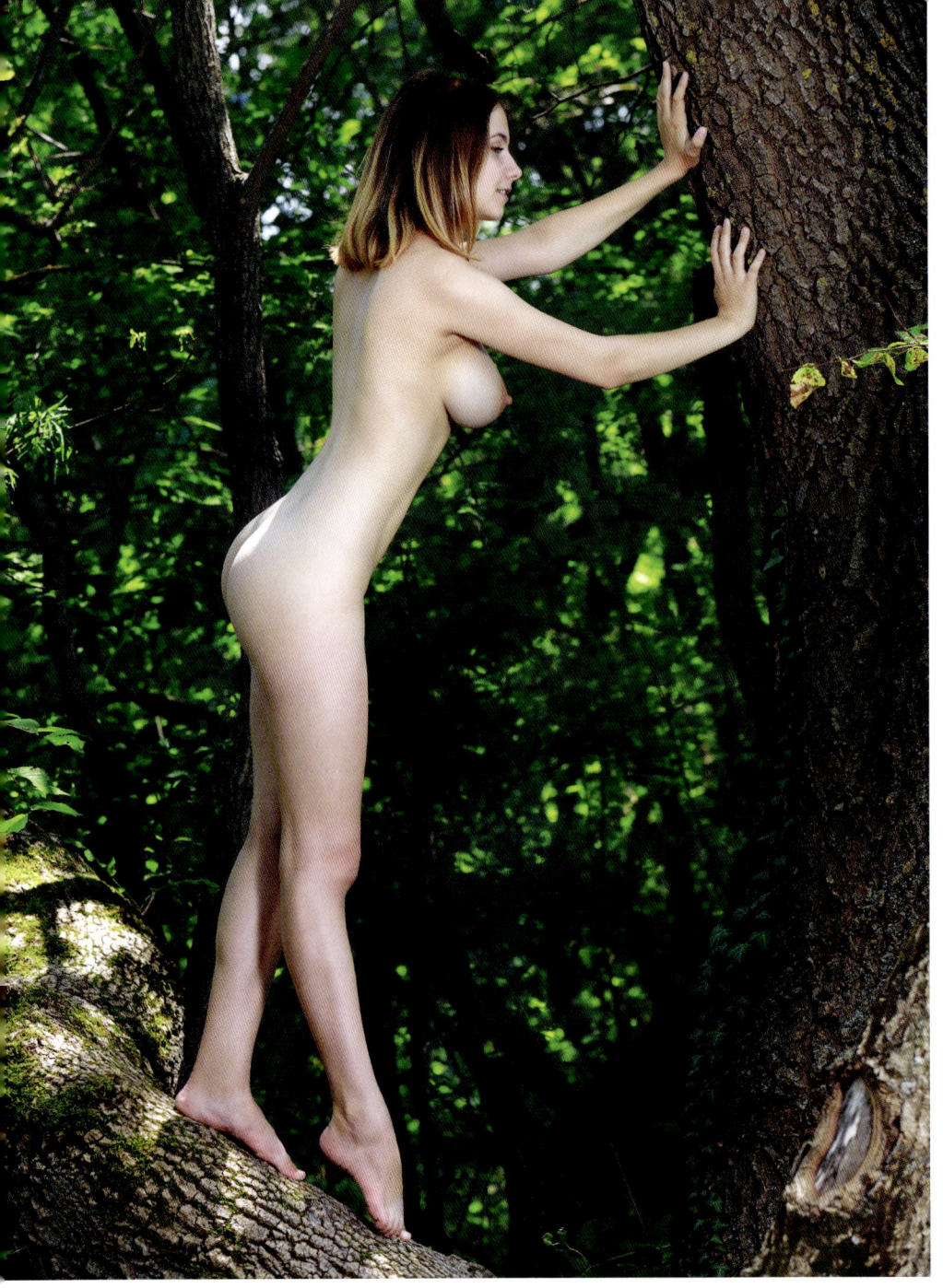

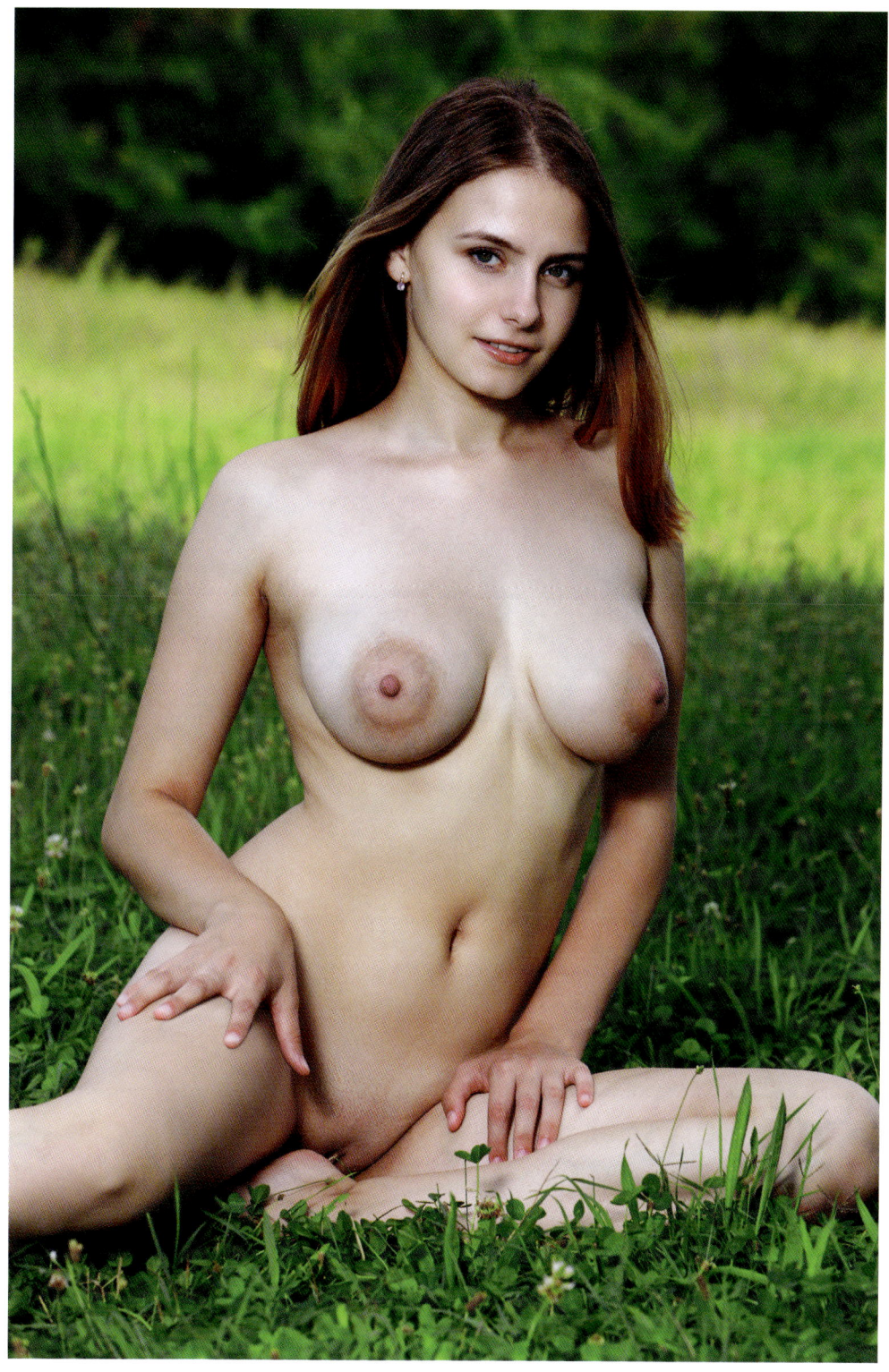

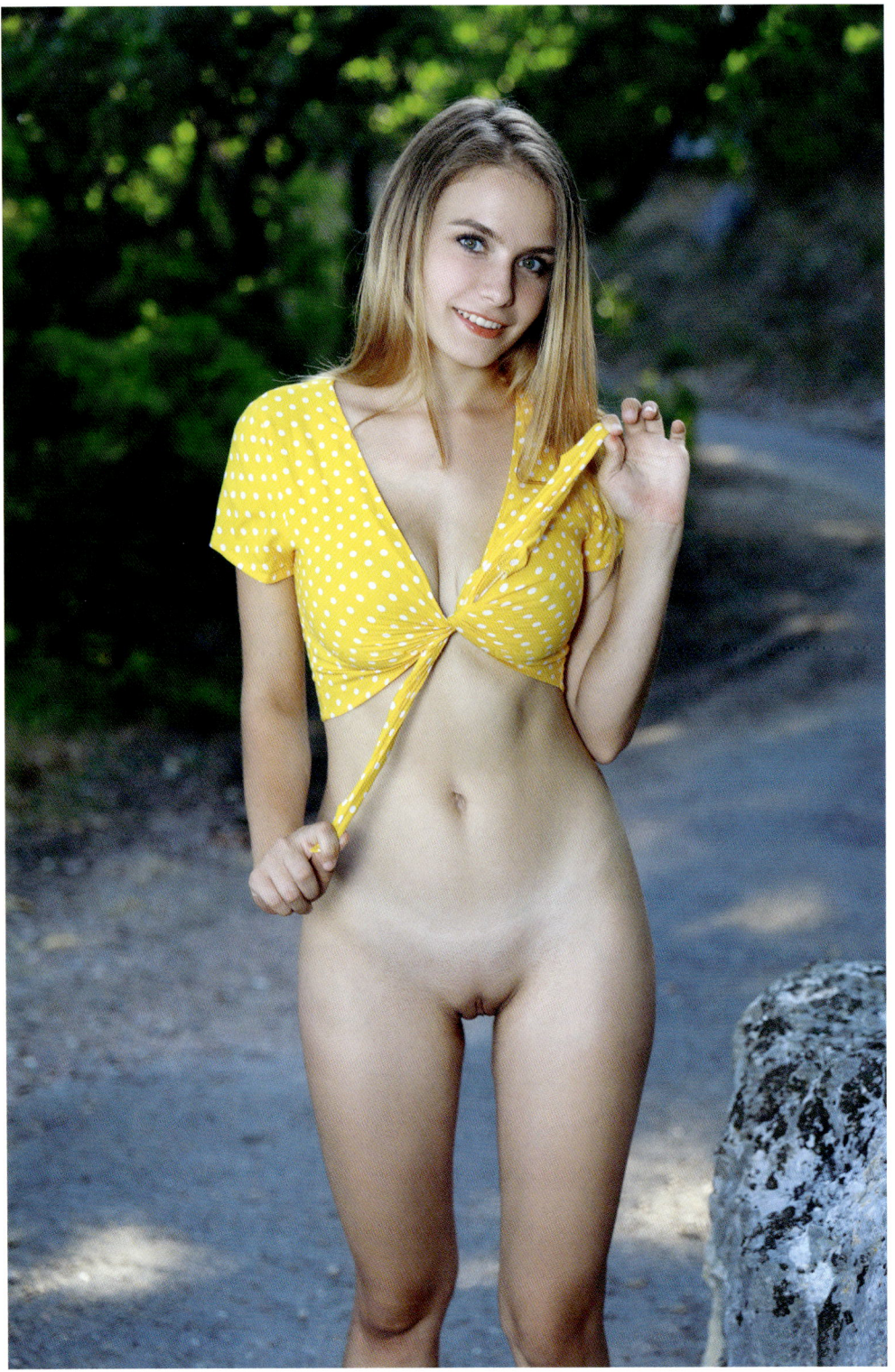

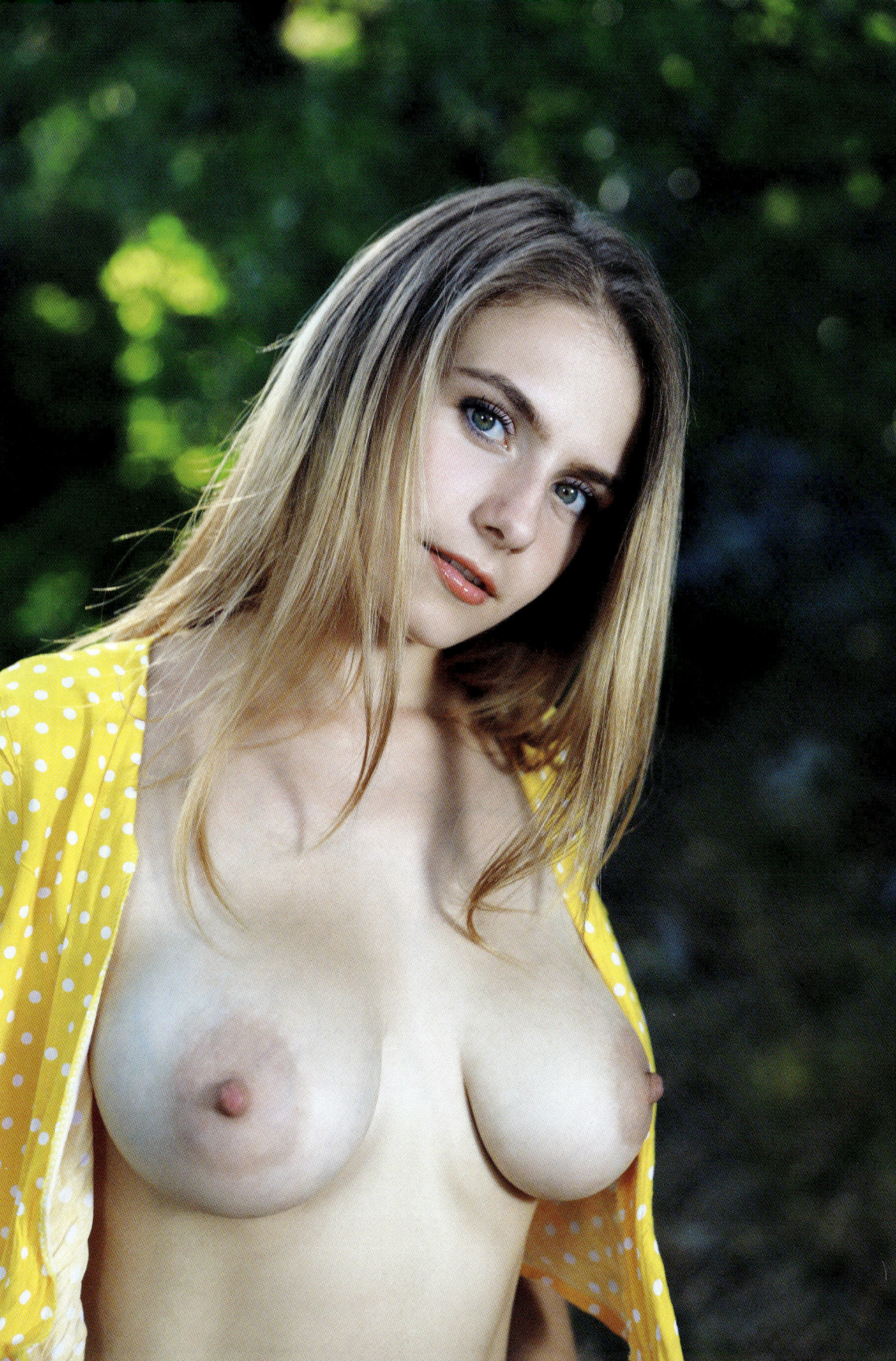

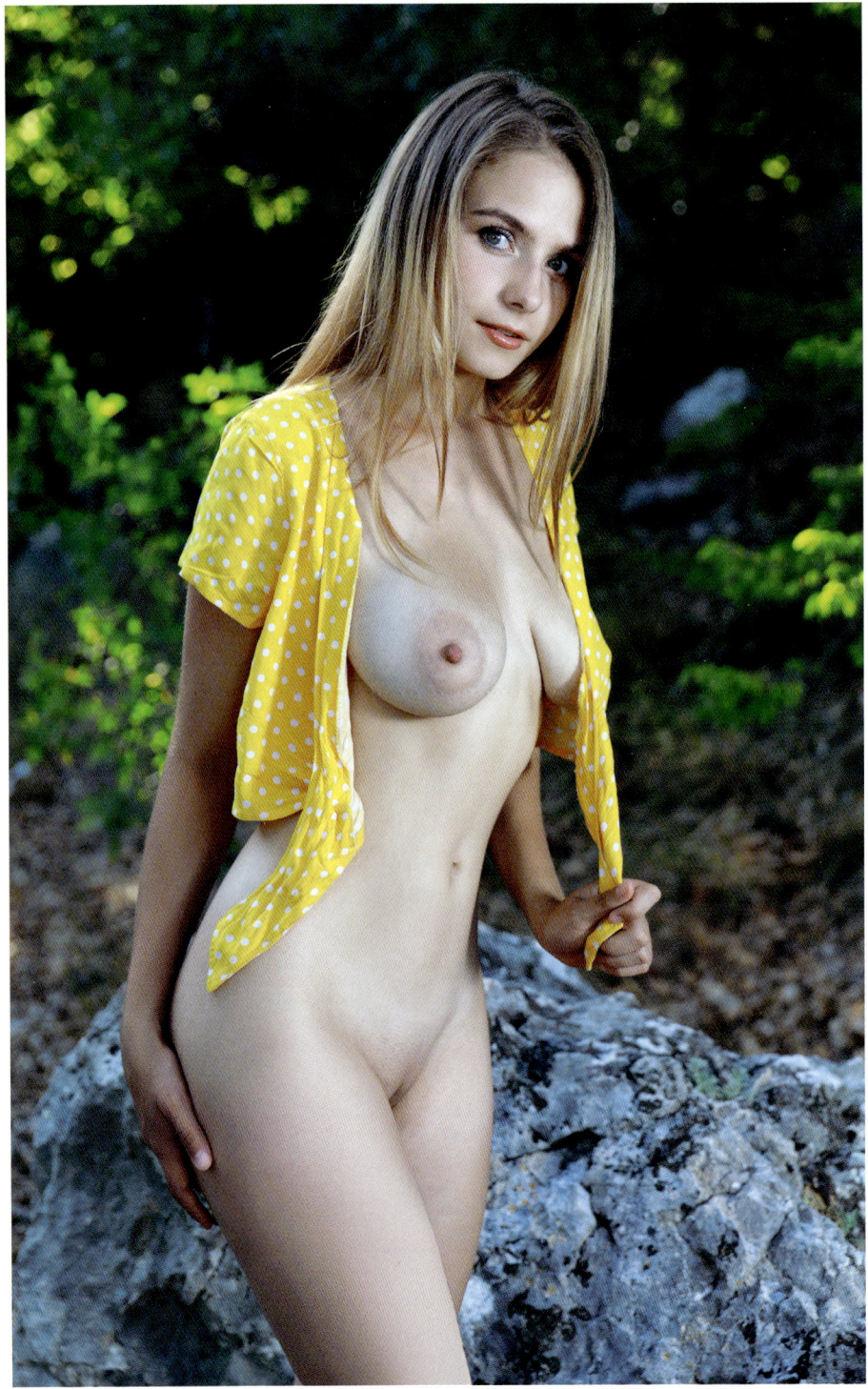

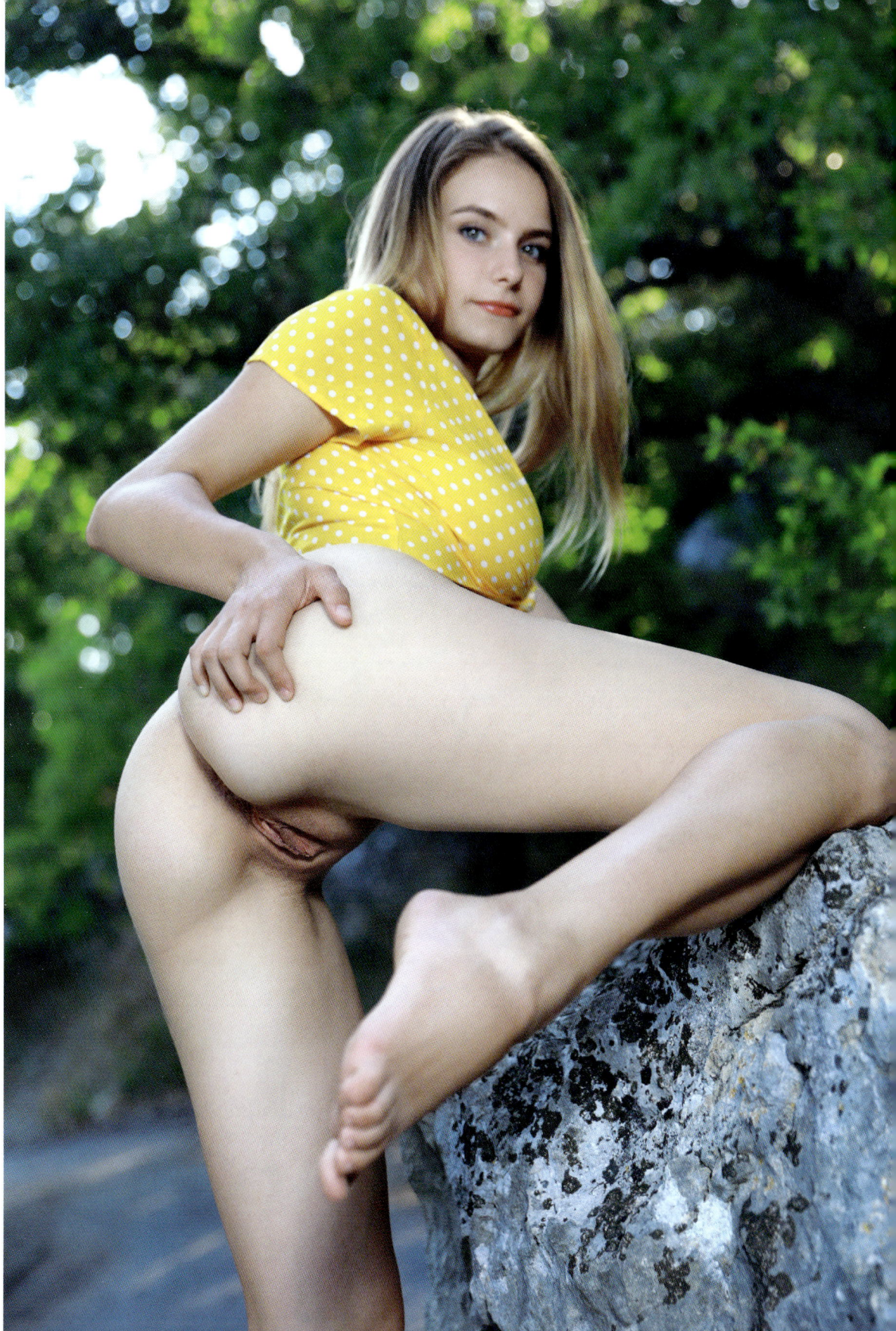

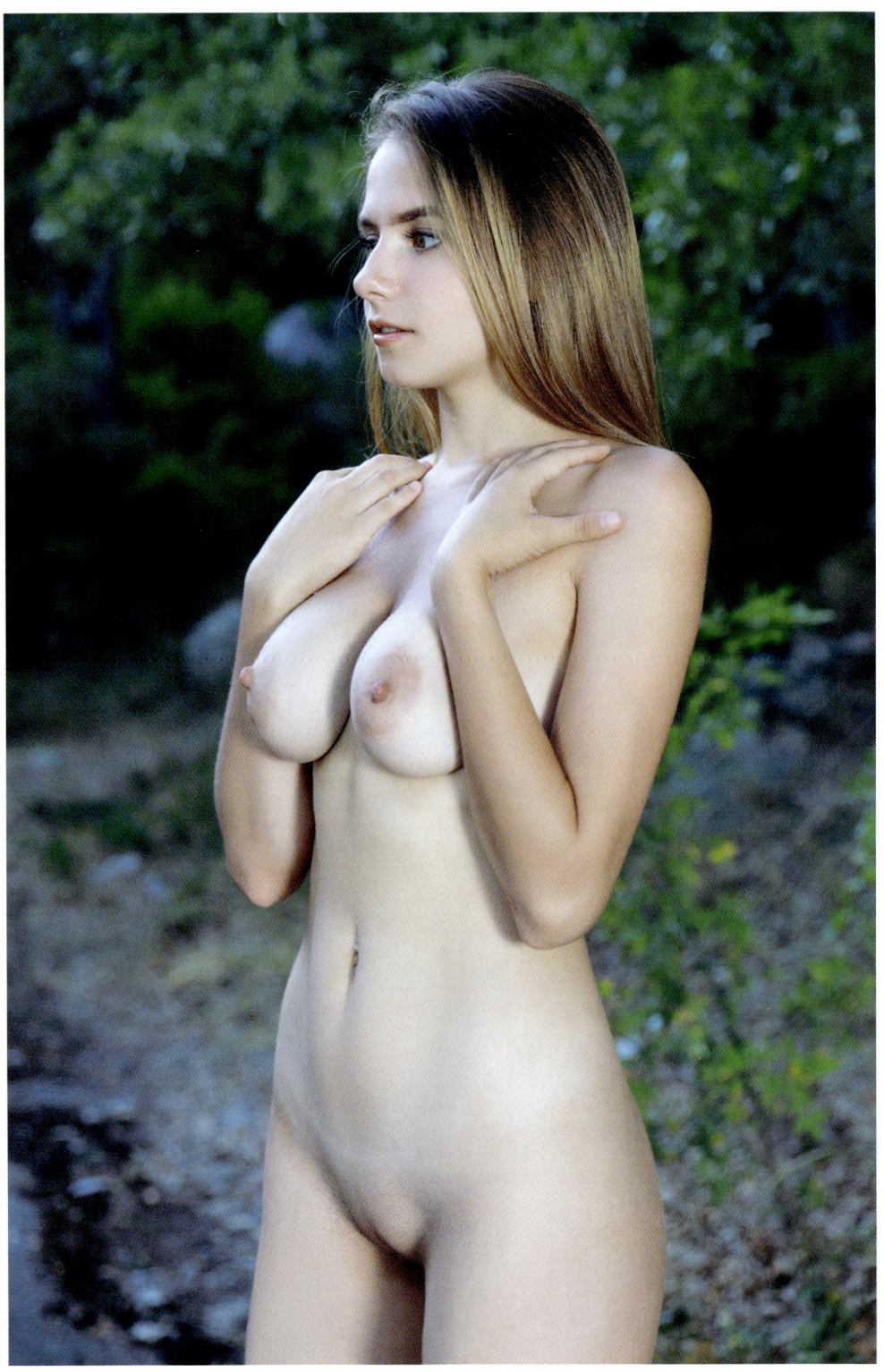

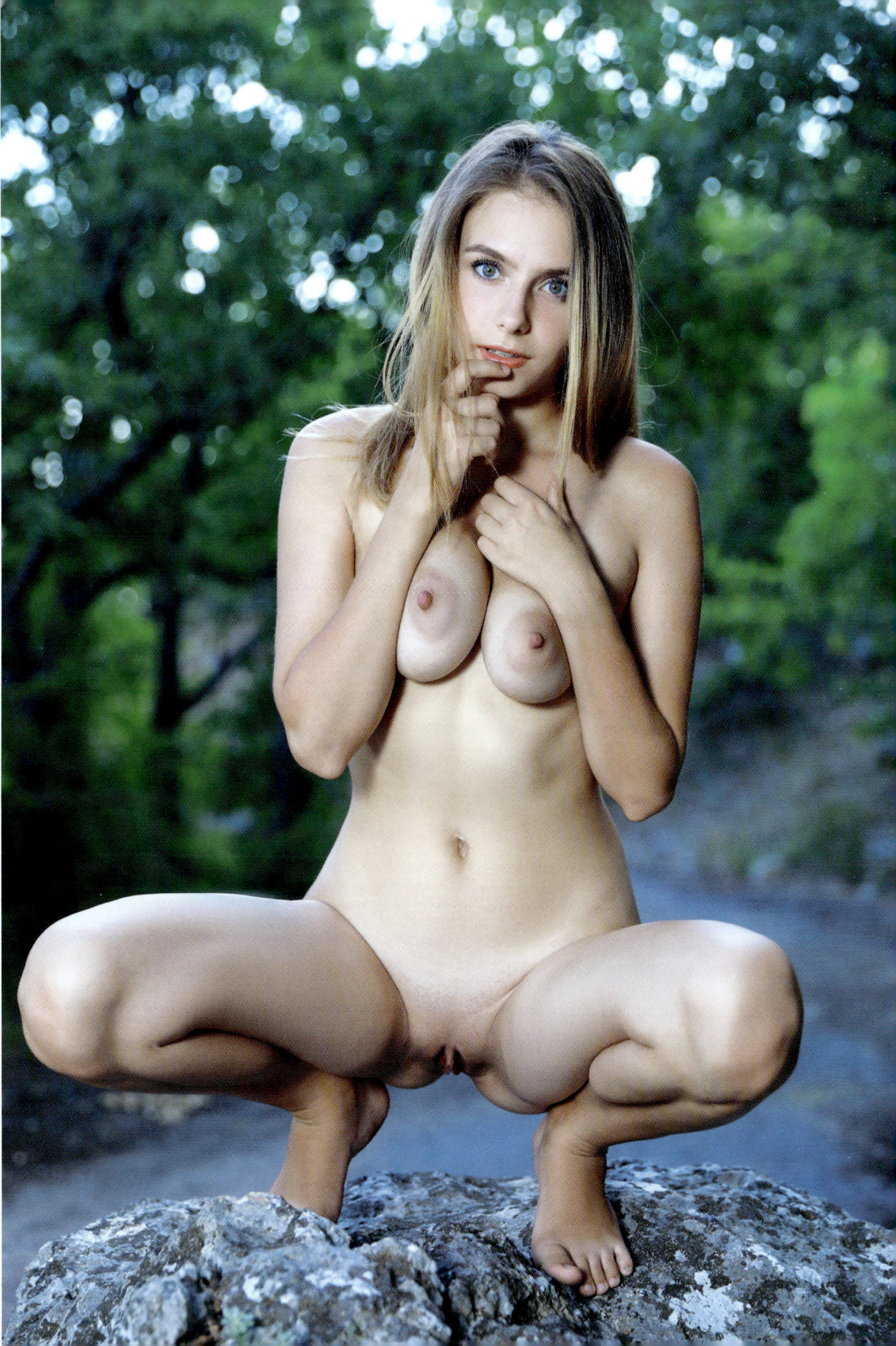

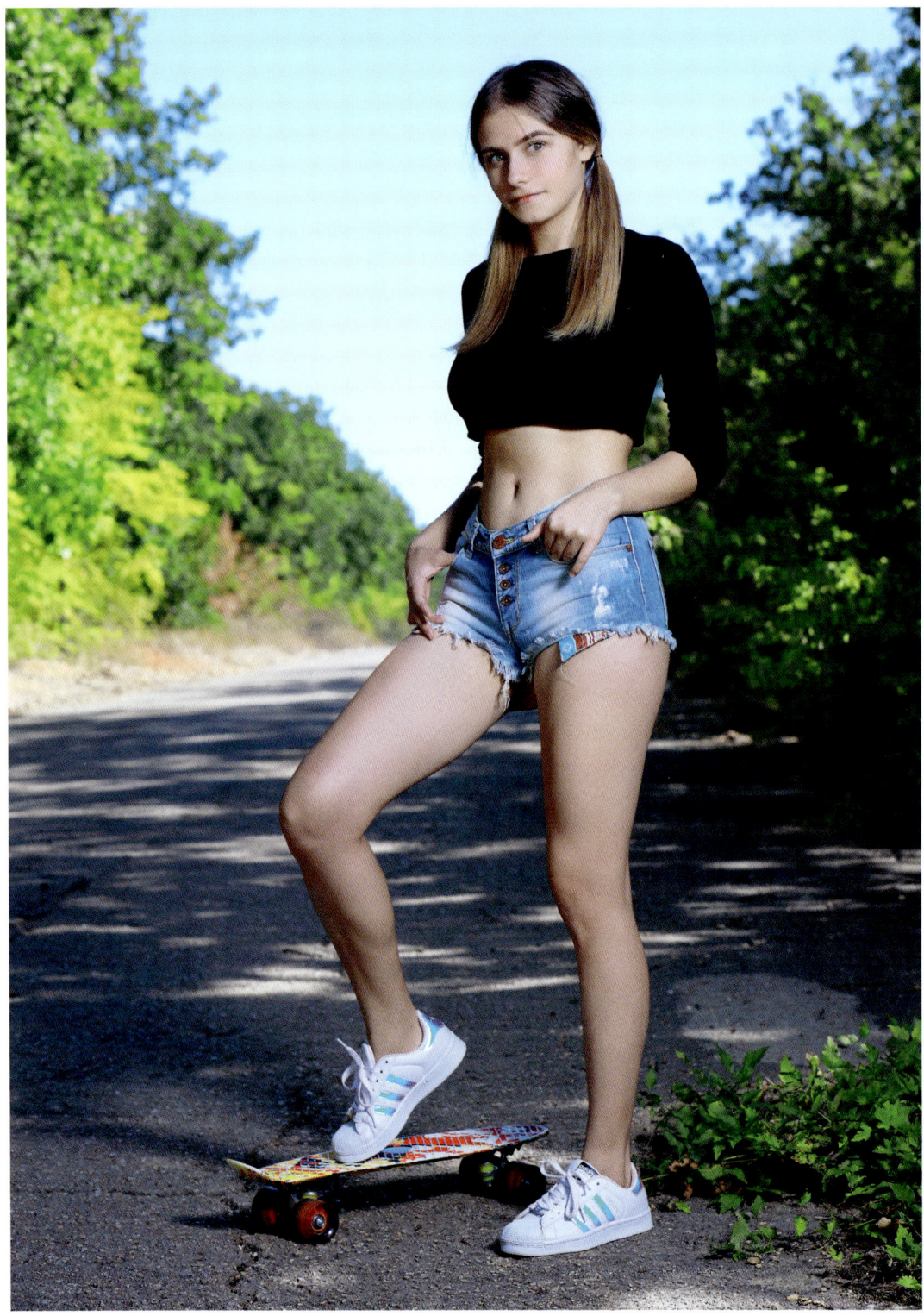

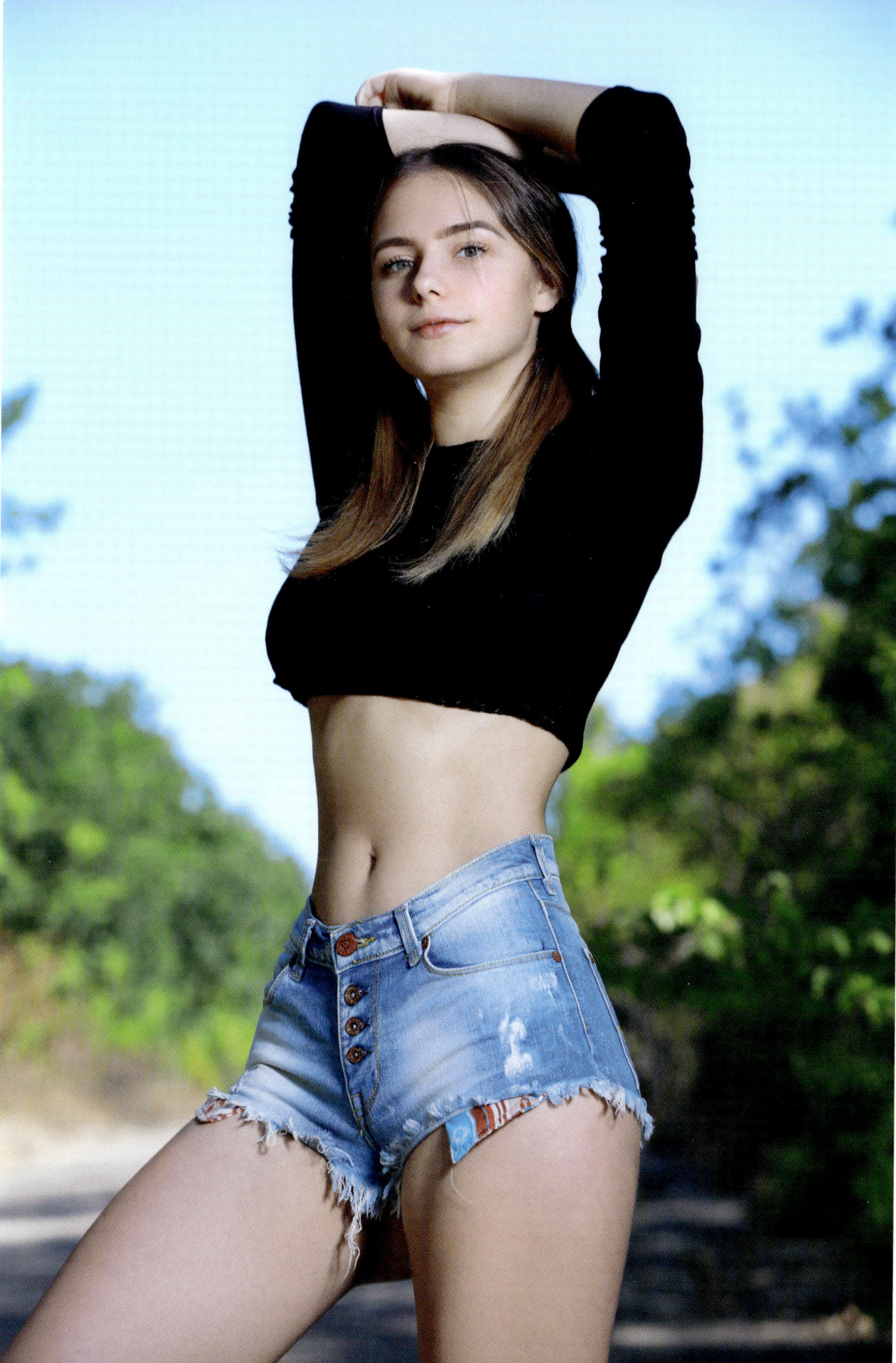

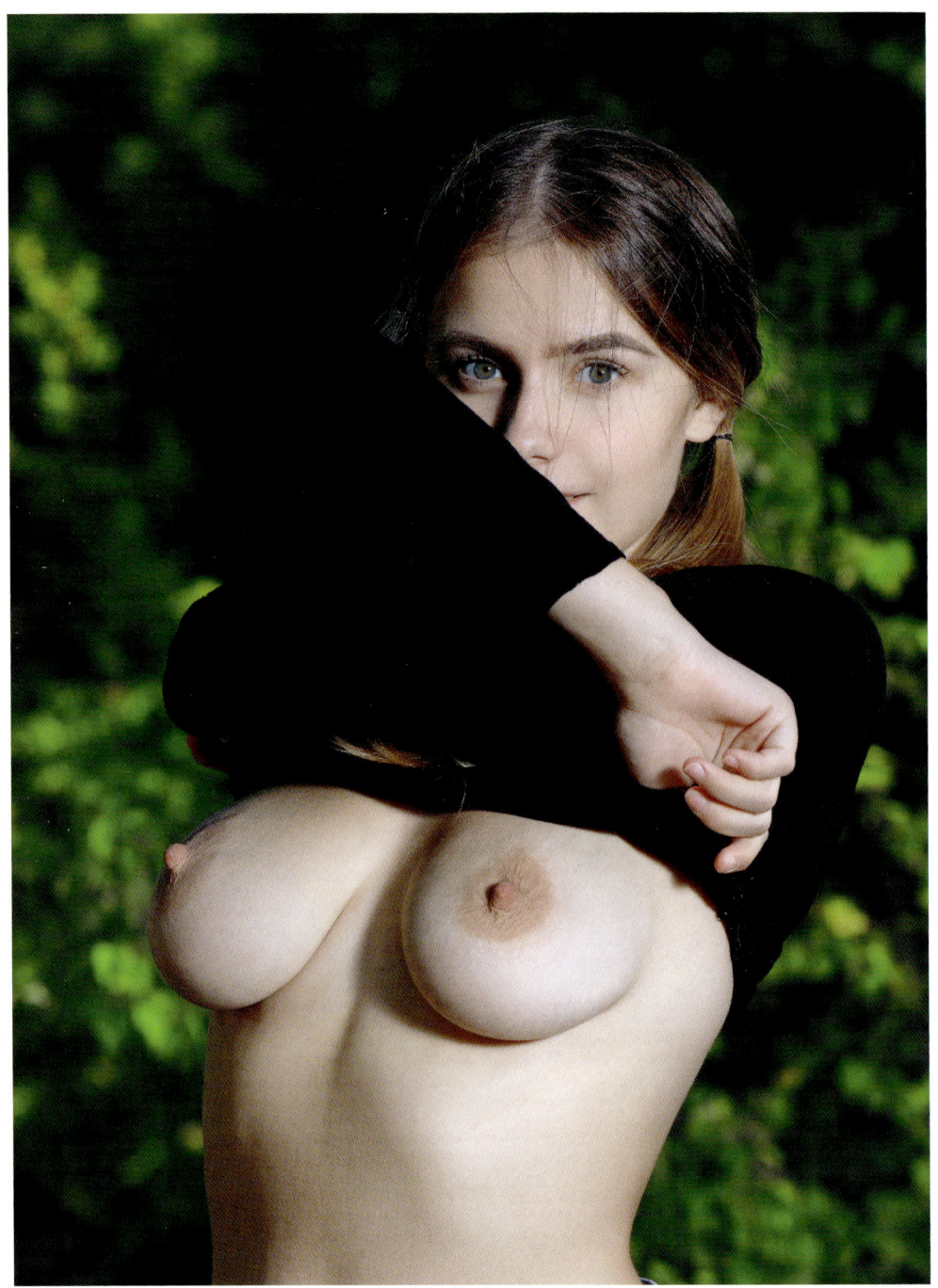

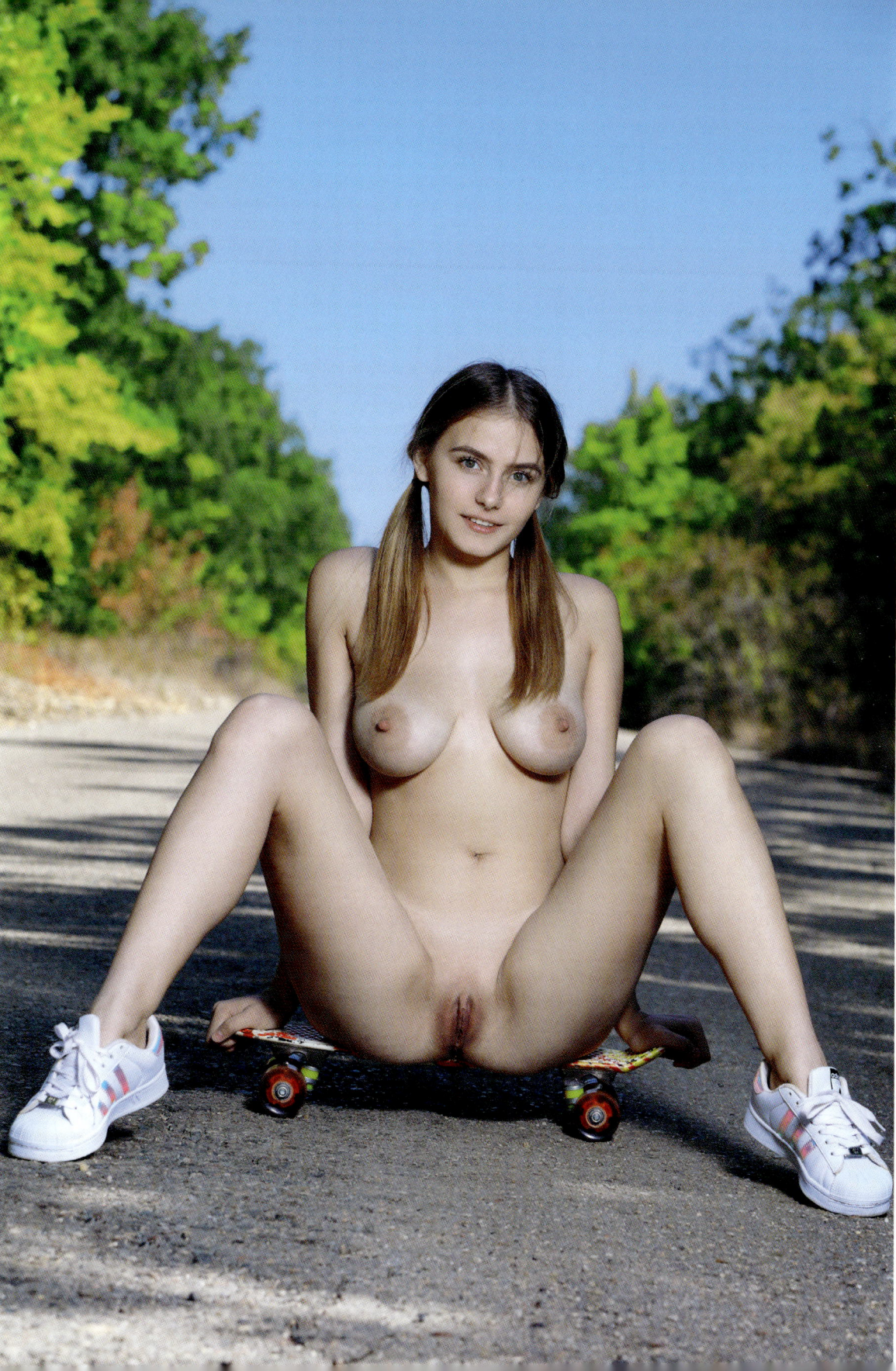

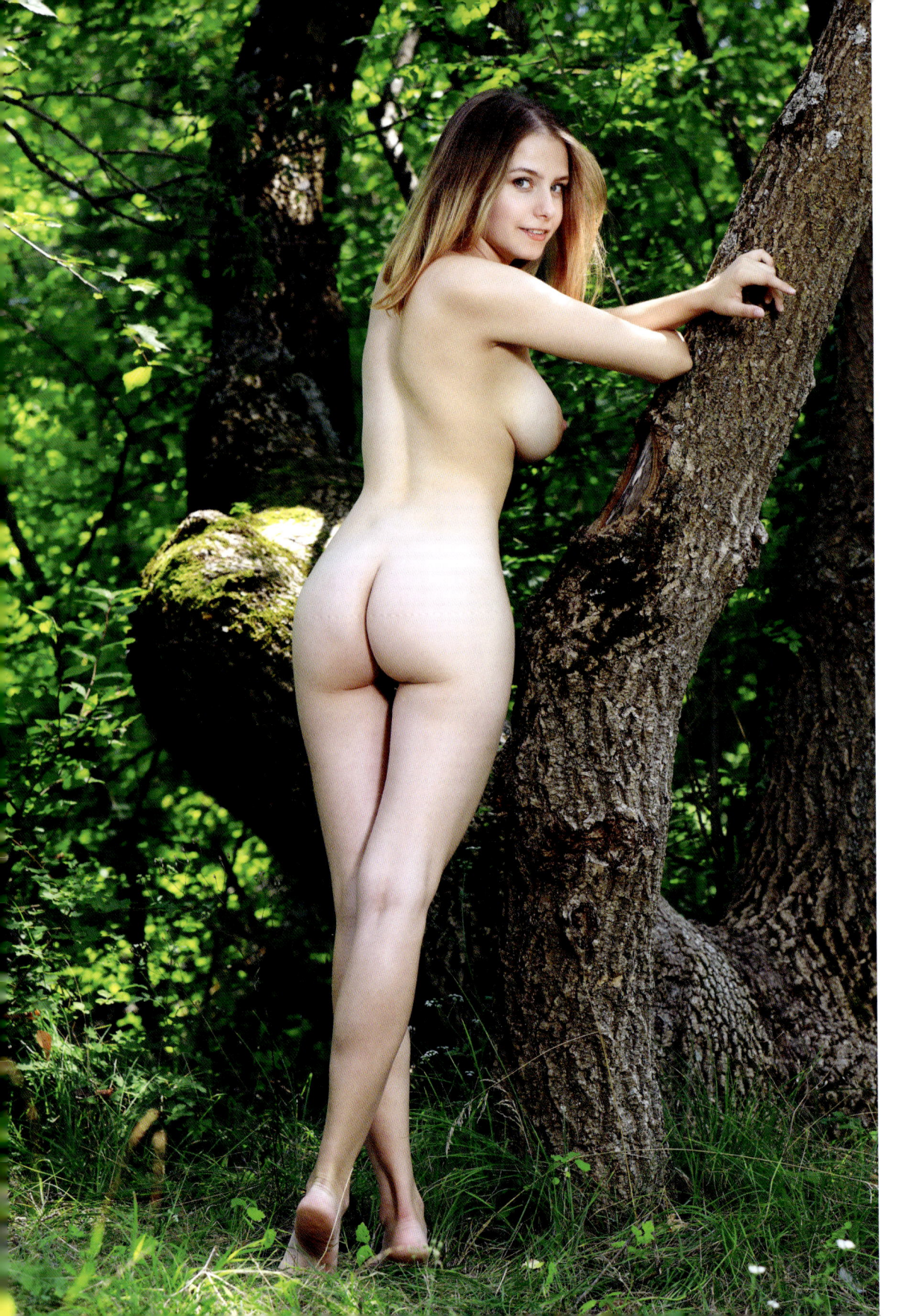

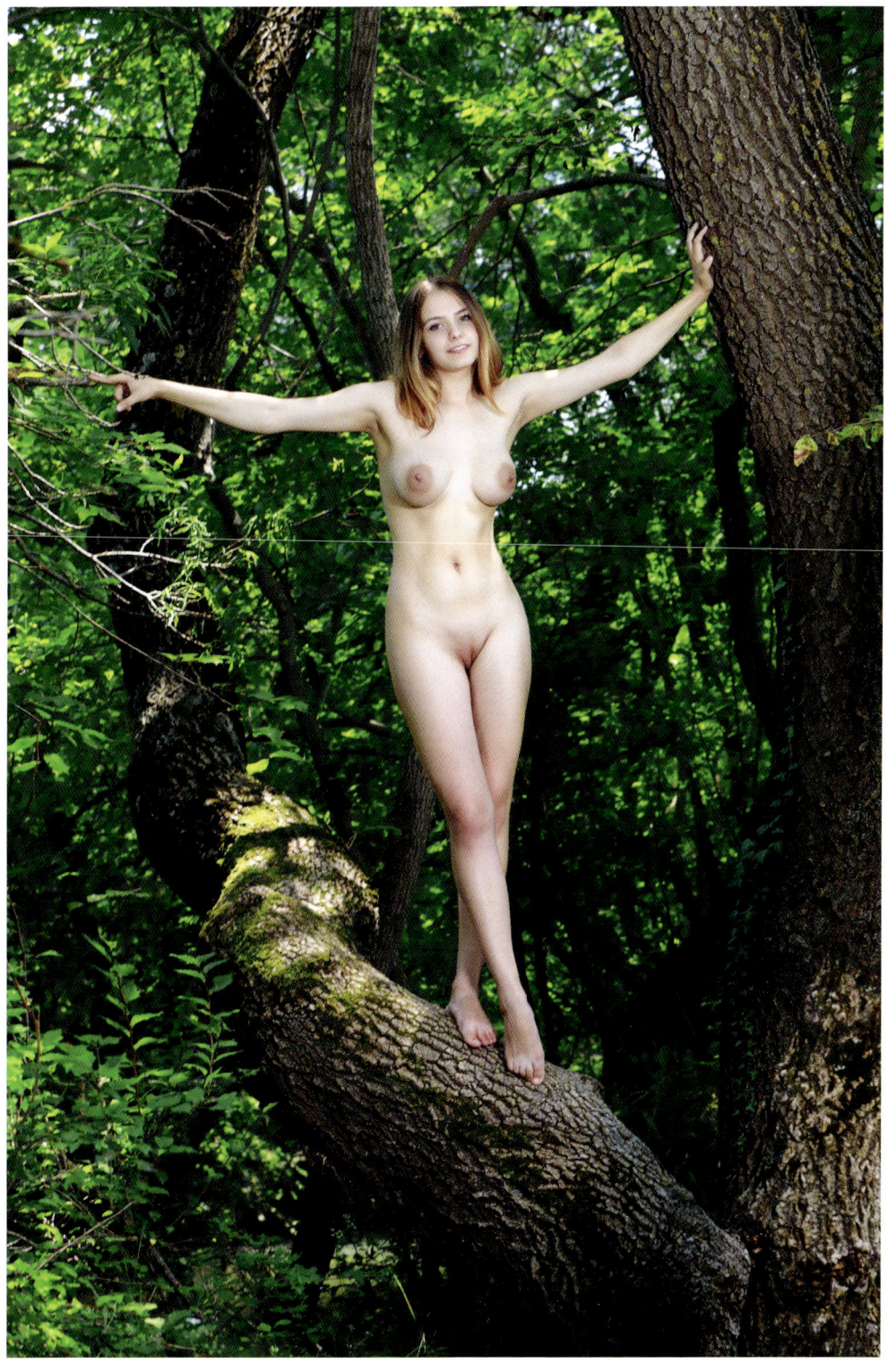

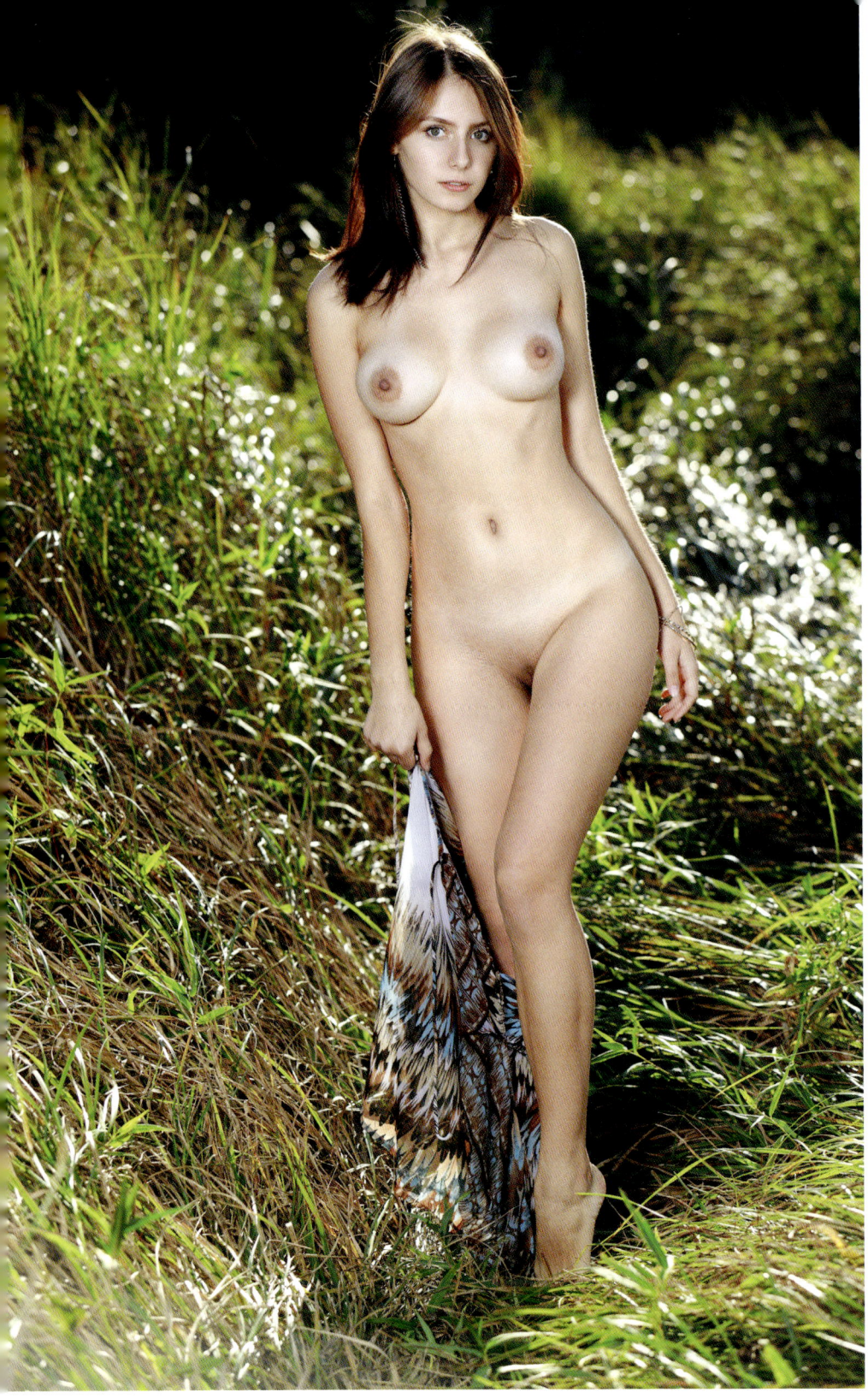

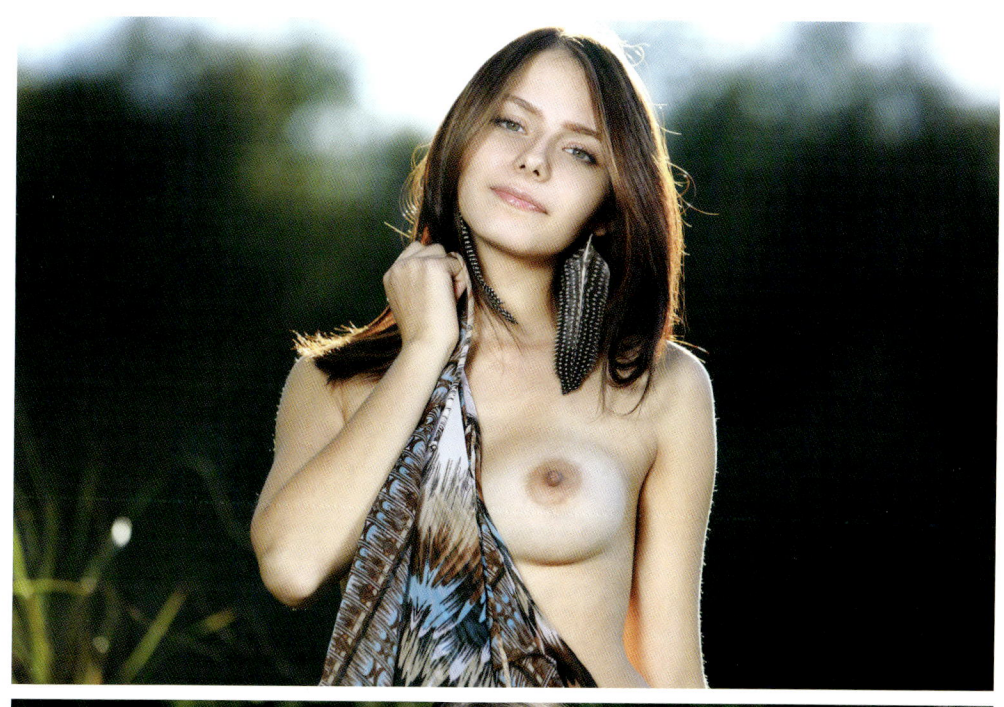

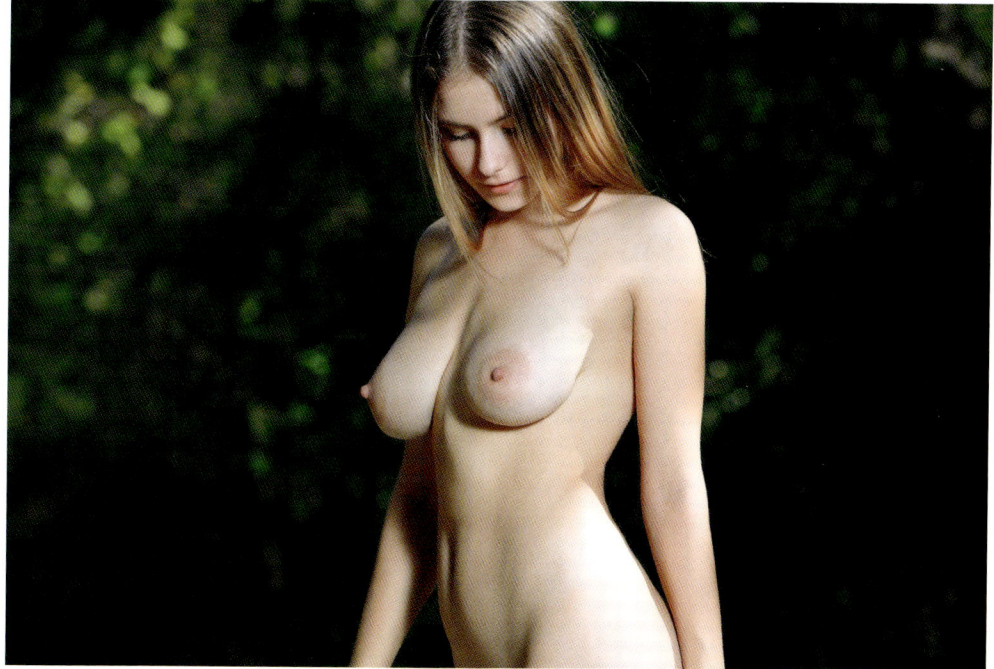

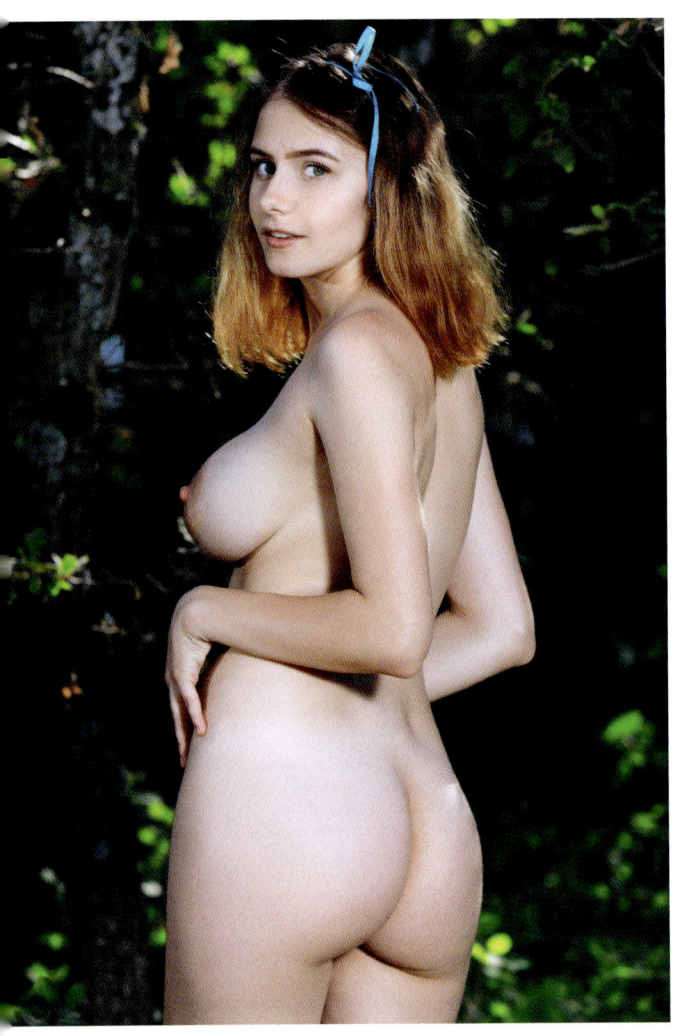
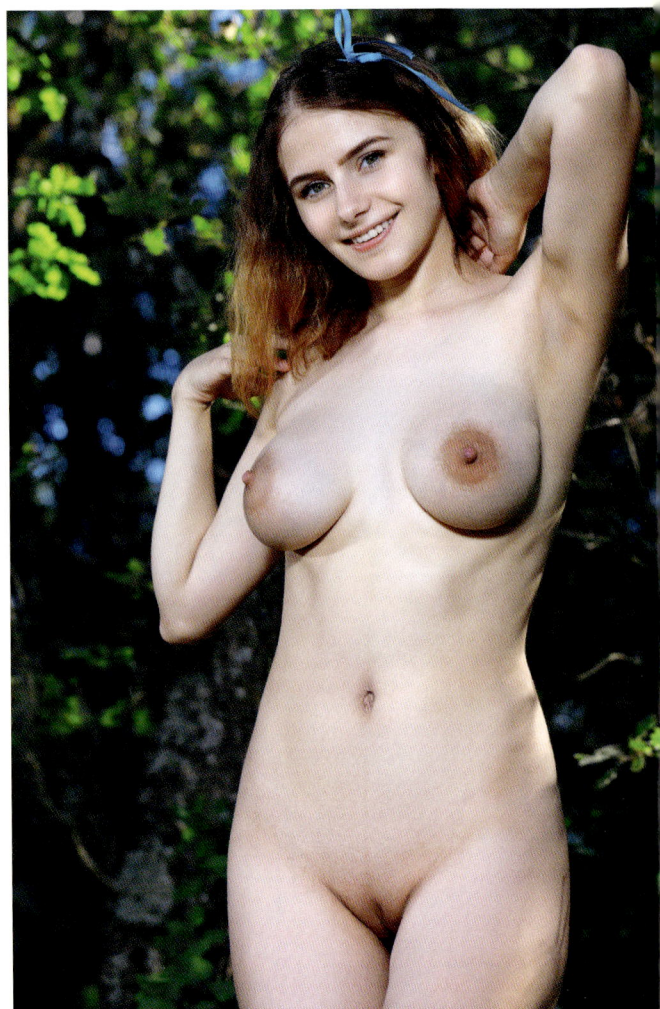

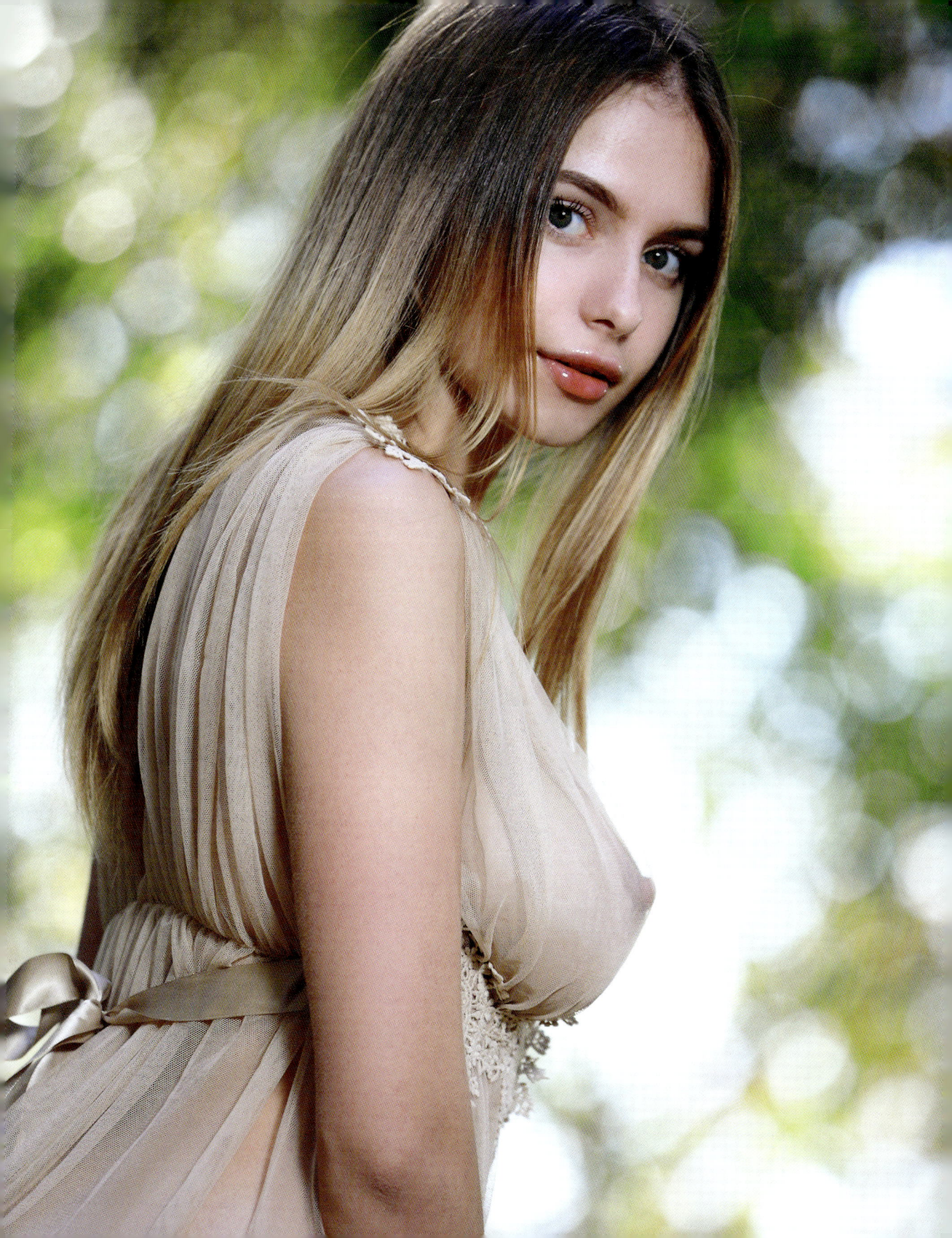

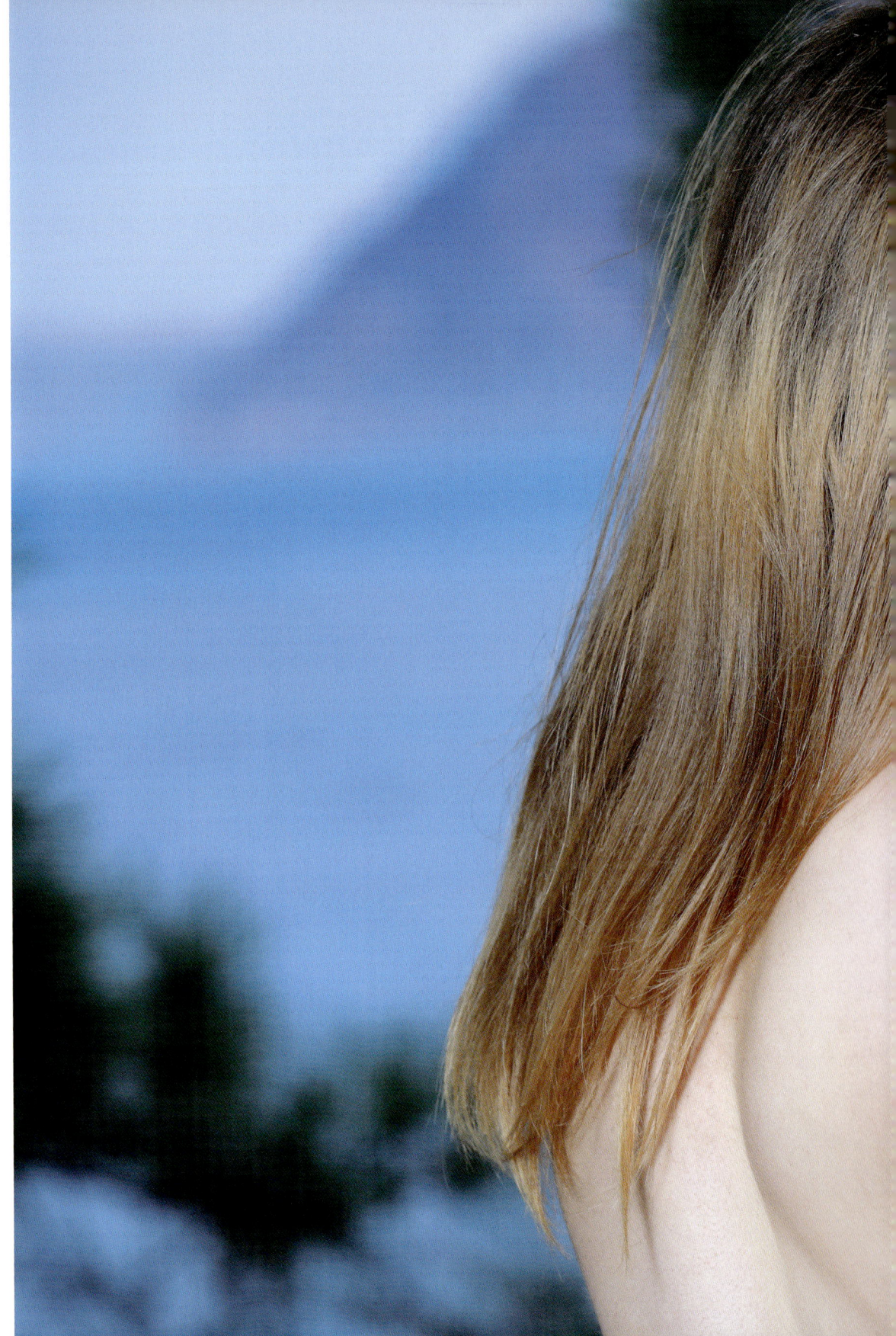

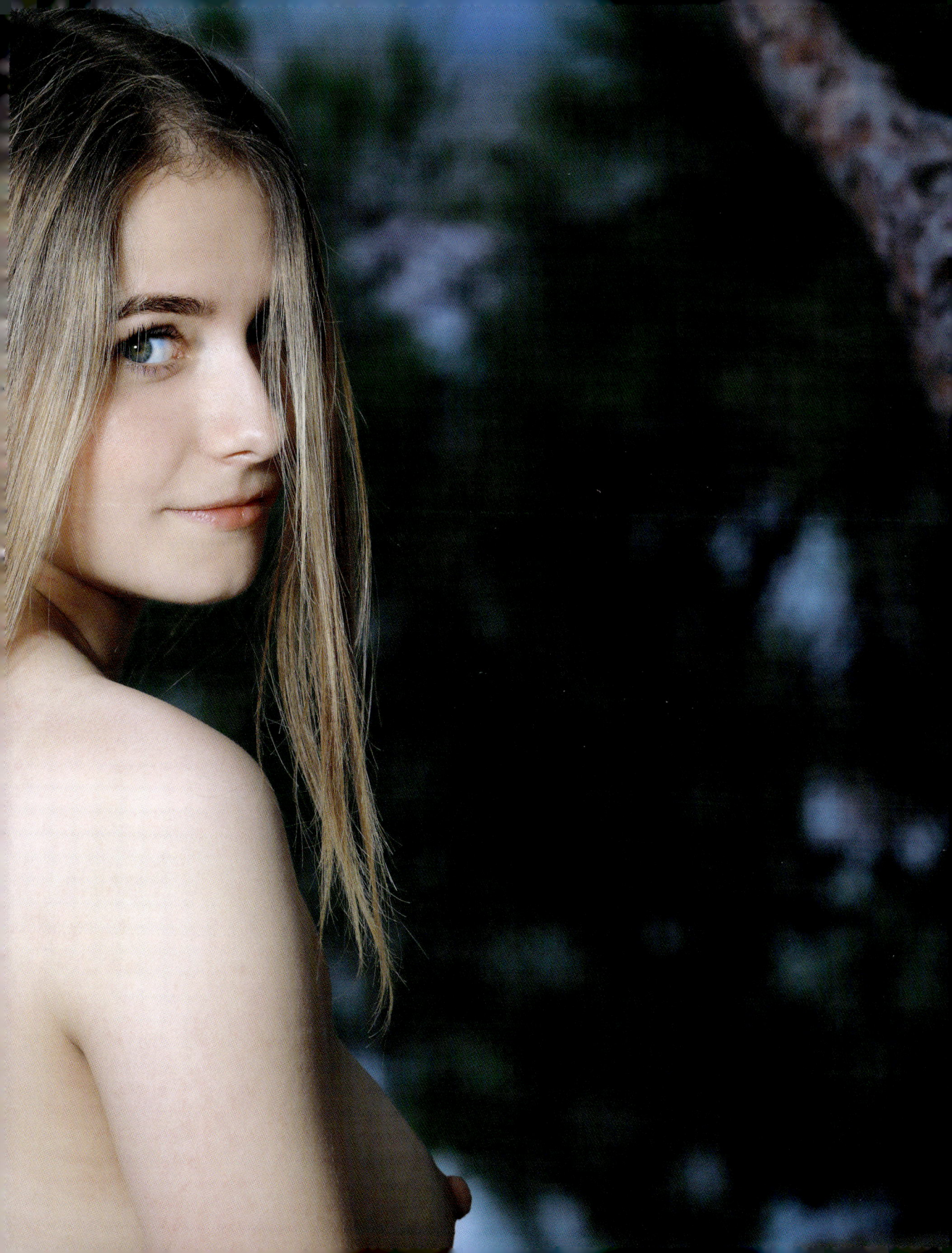

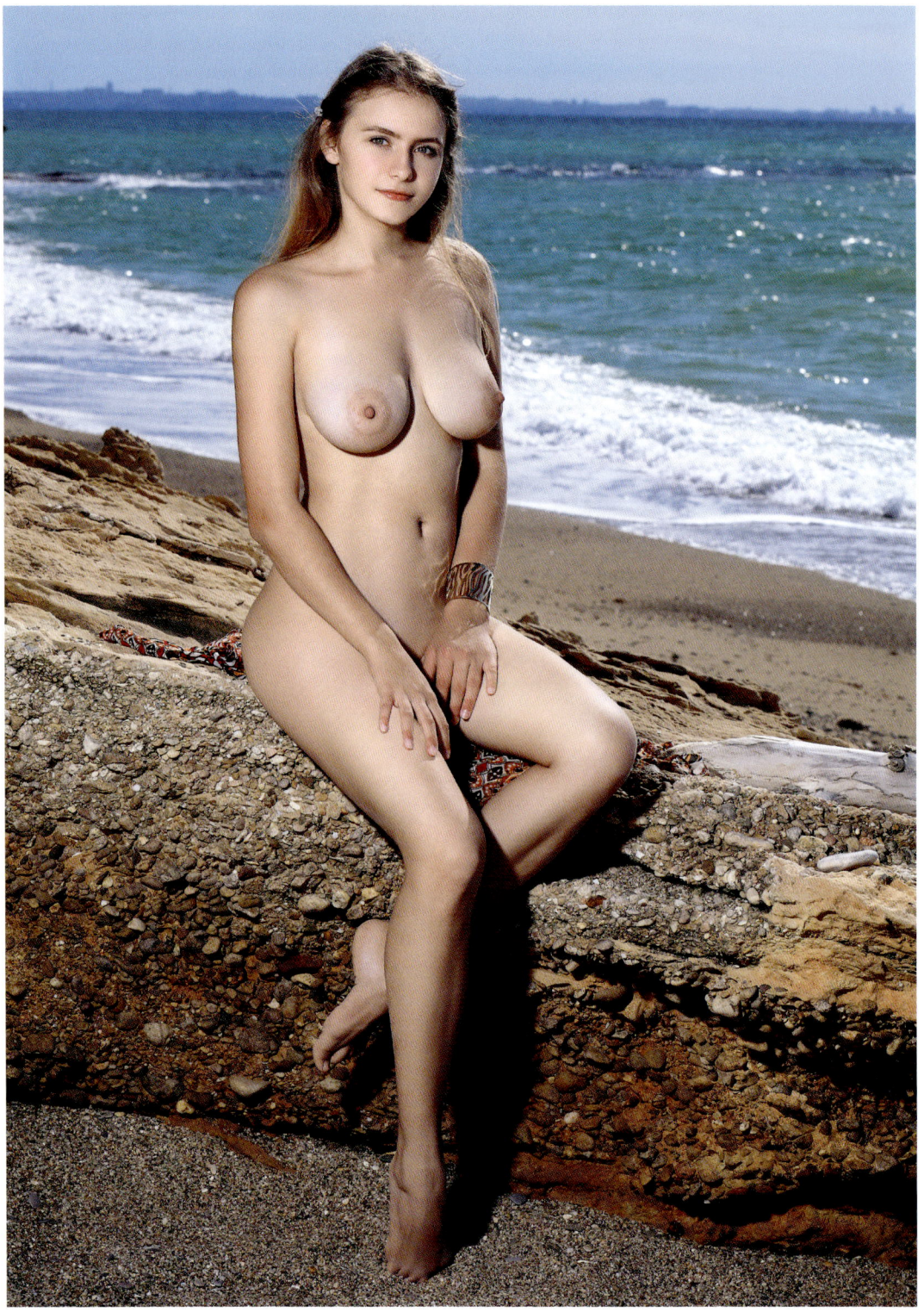

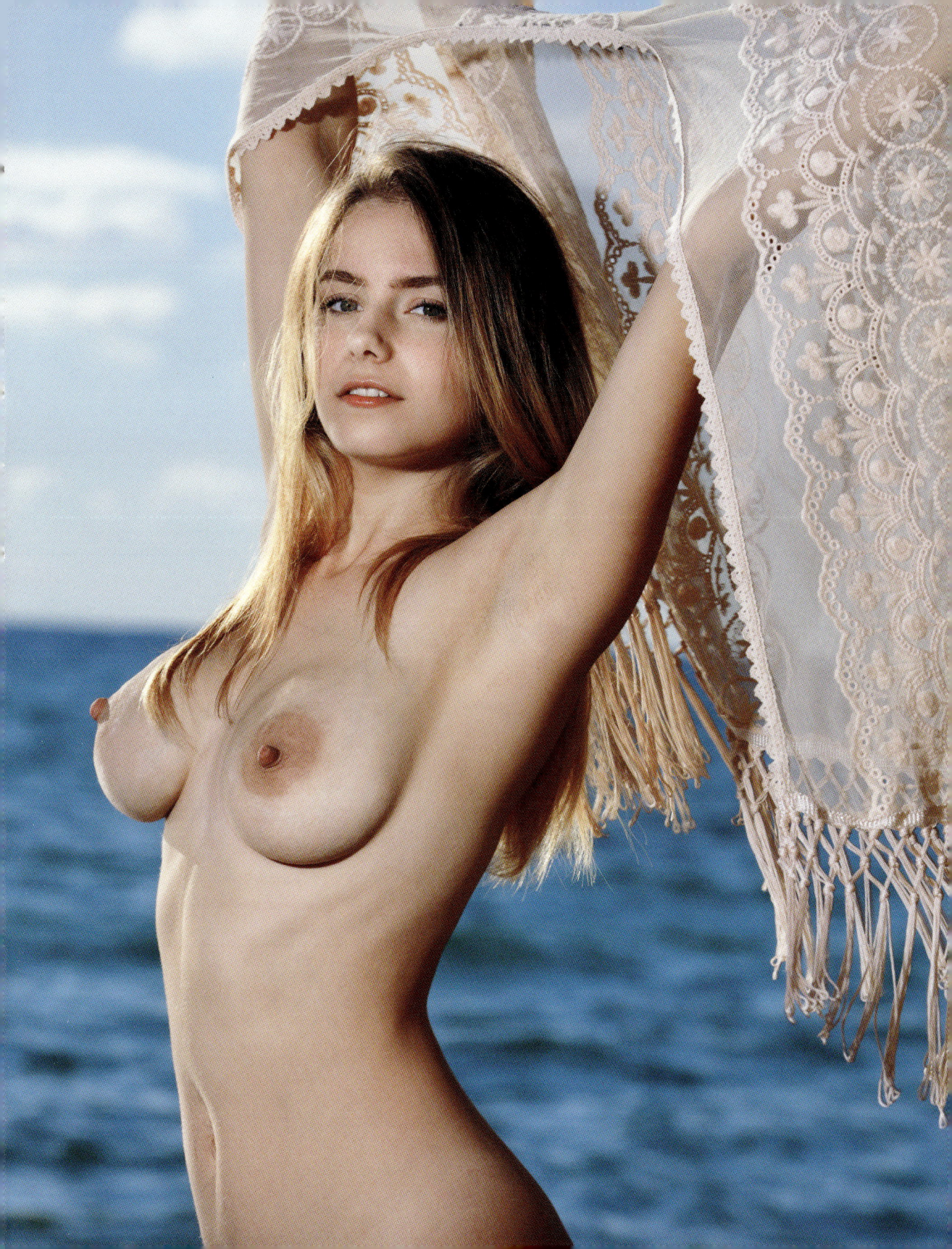

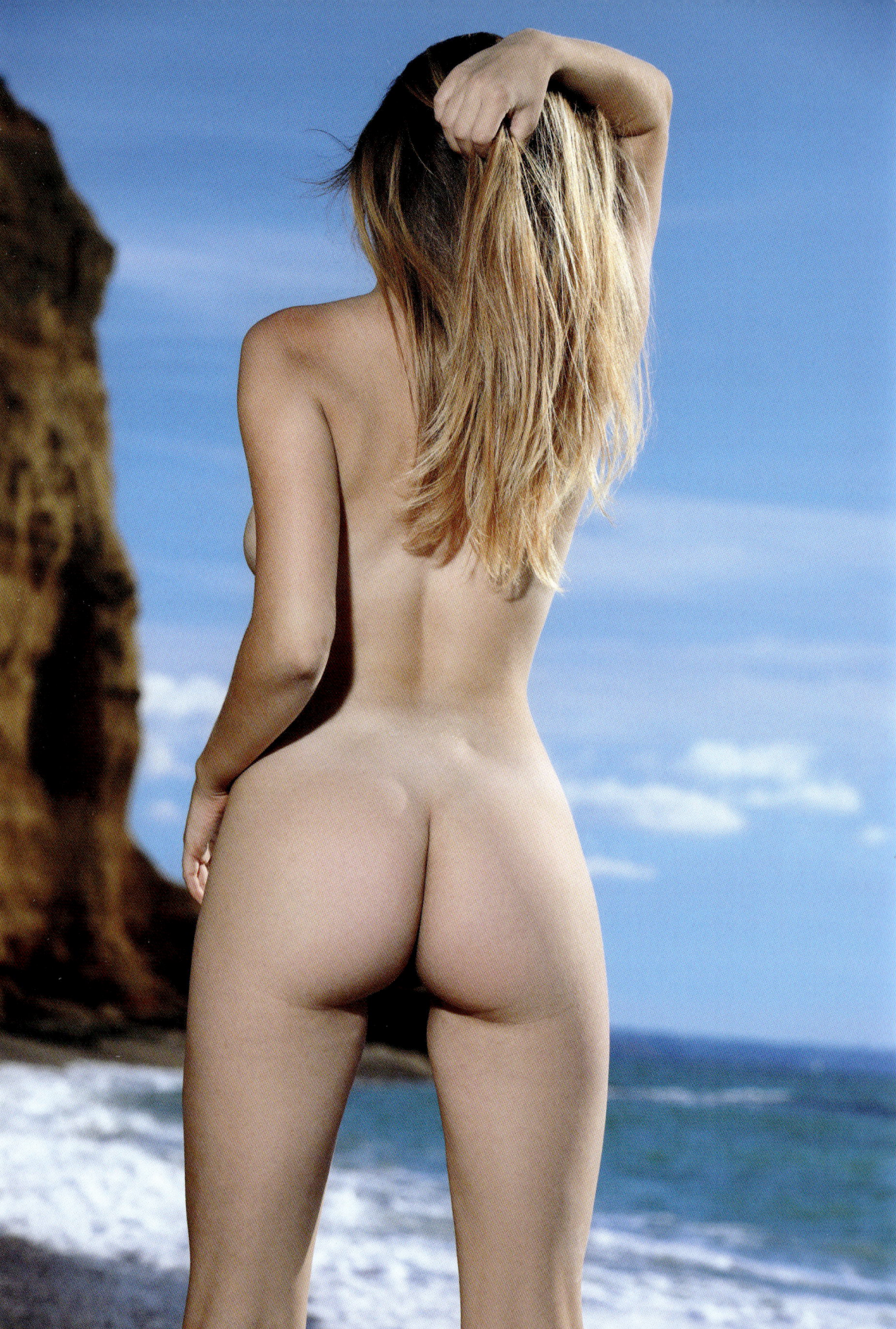

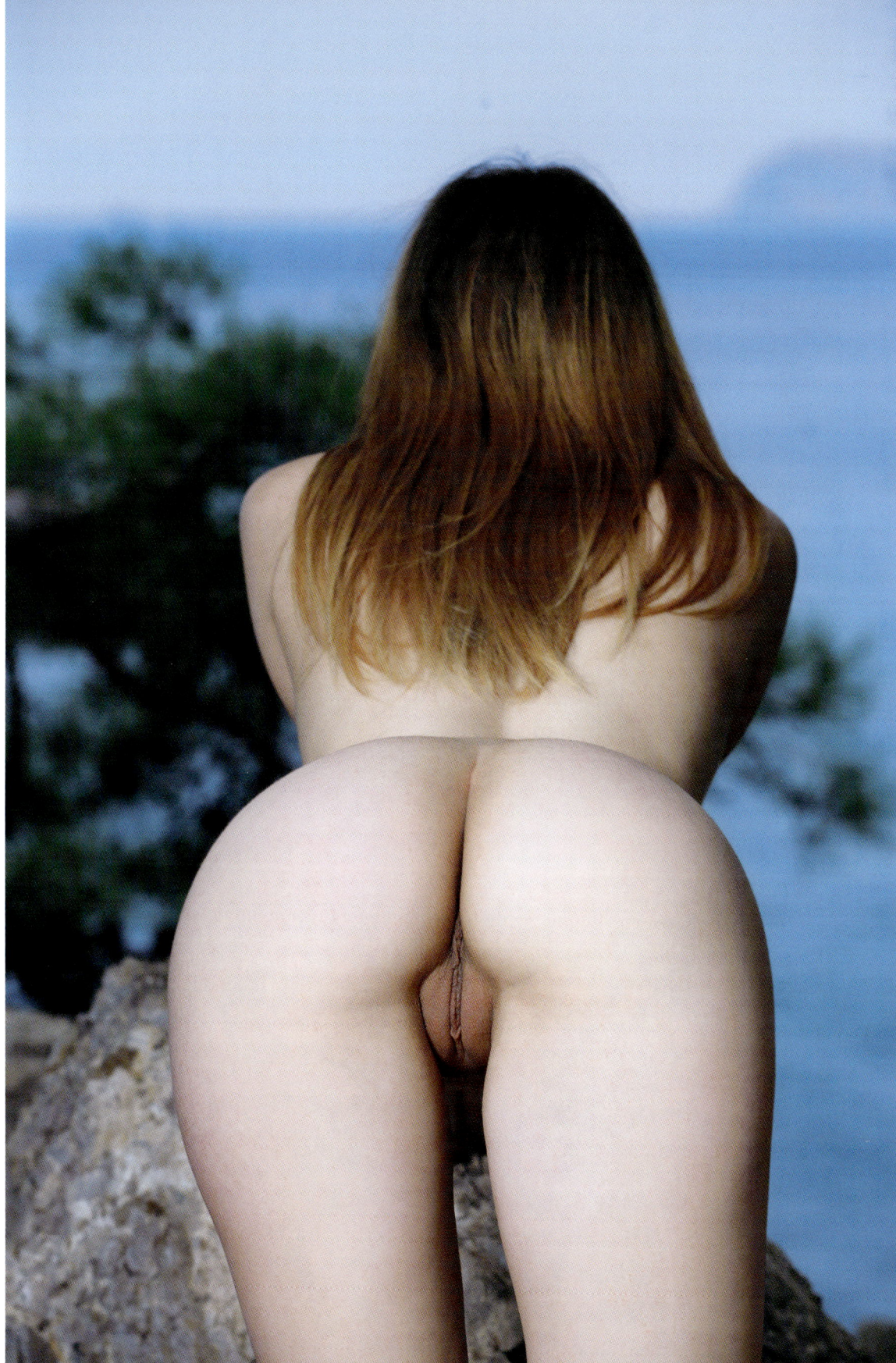

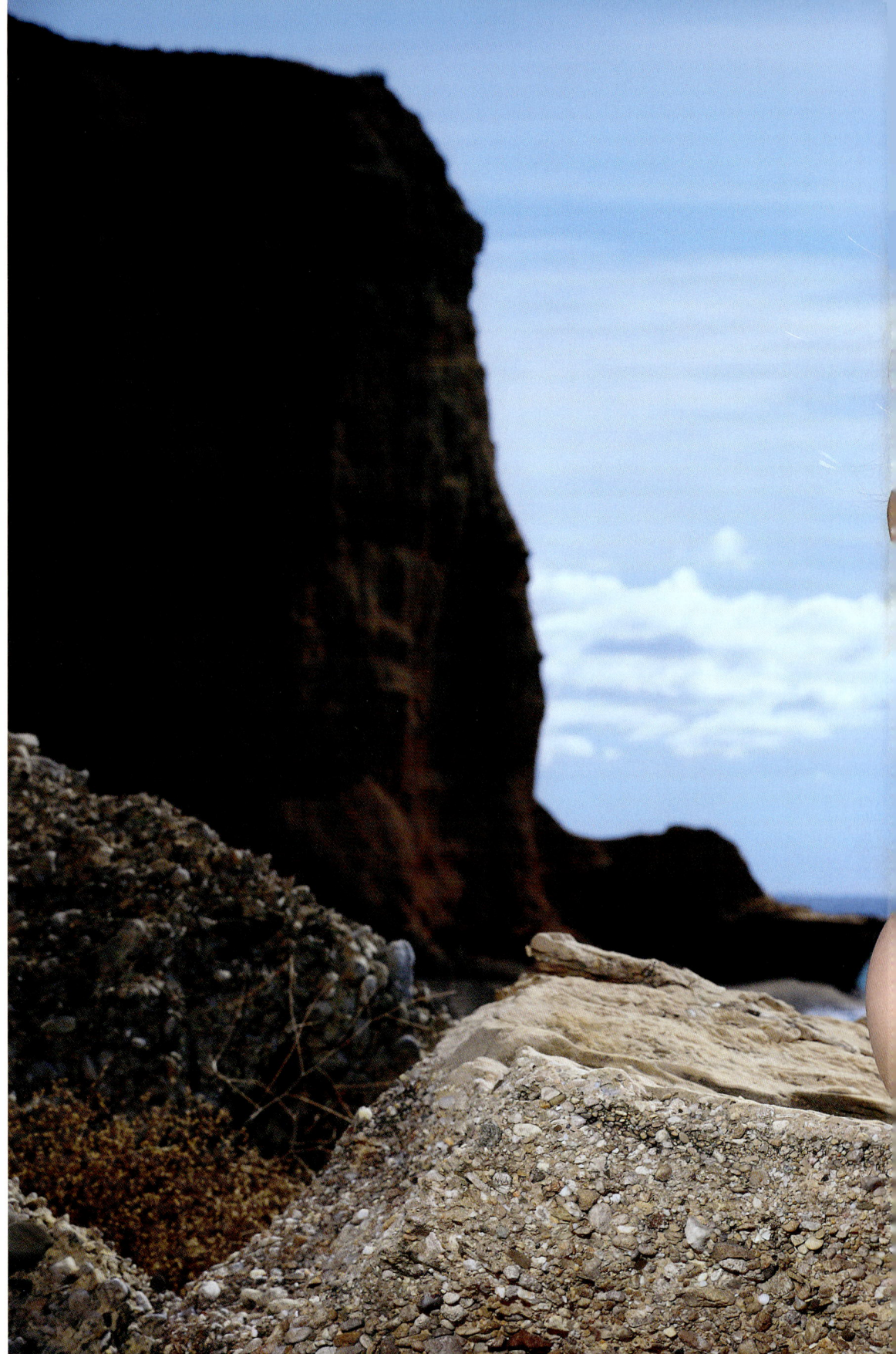

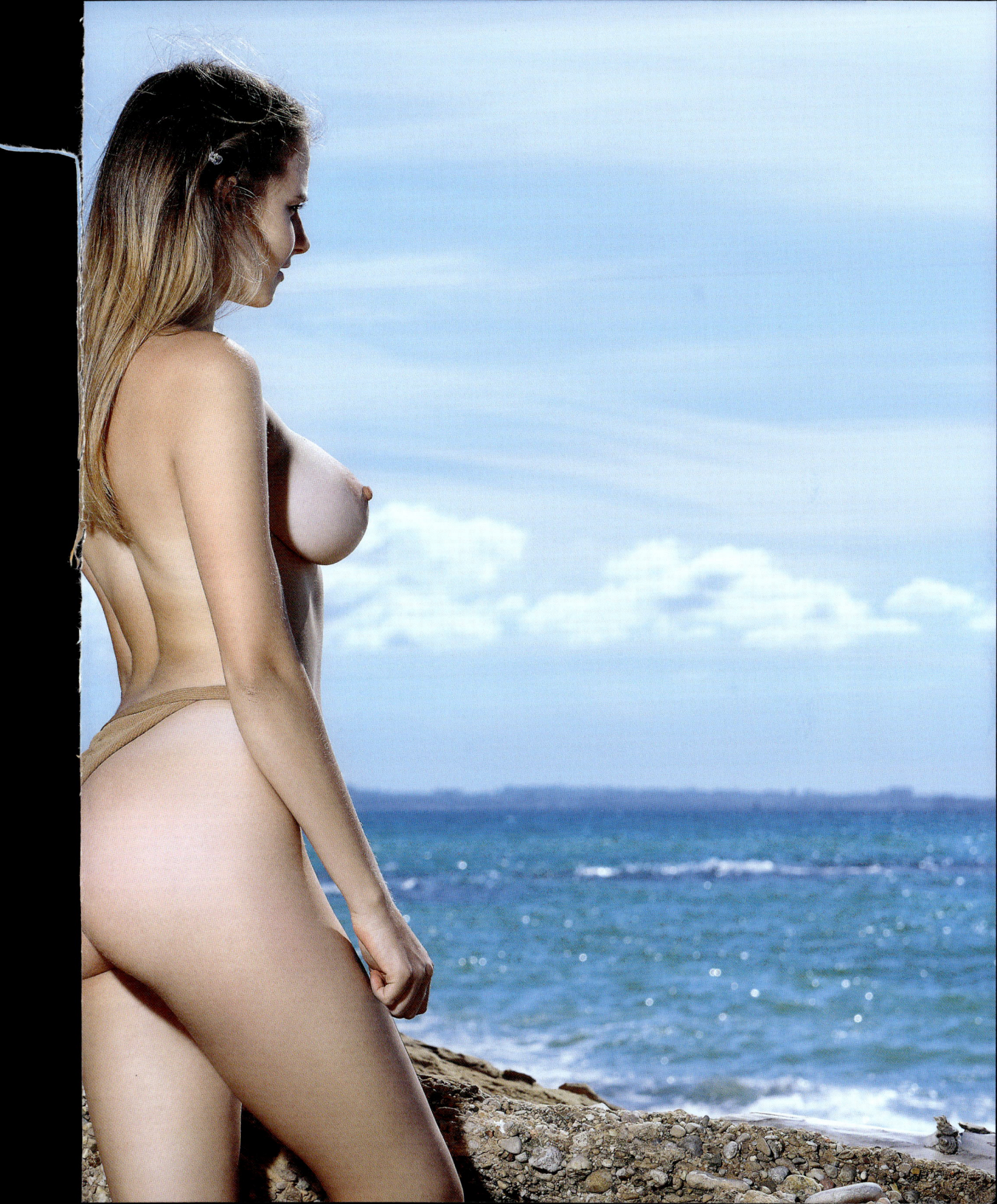

COLLECT THEM ALL: OUR MOST BEAUTIFUL

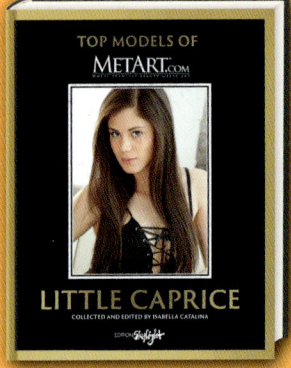

ISBN 978-3-03766-659-3

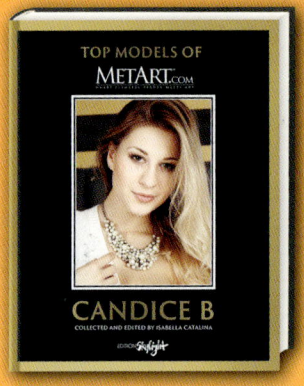

ISBN 978-3-03766-660-9

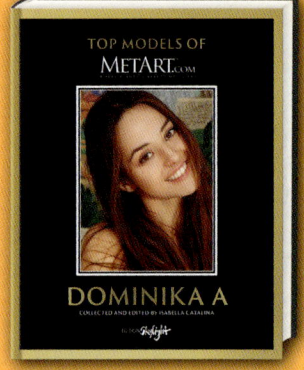

ISBN 978-3-03766-679-1

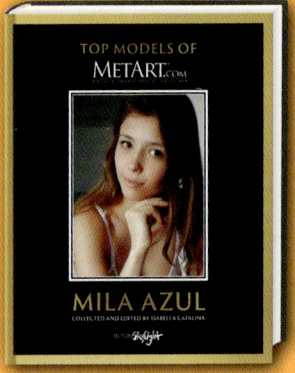

ISBN 978-3-03766-680-7

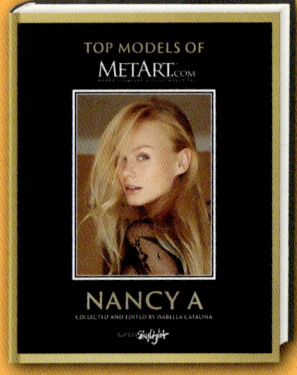

ISBN 978-3-03766-687-6

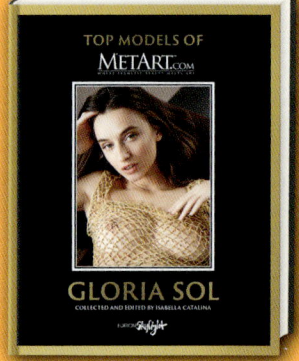

ISBN 978-3-03766-688-3

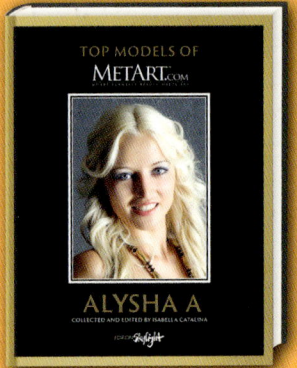

ISBN 978-3-03766-692-0

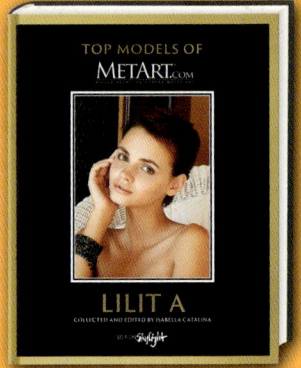

ISBN 978-3-03766-693-7

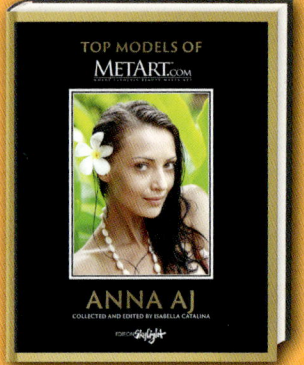

ISBN 978-3-03766-695-1